A Summer with Freeman

Daniel Geery

2013

Dedicated to my grandson, Gabriel Geery.

May he and his generation live to see a happier, healthier planet than the one we are leaving behind so far.

Acknowledgements

I am extremely grateful to my family, present and past, who endured all too many years with an aspiring writer. I am well aware it is no simple matter to live with a "Creative Hopeful." Although I have been accused of being "obsessive and compulsive," I prefer to see this as being "focused and motivated."

I owe a huge debt of thanks to Ruth Stanley, my editor, whose experienced, well-trained, and appropriately nit-picking eyes pointed out probably thousands of typos, grammatical errors, poor wording, and so on. Any errors in this regard should be attributed to the author. I am likewise grateful to Christine, my warm and loving wife, who I mentored in writing just three years ago, and who wrote and published her own book, *Heart Full of Hope*, before I finished this one. She now mentors me, in writing as well as other areas. Christine's unfailing encouragement and original exclamation that, "This should be a movie before it's a book!" is ultimately responsible for your holding this story in your hands. Many thanks also to those editors who would prefer to remain unnamed, but who I fully and forever appreciate, for their hard work, insights, and multitude of ideas, including the title.

Love and thanks to my Best Bud, Cooper, who lived with me through the years it took to compose the manuscript, wanting nothing more than to lie at my feet for hours on end. I thank him also for taking me on what seems like millions of miles of walks on this beautiful planet, in city and country, and likewise for chasing me around Salt Lake City on my rollerblades, over the course of many years. This helped me stay connected, at least marginally, to reality. Eternal peace to my unconditionally loving canine friend.

Similar thanks to Daphne, my present canine bud, who at the moment is lying at my feet on our bed on a snowy January morning. She loves to walk with me in our local park, or gallop beside me when I rollerblade the Jordan River Parkway. I also thank her for loving me most when I neglect to shower, even though Christine loves me most when I do (writing does seem to have a way of monkeying with all aspects of my life).

Deral Barton, who created the cover from scratch and brought it to life, and worked through many iterations to appease me, gets my unconditional round of applause--particularly because, as we all know, almost everyone judges a book by its cover.

I thank Create Space and the folks there who made this book possible, along with the countless unknown humans who helped make Kindle a reality, one that has altered my life for the better. I now carry a library in my pocket, read easily at night, don't waste time in doctors' offices (especially those with two year old magazines), and just last night downloaded *The Complete Works of Mark Twain*, my favorite author, for $2.99—a fact I realize might make him writhe in his grave, which of course is last thing in the world I would want him to have to do.

Last but not least, my thanks to the National Education Association and the folks therein, who helped provide the time necessary to turn the seed of an idea into the reality of this book.

1

It was a Saturday morning the first time I saw her. I was standing in an aisle at the grocery store, getting bread for my mom, squeezing the loaves to find a fresh one, when something bumped my sneaker. I looked down and saw a big green apple rolling to a stop. I stooped to pick it up, and the most beautiful girl I'd ever seen was suddenly kneeling in front of me, like an angel who had floated down from the clouds. Our heads nearly touched, and her curly golden hair brushed across my arms. She smiled the warmest smile, with the most beautiful lips, so close to my face that I could feel her breath.

Our glances met and her lively green eyes cast a magic spell over me, while the scent of her perfume filled my head and nearly drove me insane. The soft roundness of her cheeks made me want to kiss them and never stop–never ever! Her hand touched mine as she reached for the apple, and I was overcome with her warmth and gentleness. My insides seemed to melt, and I had a feeling I had never felt before.

"It's bruised now," she said. "I guess I don't want that one anymore."

"Don't worry! I'll eat it myself!" I blurted out, chomping a large bite, for no reason other than I had turned into a complete idiot.

She laughed and spoke a few words that I can't remember, mainly because I was too stunned to hear very well. All I know for sure is that I fell madly in love, then and there, and I was certain she did too. Then in the blink of an eye, she walked off with her bag of apples, oh so graceful in her white summer dress, her curls bobbing like lively springs around her creamy, smooth shoulders.

As I stared down the empty aisle, it dawned on me that I didn't know her name or phone number or even if she lived in Sunnyville or was just passing through. I chomped on the big green apple, wondering if I'd ever see her again; mad at myself for not finding out more about her.

It was early May then, and I was still dreaming about her three weeks later when school ended for summer. It was a joy to be done with school and a huge relief to have another year of drudgery and boredom behind me, with no more nuns breathing down my neck or hounding me for homework, or announcing some new test I'd have to worry about.

But it took less than a week before I wondered what to do with myself. Summers can be a raw deal when you go to Catholic school ten miles from home, and you've got no real friends in your own neighborhood. The last two summers had been lonely and boring on account of it. I even said a prayer to St. Jude that I might find a friend this summer, though I didn't really believe it would help.

And so it was early June, on a hot, muggy morning, that I tossed and turned and tried to go back to sleep; I wanted to avoid getting up, so I could go on dreaming about my green-eyed angel. But the sun blasted through my window and one obnoxious fly circled madly around my head, driving me nuts. I glanced at the clock on my desk and saw it was nine forty-five. I rolled out of bed and slogged through my morning routines, squeezed three new pimples, and wolfed down a bowl of Rice Krispies. I nearly made it past the kitchen and the smell of fresh perked coffee, when Timmy's voice came from behind me.

"Why don't you play catch with me today, Joey?"

I turned and saw him leaning on the refrigerator, like he owned the kitchen and everyone who passed through.

"I can't. I have to be at the game at ten."

"You say that every day."

"That's when they start playing. What do you want me to do? Get up at eight?"

"That would be good. So would the afternoon." He folded his arms over his red and white striped T-shirt and reminded me of a little drill sergeant.

"Go play with Ryan." I was grateful when Ryan moved into the neighborhood last year. He was Timmy's age, and he went to Saint Frances like we did. This took a lot of pressure off me, and kept Timmy out of my hair most of the time. A kid my age doesn't need his younger brother following him around all the time.

"But he's going to his grandparents today!"

"Another time, okay, Timmy?"

It was bad enough having to share a room with Timmy, but if he had his way, I'd be playing with him all day long. And if it wasn't him chasing after me, it was the twins, Patrick and Mary, who were nine.

Pestering, pestering, always pestering! Do this, do that, help me now! Being oldest is like breaking a trail through the forest, with everyone depending on you, expecting you to lead the way and behave like Superman, when the truth is it's all you can do to get through the day sometimes.

Not that I was actually excited about where I was headed. In fact, I was only going to escape from Timmy and the twins and staring at my bedroom walls. And it wasn't that I don't like the idea of baseball–it's the rejects who play and how they play, forever quibbling about everything that doesn't matter, spending more time fighting than actually playing.

"C'mon, Joey! I got no one to play with today!" He stepped toward me and clasped his hands like he was praying.

"No! Now stop bugging me, will you? I have important things to do!" I raised my voice to shut him up, at the same time feeling like a miserable excuse for a brother. Yet what choice did I have? I wasn't about to waste my day messing around with him. "Go play with the twins," I hollered over my shoulder as the screen door slammed shut.

I stepped onto the porch and warm sunshine washed over me. I squinted and breathed the smells of early summer. A robin twittered in a maple tree and a dog barked in the distance. Not a bad day really, except for my own sorry life, and my half-crazed condition because I didn't even know the name of the girl I was madly in love with.

I trudged to the ball field, kicking rocks and wishing for a better way to spend my time. A large pink car pulled to a stop sign beside me, the radio blasting, *I'm just a lonely boy, lonely and blue; I'm all alone, with nothing to do …* Like they were playing that song just for me, I thought. The driver looked about twenty, and had one arm resting on the window, his other arm around a pretty girl with a ponytail. He glanced my way and nodded, as if to say when I grew up maybe I could be like him. Then he winked as the wheels spun in the gravel.

The car drove off, and it crossed my mind that that could be my theme song. I didn't think it was possible for a person to get much lonelier and bluer than I felt.

"Wouldn't you know it?" some kid shouted meanly when I got near the ball field.

"Simpleton's late again!"

That's the nickname I got in third grade when two fifth-grade bullies were looking for someone to pick on. I pretended to ignore him and took my usual place in left field, out near the sycamore trees. I found out long ago that ignoring bullies was the best way to avoid them, and this loudmouth was no exception. So there I stood in left field with no one but myself and the squirrels for company; it wasn't long before my hat was slumped over my eyes, blocking the sun and making me as useful as a fence post. But I could think better like that, and what else can you do in left field, besides pick your nose or talk to the squirrels?

By and by someone hollered and made me jump. "Hey, dog breath! Wake up!"

Evidently I'd nodded off, dreaming about my true love. I shoved my hat back and blinked in the direction of the noise. A swarming mass of teenagers was jumping up and down, howling and swearing and pointing to where I stood. And there was that white streak of a ball, whizzing through the grass like a rattlesnake, not twenty feet away. My heart started pounding like a washing machine, and my brain sprang to life. I stuck my mitt in its path pleased it was a grounder. "Gotcha, buster!" I said to myself.

In that same instant a hissing flash of white shot up, like a fist without an arm, and whacked me soundly in the forehead. A dull *klonk* echoed through my skull, followed by enormous pain. I fell to my knees, dropped my mitt, and clamped two hands to my head.

But what hurt worse than the ball was all the screaming to get the ball and toss it back, because a kid named Donald Donnelly was flying around the bases, about to make a home run. As if it was my fault the pitcher screwed up and this guy got lucky!

The bump flared like a marshmallow in a campfire, yet no one cared about that, or the fact that I could have been dying right before their eyes. I imagined I was dying, too.

"Hurry up, you baboon!" some kid shrieked, his arms flapping like misshapen wings.

I had an urge to punch his lights out, but I chased after the ball instead, like a dog after a bone, since it was still rolling along. Somehow I managed to retrieve it and lob the thing home.

That put Donnelly out, by one hair at home plate, and settled my team down, though it got his side all fired up and anxious to kill me. They hollered and made hostile threats for a while, but soon enough they dropped it, due to their puny attention span and other kids to worry about.

I softly touched the bump and found half a golf ball sticking out of my forehead, and for a moment I wondered if your brain could actually start growing out of your head. But the pain died down after a while, and I soon came to my senses and remembered why I nodded off in the first place.

It had turned into a roaring beast of a day, humid and hot, with the sun bearing down like breath from a dragon. Streams of sweat rolled down my head and neck and shoulders, and my soggy undies were wedged up my behind, a situation I hate almost worse than homework. My stomach was grumbling and filled with hunger pains, and shiny green flies hummed around my ears, taking occasional chunks of meat from my neck and shoulders. I had a scorcher of a sunburn, and my team was losing eleven to five, though I didn't honestly give a hoot. "What's the point of being out of school, if this is how I'm going to be spending the time?" I wondered. "Summers are supposed to be fun, yet mine have been going downhill a little further each year. Is it my lack of friends, or do things really get worse as we get older?"

It was a horrible thought and for a moment I pictured myself hanging on the end of a fuzzy manila rope, with a long spiral knot, swinging from a rafter in my garage, all my earthly troubles ended. But that was a worse thought, and the idea of roasting in hell forever was utterly unacceptable. I'd have to go on living, rotten as the idea seemed.

"C'mon you dingleberry! Put the ball over the plate!" the batter shouted.

I looked toward home and saw Justin Clancy standing there, the bat cocked over his left shoulder. "Right now! I'm gonna knock that thing over the school and walk home!"

It seemed most unlikely. We'd all heard Clancy's boasting before. It was hard to believe he used to be my best friend, or that he'd turned into such a meathead in the last few years.

The pitcher was Herman Berkowitz, a scrawny character with glasses that were forever crooked, and lenses like powerful magnifying glasses. He was the only one with his shirt still on, though I imagined I'd have mine on too if I was a sack of bones like him.

Herman shifted his feet on the pitcher's mound, ignoring Clancy. I felt sorry for him and supposed most kids did, even if they didn't show it. He obviously wasn't much on self-defense, which is part of what caused the pity; though rumor had it he was a brain in school. Which I suppose counts for something, though I don't know what, considering how much I hate the place.

Herman heaved another one out that looked good to me, square over home plate.

"You cockeyed bookworm!" Clancy wailed. "I can't hit 'em when they're ten feet off the plate! Where'd you learn to throw, anyway?"

It was Clancy's third time at bat; even though many kids hadn't been up at all yet, a situation not too uncommon. All eyes were glued on him, the way he seemed to like it, except for Herman's. Herman stood still as a parked bicycle, eyes on the ground as if he was deep in thought, or fear maybe. Silence filled the air while we waited to see what Herman would do next.

A memory flashed into my head right then of the day Justin Clancy had moved to our neighborhood, several years ago, from New York City. Within a week my mom had invited his family to dinner, since they were new Catholics in the neighborhood. I showed Clancy my electric trains that evening in the basement, the big Virginian engine, the crane you could control from the switchboard, the double trestles, and the automatic coupler. I was in the midst of demonstrating how everything worked, when he asked if I wanted to see something interesting.

"Sure," I replied, unable to imagine what could be more interesting than my trains.

He made me swear on a stack of Bibles I wouldn't tell anyone, not one soul in my entire life.

"I'll even give my Cub Scout's honor."

He made me do that, too. Then he made me swear again that I wouldn't break my Cub Scout's honor. It seemed ridiculous, but I did it anyway.

He fished around in his back pocket, and then pulled out a wrinkled, folded piece of paper that looked about five hundred years old and seemed worn thin from use. He glanced to the basement stairs and whispered for me to be quiet, "absolutely perfectly quiet," to be sure no one was coming. We listened and heard nothing.

His eyes locked on mine. "If ya tell anyone, I'm gonna kill ya!"

He had dark brown eyes that seemed like pools of wisdom then; though later on I found out they were more like cesspools. He set his treasure on the control panel and opened the folds slowly, pressing back the paper like a magician performing a magic trick. As the picture opened up I could see arms and legs and two heads, and a whole lot of skin, though it wasn't till the paper was flattened out that things came into focus.

A lady my mom's age with short blond hair had her arms around the neck of some muscular, hairy guy, who looked like he might be in the navy or the air force, though it wasn't possible to tell since neither one had a stitch of clothes on. Clancy and I stood statue-like, our eyes bulging as we took in the scenery, and I tried to figure out what the picture was all about.

"See what they're doin'?" Justin spoke after a time, tapping his finger near the center of the picture. You gotta look close."

I was still in shock about the fact that they were both naked, and I hadn't made out too many details. But then I squinted and looked into the shadows where Clancy pointed, and it was a horrifying sight, one that made my neck hairs tingle.

"That's sick!" I informed him. "Why would anyone want to do that?"

He rolled his eyes and looked at the ceiling. "That's how you got here, dum-dum."

"That's a big fat lie!" I exclaimed loudly.

Even so, some part of me said that would explain a whole lot of mysteries, like why the door was always locked on my parents' bed-room, and why I never saw a stork in my life, even though I always kept a pretty good eye out.

The next day I slipped my *National Geographic* collection into a neighbor's garbage can since it no longer seemed worth keeping. Many times I wanted to see that picture again, but I always worried that Clancy would think I was a pervert, so I never asked.

We hung around together for two more years, playing cowboys and Indians, roller-skating, making cardboard huts, and doing things kids do. But he was difficult to be around, and he started getting more uppity and bossy as time went by. I wasn't sure why, though I won-dered if it had to do with the way nuns bossed him around and treated him, making him stand in the corner much of the time, or yanking him around by the ear, or banging his head on the chalkboard, as I'd seen happen on several occasions.

It seemed like he was in trouble every day for one reason or an-other. Schoolwork was part of it. For example, he spelled "when" as "w-e-n-e" in a note he left for me to meet him after school one day. Even first graders can spell that one. And he never did any homework, a behavior that would have brought a swift end to my life.

Clancy's parents were always being called in, sometimes for bad grades but more often for the fights he seemed to start on a regular basis. I once heard Sister Boneventure screeching at him in the hall, "It won't be long before no one in the world wants to be around you, Mr. Clancy!" And that might have well been true, except for a handful of losers who banded together with him, the way losers often do.

It was a mystery to me how Clancy could be so smart about girls and fixing bikes and important things like that, yet so dumb in school, almost like he had no brain at all. But the real issue was how he treated me. The final straw came when he ridiculed me in front of two girls one day when I wore my scout uniform.

"Oh look! What a cute little Boy Scout!" he said to get their attention. They laughed with him, and I decided then and there that Clancy was no longer a friend of mine. And it wasn't much longer before I quit scouts since I was too embarrassed to wear the uniform, though afterward I was embarrassed that I had quit.

He asked me to call him "JC" back then, which I've called him ever since, though now I think "Jezum Crezum!" whenever his name comes up.

"You skinny twerp, get the ball over the plate, will ya?" JC was yelling now at Herman in the most insulting manner.

Herman was still looking silently at the ground and you had to wonder what was running through his little straight-A brain, though there was no way to find out. The catcher, Freddie Freeman, heaved the ball back to Herman, a few feet too high. Herman leaped and caught it smoothly, one hand extended in the air. Herman's a good thrower and catcher, like skinny kids often are for some unexplainable reason.

He held the ball and studied it slowly, like he expected it to say something. He turned it over a time or two, brushed it on his left side, then on his right. Everyone watched with great interest, even JC, who had shut up for once. Then Herman stood still, glaring at JC, and you could almost feel the anger in him. JC froze too, and I sensed that something unusual or even terrible was about to happen, though I didn't know what.

Next thing we heard was Herman's voice, loud and screechy as a girl's: "Okay, pimple puss! Hit this!"

He wound up like a windmill, and the ball flashed like lightning toward JC. It nailed him in the neck, near his Adam's apple, and a fleshy *thwack* filled the air. JC dropped the bat, stumbled toward the backstop, and fell on his back, one hand clamped to his neck. There he lay, not moving a twitch. Stillness came over the place and every eyeball was fastened on the body.

"He's dead!" someone announced.

Everyone but Herman moved closer to check it out. I don't think anyone had ever seen a dead person before. But he wasn't dead, not by a long shot; and after a few moments he wiggled around a little, like a boy in great pain. He slowly rolled to his stomach, and shouted as he did so. "You bony four-eyed runt! What the hell's wrong with you?"

Herman quietly gazed toward JC, as if he were on a field trip studying a museum piece. I was proud of Herman, but at the same time mighty glad not to be in his shoes. JC was close to six feet, and he'd been lifting weights for years. Plus it was no secret that he fought dirty, so it did not look like a very serious contest.

JC began crawling on all fours, dog that he is, and picked up the bat. He stood up and began swinging it madly, a crazed look in his eyes, while he advanced in the direction of the pitcher's mound.

"C'mon, you pinhead," he wailed, "let's see if your head can fly like a baseball!"

JC was wacko enough to do it, and I didn't see one sign of life coming from Herman.

He appeared to be in paralysis the way he stood there gaping stupidly. Who could believe he was a straight-A student?

But then out of the blue, Herman came to life. He wound his arm up and let loose with a rock the size of a ping-pong ball, which flew out with a deadly *whoooooosh!*

It sailed fast and straight as an arrow, until it glanced off JC's sun-burned forehead and plunked to the ground. It made my own head suddenly feel a little better as I grimaced and felt a pang of sorrow for JC.

That big oaf dropped the bat and grabbed his head, swearing and cursing in a way I'd never heard before, which is mighty unusual. But he stayed upright and danced in circles several times, shouting out new combinations of words for Herman's benefit, and giving us all a good education in the process. His hands and face grew redder as blood gushed from his forehead.

He soon stopped dancing and lunged after the bat, wrapping two bloody hands near the base. Then he arose and continued swinging it madly, moving toward Herman. Blood streamed from above his right eye and flowed down his face and neck, till it mixed with shiny sweat and black chest hairs.

Herman remained on the pitcher's mound, a fact I wouldn't have believed if I didn't see it for myself. I would have worn my sneakers out, getting clear out of Sunnyville and the State of New York, though I have no idea where I would've gone.

But Herman had become a source of never-ending surprises. He cranked up and let another rock sail, one I didn't even know he had. But JC ducked and the rock flew past, then continued flying till it rolled to a stop in the field beyond.

This caused JC to come on faster with the bat, swinging it to and fro, mad as a wet hornet. I said a short prayer to Saint Jude—"Please help Herman as soon as possible!"—since it looked like a very, very lost cause, and I was worried sick about what might happen next.

Prayers work about half the time for me, but I never know for sure which half. The nuns say prayers are answered in ways we can't understand, though I never could quite grasp the value of that. So I save them for times like this, when there's really not much hope for anything else. And it looked like a serious test—JC had turned into a wild bull, only more dangerous and not so smart.

Herman stood looking at him like nothing ever happened, just happily waiting to be pounded into hamburger meat by the rapidly slashing bat.

To everyone's surprise, a new voice suddenly boomed from the other direction, behind the batter's mound: "Hey! JC!"

Everyone turned, and there stood the catcher, Freddie Freeman, gazing steadily at JC.

His mitt and hat lay by his feet, his hands rested on his waist, his legs parted in a V; sunburn reddened his upper body, and sweat glistened on top of that. His flattop haircut appeared bright yellow in the sun.

JC looked surprised as everyone else when he turned and shouted, "What?!"

"Put the bat down," instructed Freeman, addressing JC like a little kid. "Now."

Under the circumstances this would be a remarkable statement coming from anybody. But to hear it from Freddie Freeman was like seeing a pink giraffe fly by your window, or the three little pigs roller-skate up your driveway; it just wasn't the kind of thing you'd expect in a hundred years, for a number of reasons.

Freeman was big enough for the job, it was true, maybe a hair bigger than JC. But JC had friends and followers likely to come to his rescue. Freeman was a loner and an outcast, in addition to the brunt of many a joke over the years. I knew this well: he lived right next door to me, and his bedroom window was directly across from mine, on the second floor. He was a year ahead of me in school, though he went to the Piney Wood Public School rather than Saint Frances.

We never made friends during the several years he lived there. In part this was my mom's doing. His family wasn't Catholic, so it seemed unlikely to her that Freddie Freeman or either of his two brothers would ever be a good influence for me.

"They don't even go to church!" she once exclaimed. "I've watched for several Sundays now—they're heathens, Joseph!"

I didn't know what that meant, but it discouraged any interest I might have had in playing with them, though my mom never actually forbade it.

My dad had reservations too, though they had more to do with the Freemans' physical surroundings. "They bring down the value of the neighborhood!" he once griped at the dinner table. "Just look at the house! It's a slum! In the middle of a junkyard! They're white trash!" he exclaimed.

As near as I could tell, the Freemans were simply poor, and the parents weren't there to take care of things because they had to work all the time. It was an ideal setup for the kids, I thought, one that would make life ever so pleasant. But it also fueled nasty rumors about the Freeman kids and sometimes it was hard to tell where the facts ended and the rumors began.

Freddie—who most kids referred to as "Freeman," even though for some unknown reason they called his brothers by their first names—had several strikes against him in the narrow little minds of the neighborhood kids, including my own. One was the way he walked, bouncing on his toes like his undies were too tight. Another was the girlish way he winged a ball, even though it generally went where it was supposed to, and even though he did okay as catcher. Added to this were his hand-me-down clothes, which always made him look too big for his own body, in addition to poor.

Plus he had large ears that from the back looked like open doors on a car, and this earned him the nickname of Dumbo, in addition to other degrading names kids employed now and then. His failure to defend himself did not help the situation. This failure seemed mainly due to his shyness, which as near as I could tell was as bad as my own. All these factors made him a likely target for anyone who needed a target, and that included most kids in the neighborhood.

Then there was James, Freeman's younger brother. James went to a special school for retarded kids, in one of those sawed-off school buses for kids like that. I liked James. He always waved and smiled at me, and was certainly friendly enough. The only odd thing about him, as near as I could tell, was the way he flapped his hands like a bird now and then, for no apparent reason.

"That means he's cuttin' farts and liking 'em," Timmy once informed me.

"I think it means he's getting good ideas and being excited by them," I argued, though Timmy never bought that argument.

But it didn't matter. People acted like whatever James had was contagious, and like his two brothers might spread it. It was cruel and mean and I didn't like it, but what could a kid like me do?

Freeman's older brother was Matt. Matt was not retarded, but at sixteen he still played with go-carts, collected junk from garbage cans and everywhere else, and built tree forts—things normal kids outgrow by his age, when they're busy trying to make money, find girlfriends, and get a real car.

Plus Matt wore no underwear. I noticed this by accident one day when he stopped to watch me and Timmy play Monopoly in our front yard. He sat down in his baggy shorts, right beside us, and his dangling participles hung out in full bloom, embarrassing Timmy and me, though Matt didn't even notice. Timmy later said it proved he was a homo.

"All it means is that his undies are in the wash," I replied. "And if you think that, maybe you're a homo yourself."

Thus nasty things were often said about all the Freeman kids, Freddie, Matt, and James, and while I had no personal gripe, I never tried to make friends, either.

So Freddie Freeman seemed to be on thin ice, having attracted everyone's attention by telling JC to put the bat down. It was trouble brewing, if ever there was any.

"You wanna repeat that, Dumbo?"

"Put the bat down," repeated Freeman, politely yet firmly, serious as a heart attack.

"Who's gonna make me?!" JC inquired, swinging the bat in Freeman's direction and walking toward him as if to use his head for a baseball now, instead of Herman's.

My hands grew sweaty as JC got closer. Everyone was inching in for a better look, like a flock of disgusting vultures. I moved up just a little, because some chunky kid named Billy Hampton was blocking my view, shouting encouragement, like a few other kids were doing.

JC continued swinging the bat and shortening the distance, repeating over and over, "C'mon, ya queer! Make me put the bat down!"

Freeman circled JC, his arms moving like a karate fighter, or maybe an old lady knitting, I couldn't tell which. His eyes were fixed on JC, whose face was red with smeared blood, and whose body was covered with red splotches, wet and shiny in the sun.

Ten feet lay between them. JC slowed down, though he kept swishing the bat in threatening patterns showing every intention of making a home run with Freeman's head.

And ten or so of his own fans goaded him on chanting, "Smear the Queer! Smear the Queer! Smear the Queer!"

Billy's blubber bounced to the rhythm in front of me, and the whole scene made me woozy and ill.

JC moved in suddenly, executing a powerful swing that might well have knocked Freeman's block clear off his neck, but Freeman ducked in the nick of time. Then in a flash, Freeman dived low, wrapping himself around JC's knees, knocking that ugly brute over backward. JC's head thumped to the ground and made a noise like a coconut. The bloodstained bat flew from his hands and whirled through the air, before it slammed into the crowd.

"Damn!" someone exclaimed as the bat dropped to the ground.

Freeman took advantage and jumped on top of JC, pinning his knees on JC's arms.

Then he slapped JC's face back and forth, as if it were bread dough. After four or five slaps, JC made an animal grunt, heaved up and rolled to his stomach, pulling his knees under himself. He arched to a kneeling position, flipped his head back and clomped Freeman in the nose.

Freeman grabbed his face, giving JC a second to scramble to his feet. JC turned and faced Freeman, who was still kneeling, then pounded down with white-knuckled fists, boxing the sides of Freeman's head.

The vulture choir altered its refrain: "Kill him! Kill him! Kill him!"

I wished there were a few harps around to mix in some heavenly music with these saintly thoughts.

Freeman drew his right arm back with a tight fist, then punched forward into JC's crotch. JC flew back folded over, hands clinging to the sore spot, making deep noises from his throat. He hit the ground doubled up like a jackknife.

Freeman scrambled from his knees and walked toward JC, stopping a few feet away.

"Thanks for puttin' the bat down, JC."

Several kids laughed, though Freeman hadn't meant it as a joke. But JC appeared too preoccupied to hear him.

The next surprise came from behind. One of JC's slimy little friends, Tony Angeli, had been slinking around like a weasel. Now he leapt up from behind and wrapped his legs around Freeman's waist, and his arms around Freeman's neck, and began choking him. Freeman emitted gurgling noises and tried to shake this greaseball off but couldn't because Tony was stuck on like an octopus.

Meanwhile, JC was getting up, still holding the source of the pain with one hand. He was doubled forward, but his other hand was cocked, ready to strike.

Freeman stumbled backward under Tony's weight. Two veins protruded from his forehead, his face was turning purple, and it seemed urgent that he shake Tony off.

The crowd backed away to make room. JC stepped in front of Freeman and let go with his fist jabbing Freeman under his rib cage, knocking his wind out. Freeman flipped forward, as a natural reaction, and Tony somersaulted over his shoulders and landed on JC. Both of them went down and floundered on the ground. Freeman stood up straight, gasping for air.

The vultures were chanting: "Kill Dumbo! Kill Dumbo! Kill Dumbo!" A tall lanky kid, Jason Weaver, seemed to be leading them. I was pleased that at least a few of the kids did not seem too enthusiastic.

Then came the Big Surprise. Herman had picked up the bat while everyone else was watching JC, Freeman, and Tony. I saw him slink around the outside of the huddle, that white club resting on his shoulder.

JC and Tony had disentangled themselves and were now dragging Freeman to the ground. He was still recovering from the choking when the two thugs landed him on his chest, evidently ready to start pounding on him.

Herman was in back of JC when he announced in a siren-like voice, "Get off of Freeman, now!"

JC and Tony ignored him and began pounding upon Freeman's head with clenched fists.

"Leave him alone!" Herman squealed.

JC kept pounding, but turned for a second to look, the same second that Herman's bat was progressing around, level with JC's head. He had no time to duck. The outer end of the bat slammed into JC's teeth with a terrible *craack*! JC slumped to the ground like a rag doll.

That choir of vultures finally clammed up, and everyone became quiet as pallbearers, staring in horror at JC. But JC wasn't out of steam yet—you could tell because he was getting up again, hands over his mouth, blood running in streams over his shoulders and down his chest and back. Even his blue jeans were turning wet and sickly red.

What he said to Herman sounded something like, "You muha huka! You muha huka!!"

His pronunciation was poor, because in addition to spitting out teeth, he was swallowing blood and crying, all at the same time. I wouldn't have thought it possible to see JC cry, yet there he was doing it.

Still, I thought, JC got what was owed him, and if anything it was long overdue.

Herman had done the only sensible thing some runt like that could do. Now he stood with his eyes wide, his mouth in an O and the bat back on his shoulder while he contemplated his handiwork, which appeared to be a good bit more than he had bargained for. The rest of the audience seemed to be in shock for once, which was one small thing to be thankful about.

Freeman spoke in a low soft voice, "I'm real sorry, JC," even though he wasn't the party who'd done the damage. He attempted to help JC up, but that bloody freak swatted Freeman's hands away like mosquitoes, still crying out, "You muha huka! You muha huka!"

JC stumbled onto his feet, his hands cupped over the ugly mess where his teeth used to be. He shook his head as if he couldn't believe what happened, then sulked off in the direction of his home. He looked as miserable and downcast as I suppose anyone ever can be with all his friends hanging around.

Tony grabbed JC's things and took off after him, but first went up to Freeman where I heard him hiss, "You're gonna pay for this! Mark my words!"

They had barely made it to the edge of earshot, when some knucklehead yelled, "Okay guys! Let's play ball!"

Freeman glared at this kid, who I turned and saw was Jason Weaver again, acting as if he had escaped from the Bellview Nuthouse. Freeman spoke, pronouncing each word with great emphasis: "Drop! Dead!"

This summarized my thinking exactly, and I hoped some of the other kids' too.

Weaver looked down and mumbled, "Jeez, can't ya take a joke?"

Freeman scooped up his T-shirt, shook out a cloud of dust and flipped it over his shoulder. He dangled his catcher's mitt from a pinky, and bounced off in his oddball walk.

Everyone moved as if on signal, scampering around the bases and gathering up equipment. They were all quiet for once, as they scattered in different directions, heads down like they might even be filled with repentant, sorry thoughts.

Halfway home, thinking about JC and not watching where I was going, I stepped in a huge dog turd. It was fresh and ripe as they come, large as three or four flashlight batteries, and reeked to high heaven. Yet I imagined it was totally appropriate, once I got past the initial squish. "Doesn't that sum up my whole life just about right?" I thought, as I dragged my smelly sneaker though the grass, trying to scrape it clean.

2

Summer was already flying by, and I didn't know one kid I could hang around with, or that I wanted to hang around with; I had a purple golf ball growing out of my forehead; JC's mom would surely be after mine in the near future, then my mom would be after me about what happened to JC, which I couldn't even imagine trying to explain; I was sunburnt as a french fry under a heat lamp; my right sneaker stunk something terrible; the afternoon air was hot and soggy; and I didn't even know the name of the girl I was madly in love with, let alone whether I'd see her again. In short, there was not much to be enthused about in my weary, dreary life.

These gloomy facts swept around my head like a hurricane, and I wanted to lie on my bed and wallow in despair. But I forced myself to grab a comic, hoping that it might ease my mind, the way comics do. I was snatching one from my desk when I happened to glance out my window.

There was Freeman, across the driveway, sitting in his bedroom window, reading a comic himself. He was scrunched up like an embryo, half inside the frame, half out. I had a brainstorm and didn't stop to think.

I grabbed a desk chair and sat by the window with my comic, identical to Freeman as I could, given that there was a screen on my window. I pretended to be reading just like he was. I reckoned that after a while he'd look over and see me and say something, and we could strike up a conversation and who knows? Maybe here was the friend I needed all along. It was obvious that Freeman had at least half a brain in his head, and I really didn't care anymore what anyone else might think about him.

Several minutes went by. He turned some pages and readjusted his rear end, shifting more weight to the inside ledge, which at least was safer. I figured he couldn't see me because of the darkness of my window screen. I would have yanked it out and trashed it, except my dad would have done the same to me if he ever found out.

So I mustered up an ounce of courage and called out, "Hey!"

He looked over, surprised, and squinted to see what was going on, his bright blue eyes beaming at me, his ears protruding on the sides.

"Whatchya reading?" I said, my heart banging like a trapped bird in my rib cage.

"*Archie*," he replied, holding it up, as if I might not believe him. "How 'bout you?"

I looked to see what was in my hand, because till then I hadn't noticed.

"*Porky Pig*!" My face got warm, since that particular comic seemed a bit juvenile for the occasion. "But I've got *Archies* here too! Tons of 'em!" I held up a stack of maybe a hundred comics. "This is one little pile. How many do you have?"

He disappeared into his room, and after a while I began to wonder if he was coming back. But then he did come back, hands locked together, arms wrapped around a bulging heap of comics two feet high. Two or three slid out the back, and another slipped out the window and fluttered to the ground, landing on the porch beneath his bedroom window, though he didn't seem to notice.

"Oh, a few!" he shouted, giving off a wide, dumb grin.

"I've been looking for someone to trade with for three years!" I hollered.

"Prob'ly we got a lot of the same ones, huh?"

"Well, maybe so," I pointed out, "and maybe no." I scrunched my face to the screen to be sure he could see me. "But I know a good way to find out!"

He gave me a wild grin, and kept grinning for a while, till I wondered if I'd made a mistake—maybe he was retarded like James after all. Then I realized he was probably having the same idea I was having, and I smiled back. Still, I was relieved when he finally spoke.

"Baseball sucks, don't it?"

"You bet your family jewels!" I blurted out. "I hate it!"

"So where do you want to meet to share these comics?"

"Your place looks good to me!" I knew my mom would find a way to ruin everything if he came to my place.

"Meet you by the door below in two minutes, Porky!" he laughed loudly, and I believed a bit unnecessarily. "Bring as many as you can!"

I stood by his back door toting an apple box of comics. I picked up the one he'd dropped, *Little Lulu*, and handed it to him as he opened the door. He looked it over like it was a long-lost treasure, then said slowly, "Wouldn't you know it? One of my favorites!"

He put it to his lips and gave a loud, smacking kiss, and once again I thought maybe I was making a big mistake. But then he smiled like I must be an idiot to think he was serious, and it was a great relief to see he was pulling my leg.

And so began our friendship, after all the years we'd been neighbors and strangers, and along with it the summer of 1959, the most interesting summer in all my fourteen years.

We soon migrated to his garage, where Matt had strung two hammocks wall to wall that Freeman said were rescued from someone's garbage only the week before. The one I used was green canvas and extra comfortable, due to a one-foot hole that had been worn through where your rear end could hang out and catch some air. Freeman's looked like an ancient fishnet, and smelled like maybe it was one. Scattered over the floor were boxes and armloads of comics, each of us claiming to have more in our rooms. We were happy as pigs rolling in cowpies, not only for doubling our comic supplies, but also for that wonderful hope of having a genuine friend to hang out with all summer long.

We loafed around like bumps on a log, reading comics hour after hour. I began to worry that my eyes might start protruding, but Freeman claimed that was ridiculous. "I've been readin' 'em all these years, and nothin' ever happened to me."

But I made him check anyway. He said they looked okay to him, though he couldn't be certain since he never saw my eyes close up before, let alone "when they was fresh and new and not used up so much.

"But there's no point worryin'," he continued, "'cause there's nothin' you can do about it anyway," and I realized he was right.

We ended up in his bedroom on the afternoon of the second day, so we could stretch out on the beds. He said his mom never came there, due to back problems when she climbed the stairs, so it didn't matter how much we messed the place up. That seemed true enough; it looked like several tornadoes had passed through since anyone had done any cleaning.

It was also a good hideout because my mom believed I was still playing baseball, and I wasn't anxious to find out if she still objected to my palling around with Freeman.

Piles of comics slowly spread around the place until the floor was hidden from view and you couldn't walk anywhere without stepping on them.

"It's like a newfangled carpet for kids, ain't it Joey?" Freeman asked, obviously pleased with the arrangement.

We talked about all kinds of things, and I found I wasn't my usual clamshell self. In fact, I discovered I didn't have time to feel pity or sorrow for Joseph Daniel Simpson anymore—I was too busy chitchatting away, and having a grand old time!

One topic was James, who I learned had been retarded since he was three. Freeman said it was the result of a plastic bag he had stuck over James' head long ago. He was just playing around and looking for a good time, the way kids do, but didn't take it off till James's face turned purple. Freeman was seven then, and of course he was sorry now, like people often are after having too much fun. He claimed he took good care of James though, and I would have believed him except that very day he locked the bedroom door so we could read comics without being disturbed. James knocked and begged to come in twice, but went away when Freeman hollered for him to leave.

"Shouldn't we at least give him a few comics?" I asked the second time, as it seemed like a decent thing to do.

"Naw. He can't read too good. Besides he'd prob'ly lose 'em or make paper airplanes or some damn thing."

But then he called James back and gave him a baseball to play with, an old beat-up thing with strings hanging off that looked like it might be the first baseball ever made. Freeman told him to take it out in the driveway and roll it around out there, and that it would be a real exciting game for him. It seemed like a heartless lie, but I bit my tongue.

We yakked about girls, and it came as no surprise that we both wanted girlfriends real bad. "Real, real bad!" Freeman proclaimed, wrapping his arms around his shoulders and stroking the back of his head. "More than anything else I can think of!"

I laughed and told him about the object of my dreams, and the fact that I could think of little else so much of the time. "It drives me crazy," I concluded, "and I don't even know her name or where she lives."

"So what's she look like?"

I described her springy golden blond hair, her rounded face and beautiful lips, her soft voice, her smile, and how her perfume had made me so insane.

"Did she have green eyes?"

"Yea, she had the most amazing dark gr … " I stared in disbelief. "How did you know?"

"That's Maggie Engles, Joey! She moved in last April. She's in my class, one aisle over and three desks back."

"No!" I couldn't believe what I was hearing.

"But you may as well forget her now. Every guy in the world is interested in her. And she flirts with 'em all. She's nothin' but a tease, Joey. A real tease."

"But this was more than teasing! She laughed and smiled at me!"

"She smiles at everyone. And she laughs a lot, too. It ain't against the law, ya know?" He looked to see if that registered, but it didn't.

"But she touched my hand, too!"

He rolled his eyes as if such things happened every day. "You said she was reachin' to take the apple—so what's the big deal if she touched your hand?"

He hesitated, like perhaps he'd hurt my feelings, which he had. "I hate to bring ya bad news, but I think ya may be chasin' a rainbow. Or maybe a wet dream."

"No! I swear this is different! You don't understand! I could just feel the love she had for me! It was the most amazing thing!"

Freeman squirmed on the bed, as if my words somehow caused discomfort. "The thing that amazes me is how many guys sound just like you do. She uses guys, Joey—she's what my mom would call a social climber. That's the way I see it, anyways."

"Well, then … I wish she'd use me! And I wish she'd hurry up about it!"

There wasn't much more I could say. He wasn't even there that day so what could he know? I didn't hold it against him though, he was just trying to help.

But I did wonder what he meant by "social climber"—it was a new one on me. All I could imagine was it had to do with some sort of gymnastics I was unfamiliar with. I was glad to think she might be athletic, but I didn't ask for fear of sounding stupid.

As for other guys? Well, Maggie was probably a friendly person. And what of it? I wouldn't want a girl who wasn't friendly!

That night I got a diversion from my thoughts about Maggie, though it was one diversion I could have done without. My mom cornered me at the dining room table as she and I were finishing dessert after everyone else had left.

"Helen Clancy came by today, Joseph," she announced between spoonfuls of fruit cocktail.

I nearly choked on a grape. Helen is JC's mom, so it did not look like I would be enjoying what was left in my bowl.

My mom soon stopped eating and rattled on about her version of the incident with JC, getting more worked up as she went; it didn't take long before she was close to hysterical. Helen had come to her in tears, she said, bemoaning how friends had turned on JC like that. How could Christian boys behave so terribly?, both she and Helen wanted to know. What could JC have possibly done to deserve such a thing? Did I know he had three teeth knocked out, and that it would cost over five hundred dollars to get them fixed?

She wailed away and I didn't have a chance to open my mouth until she was out of breath and broken down whimpering. I waited till I thought she might be able to listen.

"I had nothing to do with it," I squeaked.

She sobbed and carried on like I hadn't spoken. I had to repeat myself twice before she realized I was trying to say something.

"What did you say?" she moaned between breaths.

"I said I had nothing to do with it!" I raised my voice in hopes it might sink in.

"You didn't?" She raised her head, dabbing her eyes with a napkin.

"I didn't lay a finger on him," I explained, calmly as I could.

Her chest heaved and she looked relieved, as if her main concern was not for JC, but rather whether her own son had a hand in the deed.

"But Helen told me JC identified you as one of the culprits!"

"He's lying!" I protested.

I laid out the facts I believed she needed to hear. I mentioned Freeman hardly at all, I spoke of Herman sparingly, and I talked nonstop about Tony, implicating him as much as possible. I knew my mom was no longer as fond of JC as she had been originally, so I kept pointing an accusing finger at him too, which seemed only proper.

"It was his own fault," I kept repeating, hoping she would accept that.

I'm a miserable liar because my ears turn fire engine-red every time I try. It's a big problem too, since adults don't usually want to hear the truth. But I've gotten okay at shuffling facts around when push comes to shove, as it seemed to have done right then.

"So you see, it was Tony who was sprawled on top of him, just before someone from the crowd slugged him with the bat."

"I am so relieved to hear that you weren't involved, Joseph!"

I imagined she was as satisfied as any mother can be who has a teenage son.

"You know me, Mom. I'd never tell a lie and I'd never hurt a fly!" I shrugged my shoulders and hoped that was the end of it, then stood up to leave.

"I guess you heard what little good news there is in JC's life these days."

I stared with a blank look.

"Helen and Harold have decided to let JC get that car he's wanted so badly. Provided he gets a job. They think it will help him develop
a sense of responsibility—if he gets a privilege like that and has to
work for it. Don't you think that's a good idea, Joseph?"

I pictured JC in a car and knew right off it was a dreadful mistake.
But it also occurred to me that if he got a car, he might stay out of
the neighborhood and leave everyone in it alone. And who could say?
Perhaps he'd demolish the thing in a fatal wreck, and solve everyone's
problems.

"I think it's a great idea, Mom." I imagined JC slamming head-on
into a semi or perhaps a bridge embankment. "It just might work out
for everyone."

She smiled as if I were something to be proud of. I was gripped
by a twinge of guilt, but it passed quickly as I slipped away from the
table.

Early the next morning Freeman announced that we needed
more variety in our lives.

Whereupon he opened his closet door and marched me up a
narrow ladder to a small hole in the ceiling; then along the ceiling,
crawling on hands and knees, to a vent, which we squeezed through
out onto the roof with a handful of comics each. Sitting on the warm
shingles we had a good view in most directions.

You could see a space in the trees to the northwest where the
ball field was. Next to it was the roof of the Piney Wood School, which
Freeman went to. I imagined Maggie sitting in there, doing math, and
I wondered if she hated school like I did. Three blocks over you could
see part of JC's house, a green split-level that had been built shortly
before his family moved in. The upper third of Piney Hills could be seen
further to the west, and there was that endless sprawl of tract houses
to the east. The tops of two factories barely broke the skyline further
to the northwest. And when we slid across the ridgeline, there was my
own house, with a direct view of the screen on my own bedroom.

"When your light's on I get a real good view of you and Timmy
dancing around in your undies." Freeman grinned.

"Well, when your light's on, I get a nice view of you without your undies!" I thought of how he and his brothers often pranced around naked before going to bed. "Among other things," I added, thinking of the two times I'd seen him doing the thing guys do when he no doubt thought he was alone. He closed his eyes and grimaced, and it was one of the few times I ever saw him turn red. I imagined I was pretty red myself.

"Dadgumit!" he exclaimed, his eyes still closed.

I racked my brain for another topic to spare both of us further humiliation. I remembered what my mom had said about JC getting a car, and I told him that. "Plus he's supposed to get a job, 'to help develop a sense of responsibility,'" I mocked.

"The roads will soon be dangerous places," Freeman responded solemnly. "Very, very dangerous!"

We opened the comics finally, and I read two *Beetle Baileys* and a *Veronica* before hot shingles and a scorching sun drove us back to the bedroom.

We were not there long when a ruckus at the bedroom door disturbed us.

"Open up! What are you two weirdoes doin' in there anyway?" Matt was hollering and pounding. "I got a letter for ya, Freddie!"

Freeman unlocked the door and there stood Matt holding a long white envelope over his head, like a flag, with James standing under one arm pointing up to it.

"Feels like a ring in here. Now who could it be from, I wonder?" inquired Matt with a smirk. He began humming, "Freeman and some girl sitting in a tree … ," and James hummed along with him, off-key something terrible.

"Gimme it!" Freeman reached to yank the envelope from Matt's hand. Matt stepped back, lifting it higher.

"Why should I?"

"'Cause it's mine!"

"How do you know?"

"You said it was!"

"Let me double-check that." Matt examined the envelope above his head. "Well, I can't be positive. It says 'Screamin Freeman?' Is that your new name?"

"No, he's Freddie Freeman!" laughed James.

"Gimme it!" Freeman lunged and grabbed the letter. There was a small rip as he yanked it from Matt's hand.

"So what is it?" Matt asked while Freeman stalked back to his bed.

I glanced at the envelope and saw writing in large, uneven letters in red crayon, as if scrawled by a little kid: "Screamin Freeman."

Freeman tore the end off and three bloody teeth dropped onto the bedspread, with yellow stains on the enamel. "Jeez!" he exclaimed. "What is that nutcase sending me these for?"

"I want one! I want one!" cried James.

Freeman gave him a tooth, then pulled out a sheet of loose leaf paper with frizzy edges down one side and big messy writing in red crayon, the same as on the envelope:

We are planning to kill, you, Big Boy!
But we will cut your balls off! First.
And you will be Screamin Freddie Freeman!
Sereus!

"What a nincompoop!" I exclaimed.

"So who is she?" asked Matt.

"It ain't a she," Freeman replied. "It's that dumb-ass JC."

"Or Tony," I noted. "That numbskull used to go to St. Frances till he got kicked out for mouthing off to the nuns. I wouldn't be surprised if he sent it, or put JC up to it."

"You may be right. We're stuck with him at my school now. He's a year ahead of me."

We showed Matt the letter, and he examined the teeth carefully.

"Could be dog teeth. So what's he sending them to you for?"

We relayed the story of Herman and JC and the bat, which Matt absorbed with great interest, particularly since Herman was a friend of his. His only friend, so far as I knew, the two being brought together by their interest in tree forts, go-carts, junk collecting, and other odd things.

"Well, you don't have to worry about the last part of this, Freddie," Matt assured him in a confident tone when we got done.

We looked to Matt for clarification, and I prepared myself to hear words of wisdom that I imagined would be motivated by Matt's desire to assist his own brother who had so recently saved his good friend from destruction.

"You don't have any balls!"

Matt and I laughed and rolled on the beds and slapped our thighs, and James did likewise when he saw us do it. But Freeman didn't seem to appreciate the humor in it.

"You buttheads!"

"Jeez, Freddie," Matt managed to say between laughs. "You don't really think he's going to kill you, do ya?"

"I wouldn't put it past him. That guy might do anything," Freeman responded.

"Freddie could be partly right," I added, regretting that I couldn't stop laughing long enough to finish my thoughts. "I don't think he'd kill anyone, but he might try something stupid. JC's got brain damage or something, if you ask me."

I nearly laughed again, then I remembered James right there next to me, and I was embarrassed as all get out. "I mean, you know. His head's cracked or something. There's no telling what he'll do. It was a sorry sight, what happened to JC's teeth."

"I got brain damage too!" spouted James, like it was something to be proud of. I cringed and wanted to slide under the bed.

Matt suggested several worst-case ways that JC might try to kill Freeman, ranging from running him over to drowning and stoning and tying him to the railroad tracks.

Freeman just laid back and sulked and refused to contribute to the conversation.

"I don't really think any of those things will happen," I said when Matt got done, as much to make Freeman feel better as because I really believed it.

"Yea, I wouldn't worry too much, either," Matt agreed, evidently realizing how disturbed he was making Freeman, and trying now to cheer him up.

"That's because the letter ain't addressed to you guys!" Freeman retorted.

"Good point," Matt replied solemnly while he winked at me, like it was all a big joke. "But the main thing I want to know is: Can I have all your comics and your arrowheads, if you do get killed?"

"I want some too! I want some too!" sang out James, flapping his hands in excitement.

Freeman looked Matt over and ignored James, trying to control himself. "Sure you can have my comics. And all my arrowheads too." He shrugged his shoulders as if to say, "Why not? You're a good sport and you deserve it." Then he glared and said, "You can have my fist too, if ya want!"

He proceeded with a big sweep of his arm that ended in a sharp blow to Matt's stomach. Matt made a whooshing sound, as he folded up on the bed, arms over his stomach.

"You're a piece of shit, Matt!"

"Criminy! I was just pullin' your leg!" he gasped.

"Yea, Freddie! He was just jokin'!" added James.

There was a long silence while that sank in, and another long silence while we waited for Freeman to respond.

"You mean you'll actually help me if JC tries to do somethin'?"

"If you don't kill me first, sure! You're my own damn brother, re-member?"

"All right then. I'm sorry."

"It's okay. I think I'll live. Just don't do that again! And I don't think you need someone to defend you anyway with a punch like that."

It occurred to us on the afternoon of the next day that we were bored stiff with comics and talking about JC, not to mention lying around on our backs.

"We need to do something more physical and not so scholarly," announced Freeman as he stood up and bent to touch his toes. "Look at that! I can't hardly reach 'em no more!"

His fingers had stopped several inches short.

"I don't think adults understand how hard it is to be a kid these days." I twisted to stretch my own sore back. "They just can't imagine."

"That's the truest thing I ever heard," Freeman replied as he fluffed up his pillow and lay back down.

We stared at the ceiling and the cobwebs around the light fixture, scratching our brains for something better to do, but nothing came to mind. I started to wonder if I'd end up bored as before, the only difference being Freeman was there getting bored with me.

I was fretting over that and clogging my head with related miserable ideas, when Freeman piped up, "Why don't we make a trip to the ponds and get a little change of scenery, Joey? Not to mention a little fresh air?"

"Why, hell yes! That is a good one!" I exclaimed, sorry I hadn't thought of it myself.

The ponds he referred to are actually a series of five ponds, all connected by small streams, and fed by water from underground springs in the Piney Hills Development. The Piney Hills Development consists of several rolling hills forested in pine trees. Winding narrow roads go through the place, leading to fancy houses owned by doctors and big business types who work in New York. Railroad tracks mark the western boundary. Past the tracks to the west and north, grassy, weedy hills surround the ponds along with small groves of trees and shrubs. It's a good place for rabbits, birds, squirrels, skunks, and an occasional raccoon. And you can find tracks of foxes if you look close enough.

A billboard once claimed the ponds area was "50 plus acres," at a time when there was talk about putting in a shopping mall. But the idea never caught on, so there's still a place for kids to get away and act like kids now and then and not worry about adults. I hadn't gone for a while though, since I no longer cared to go with Timmy, whose interests seemed stranger and stranger the older I got. I admit it was odd, because we used to go there all the time and have lots of fun together. But he seemed more and more like a dumb little kid in the last year or two, and I no longer liked hanging out with him. I went by myself for a while, but that grew old and I simply stopped going. So I was excited in an instant at Freeman's suggestion.

Freeman led me to a huge Bible on his mom's desk before we set out. We put our hands on it and swore we'd never play baseball again.

It was a vow I intended to keep till the day I died, and longer if they play the game up there in heaven.

"I don't know why we didn't think of this sooner," he said with a broad smile.

"It's for boneheads and losers," I declared. "If I never see another baseball, I'll be happy as a clam in the ocean!"

"I thought ya was a clam in the ocean," he goofed, brushing the top of my baseball hat. "What with that pointy head of yours!"

We headed out with small army packs containing peanut butter sandwiches, half a pack of Oreos, canteens, extra shirts, and two slingshots, one of which I borrowed from Timmy, though I neglected to tell him about it. We followed the footpath behind Factory Alley, which skirts the northwest end of Piney Hills. From there we cut to the junkyard trail.

The junkyard is a weedy, sandy tract, dotted with trees and bushes, hidden from Cold Water Road by a wide, low sand hill, with an old broken-down snow fence on top. The trail there zigzags around ancient cars and trucks and two old school buses, all of them rusted with cracked or missing windshields and flat tires or bare rims. I told Freeman how Timmy and I used to collect things here, such as antennas and goods from under car seats. We'd found ballpoint pens, combs, maps, and coins, usually small change, though last fall Timmy found a wallet with a ten-dollar bill that I tried to talk him into splitting.

"Brothers really ought to share things," I had told him.

"Oh yea? What have you shared with me lately?" he asked. All I could think of was "brotherly love," so of course I didn't get a dime.

Freeman claimed that this was one of Matt's main junk supply areas too, and that Matt knew every square inch of the place. We stopped to rest in the weeds behind an abandoned pickup truck bed. We propped our heads on our packs and set our feet on a log that sprouted orange toadstools and patches of emerald green moss. Billowy white clouds floated above in a thousand different shapes, like creatures from another planet. The weather had finally cooled and my temperament was turned around too; it was the happiest and most cheerful I could remember being in a long, long time.

We watched clouds and took in the freshness and beauty of the place, me thinking how smart Mother Nature is to invent such peaceful settings, and how much happier it made me than sitting in a classroom with some wild nun screaming up and down the aisles.

"So you think he's really gonna cut 'em off?" Freeman broke the silence after a while.

"Of course not," I responded bravely, twisting my foot on one of the orange toadstools, the way I wanted to mush JC. "I wouldn't worry about it anyway. JC's so stupid he'll probably forget he even wrote the note in another week. You just wait and see."

We discussed Matt and why he still made go-karts and wreckers and other contraptions that seemed like a waste of time, particularly when he should have been trying to get a real car, like normal kids his age.

"He wants to be a famous inventor," Freeman explained. "Like Thomas Edison or Alexander Bell. He says any old fool could have invented the Hula-Hoop and someday he's gonna make somethin' even better."

"I could have invented the Hula-Hoop," I replied. "I just didn't think of it for some dang reason." I readjusted my backpack under my head, thankful I had two shirts in it for padding.

"Now he says he's workin' on something better and more important than a Hula-Hoop."

"Yea? Like what?"

"Some kind of underwater dealie. He says it's like a submarine, only better because it won't need any motor to move itself."

"How can anything move without a motor? That sounds ridiculous to me."

"Everything he does sounds ridiculous. Though I gotta admit every now and then he comes up with a good idea." Freeman wiggled about as if to avoid some hard object under his back, then pulled his hat over his eyes and kept on talking. "He's been working on this one for a long time. Never lets anyone see it, either."

"Sounds like baloney to me," I said.

As for the no underwear situation, Freeman admitted that he always tried to get to the wash first, which left Matt without, though sometimes it was Freeman who went without.

James was smaller and had his own undies. All that made me feel better about Matt, though it still seemed he might have a gear stuck, or at least a lubrication problem of some kind.

Freeman rambled on, and by and by he contradicted what he'd told me before by admitting what I already thought, which was that Matt was the one who actually took care of James. "It's not that I mind takin' care of him so much," he said almost as if apologizing. "It's just that most of the time those two hang out together and keep each other company. So it's easier for Matt to take care of him. And for me to let him, if you know what I mean."

The clouds continued sailing by while various insects buzzed or flapped or somersaulted past our heads. The bed of the pickup blocked the breeze, creating a calm sheltered perch. I could have laid there for days enjoying the scenery, ever so pleased I had someone to do it with, and especially someone I could talk to so easily. The subject of how to spend the rest of our summer soon came up.

"Whatever we do, we need to stay out of sight of all those idiots," I noted. "Especially JC, whether he meant what he wrote or not."

"So why don't we build a fort way back in the woods, where no one can find it and no one in the world will even know about it except you and me?" Freeman suggested.

"Aw, you don't know how many of those things I built," I said to discourage him right off. I had had enough experience with building forts to know better. "Every fort I ever built—and I built quite a few of them—got wrecked by some jerk like JC or that weasel Tony. Though you never do know for sure who wrecked it.

"And if it's not that, then there's always some other problem and you can't use the confounded things anyway. One I built with Timmy two years ago leaked like a screen door and we got soaked to the bones in a thunderstorm. And the whole reason we built it was for protection from things like that."

Freeman closed his eyes as if to mull that over. Several minutes went by and he just lay there breathing till I thought maybe he'd fallen asleep. I was all set to reach over and poke his ear with a twig when he opened his mouth and exclaimed, "I know 'bout that crap, Joey. I built a couple of 'em too. But I'm thinkin' about a serious fort no one will ever find! Make it deep in the Westwoods, out past the fields, in the densest, most secretest place we can find. Make a beauty with real lumber instead of branches and mud and all that natural crap that falls on your head." He yanked a fresh weed to chew on and it flopped in front of his face as he talked.

"Build it partway in the ground and cover the roof with tar paper. Then put dirt on top and grow grass in the dirt so no one'll ever find it, not even Russian spy planes! And don't take no one to it!" He chewed his weed faster, rose up on his elbow, and spoke with excitement. "Just you and me, and a couple of girls, Joey!"

He slapped the ground for emphasis, blowing bits of leaves and dust in the air, and he spit the weed out, so excited was he. But then he lay back as if another idea suddenly canceled his enthusiasm. "If, of course, we can ever find any, and if, of course, they actually talk to us."

I considered the scene he described and it sounded better than any fort I had ever made. But what won me over was the idea of taking girls to it. I imagined me and Maggie sneaking in some dark night, me holding her hand and leading her through the spooky woods, with a sliver of moon in the background, along some secret trail I'd know from memory; I saw her clinging to me for safety and comfort, admiring the starry sky as I pointed out the few constellations I knew from Boy Scouts, then marveling at our fort, and the fact that I built it for her. And later, me holding her in the flickery light of candles, kissing and smooching and breathing her perfume! And who could say what else?

"But we can't afford real lumber," I suddenly realized.

"No sweat. You know them houses they're buildin' over at Stoneridge?"

I nodded recalling the new development about a mile away near the railroad tracks.

I hated new developments and this one was no exception. My dad said it was a good thing, because more people would be better for businesses and increase the tax base. I had no idea what the tax base was and couldn't have cared less. All I knew was that more woods and a marsh were disappearing, and at the rate things were going, there would be absolutely no place for kids to hang out in a few more years.

"Well, they got tons of lumber at that joint," Freeman exclaimed. "I mean all we'll ever need!"

"What are they doing, giving it away or something?" As much as I hated all new developments, I had no interest in stealing lumber from one of them, although I wasn't quite sure what Freeman had in mind.

"Sure they're givin' it away!" he replied.

"What do you mean, they're giving it away?"

"I mean they're givin' it to anyone who wants it—like you and me, good buddy!

You just need to go at the right time." He stuck another weed in his mouth, aimed toward me as if to make a point.

"And when might that be?"

"At night, after the workers leave."

"You mean steal it?" I couldn't believe he was really suggesting such a thing, and I was mighty glad my mom wasn't there to hear it.

"No, not steal it, for cryin' out loud! No one talks like that in this day and age."

"What should I call it then?" I was beginning to get upset and I made sure the tone of my voice let him know it.

"Just let 'em give it to us late at night, Joey! When no one's around and they don't care so much. That's when they like to give things to kids like us. See what I mean?" He fixed me hard in his gaze as if that might help me see his point.

"Not really. In fact, not at all."

"Well, it don't matter." He laid back and set his head on his pack. "You don't need to understand it all." He spoke as if there was nothing more he could do to help me, like I was basically stupid if I didn't get what he meant. Yet it seemed all too clear what he meant. I hoped maybe he was pulling my leg again, but it sure didn't sound like it.

I had no desire to come off like a wimpy Catholic school kid, explaining how it was for someone like me, hearing about the consequences of sin, such as stealing, day after day till it drives you crazy. And I did not want him to think I was some kind of religious freak trying to discuss nutty stuff that didn't mean diddly to him.

"What if the cops caught us? We'd be hauled off and thrown into jail!" I tried to speak in terms he could grasp, and I raised my arms to help make the point.

"They can't do that! We're too young! But even if we did get caught, I could take the blame and say you was just watchin'. My parents wouldn't do nothin'. Maybe ground me for a week, but who cares? Besides, who's gonna catch us if we go after dark? That's the main thing."

I had never considered that a kid might not get the pulp beat out of him for stealing.

And I didn't know you could be too young to get thrown in jail. Freeman was smarter than I realized, or else here was a big bag of hot air in human skin sitting right beside me.

"How do we get out after dark?"

"Just sneak out. I do it all the time." He spoke as if explaining what he ate for breakfast, with a silly fresh weed jangling like a fishing pole.

I imagined our new fort, with a grassy roof, half sunk in the ground, no twigs or insects dropping from the ceiling, a twisty, private trail being the only way to it. Yet I panicked at the idea of my soul getting aimed in the wrong direction as a result of stealing a few lousy boards. What if I died before confession? Then I'd never think it was worth it. I'd be bitter and mad at myself, with all eternity to think about it when it was way too late and way too hot to make a difference.

But those thoughts were overshadowed by visions of Maggie and me in the candlelight, me looking into her eyes and getting lost in her perfume, making out all night long. The result was a throbbing in my pants, which began to cause discomfort. Freeman must have sensed my uneasiness, even if he didn't know the cause of it.

"Want a cigarette?" he asked as though a cigarette was just what I needed to get a grip on myself.

But I was no more comfortable with the new topic than the old one, never having smoked before. All my life I had heard terrible things about smoking, mainly from my parents and the nuns, though I was not anxious to bring those points up with Freeman as the audience. I'd always wondered when would be the first time someone would offer me a cigarette, and I always wondered what I'd say. This moment came sooner than I expected, and I was not well prepared.

"You got some?"

"I do." Freeman reached into the pocket of his flannel shirt and produced a small package, which he folded in his hands on his chest.

"What kind?"

"Camels."

"Where'd you get 'em?"

"My dad's dresser."

"How many you got?"

He casually held up the package in one hand. "A pack."

"Is it open yet?"

He tore off the stringy red part and let it sail away in the breeze. "Yep."

"I … uh … I don't smoke." I put my head back on my hands and gazed at the clouds.

"Why not?" he asked matter-of-factly, as if this were one of the most unusual things he'd ever heard.

"I, um … I like to run."

He put the pack on his chest, the way a cat sets a mouse in front of itself, and placed his hands behind his head. I imagined he was wondering what kind of a mamma's boy I was, and I was starting to wonder the same thing myself.

"So?"

"So? So … " I stammered, "So … " I didn't know what to say; it was thoroughly humiliating. "So I don't want to mess up my lungs," I blurted out. "I like to run a lot."

"It won't mess 'em up to smoke just a little. Besides, you'll see a whole lot more if you walk slow and don't run all the time."

How long can you argue one tiny point with a brand-new friend? How much can you argue any point and still have friends? He had a case, too. I knew a few kids who smoked all the time and still ran like jackrabbits. JC was one of them, and there were two others who were in my class.

"I'm just not in the mood right now."

"You never smoked before, huh?" he correctly observed, not rude or pointing a finger, not even looking at me, but with a tone of voice that said it might do me some good and I ought to give it a try.

"Not lately," I mumbled, still staring into space. I couldn't bear to look at him, and I couldn't bring myself to say no. I felt extremely embarrassed, though I'm not sure why; I told myself I didn't care what Freeman thought, but deep down I suppose I must have cared at least a little. Otherwise why would I feel so embarrassed?

He knocked a cigarette out like they do on TV, one popping up at a time. He pinched it in his lips, then fished around in his pocket and produced a silver lighter. The lighter made a scratchy sound and a noisy flame that sputtered in the wind. He inhaled and held the smoke, then shot it out through his nostrils, as if they were two small smokestacks. The smoke streamed away and he looked satisfied and content.

Then he tapped the pack, making another one stick up—a genuine, devilish temptation if ever there was one! He held it toward me without saying a word, and the bump on the camel pointed in my direction.

"All right," I gave in, "let me have just one. Just one though, okay?" I was pretty certain I would never get addicted if I had just one.

"Sure."

I reached over and slid the protruding cigarette from the pack. I put it nervously between my lips, trying hard to appear calm and collected while Freeman struck the lighter and cupped his hands to block the small breeze.

"Ya gotta suck a little."

I inhaled lightly into my mouth, which I'd heard somewhere was a safe way to do it if you're going to do it at all. I figured it was more like holding a cigarette in my mouth than actually smoking. Especially compared to Freeman who was wheezing away like a coal chimney. He pulled in the smoke and held it, then shot it dragon-like in pale blue clouds, and I could see he was enjoying the activity far more than I was. Eventually I sucked a few mouthfuls, one after the other, so it would look like I was doing something, though I wasn't sure Freeman was even watching. But the smoke refused to go out through my nose no matter what I did.

"You gotta pull it into your lungs first," he said as if reading my mind. Then he gave a demonstration, a slow-motion exaggeration of what he'd been doing all along.

"See? Breathe deep as you can."

I pinched the thing tight and took a humongous breath, intending to blast the smoke out my nostrils. Instead, I coughed and wheezed and nearly choked my guts out! I flailed on the ground and kicked and cursed between coughs, and it was all I could do to stay alive for the next five minutes.

"Goddamn!" Freeman said, laughing and having a grand old time, big tears welling in his eyes. "That was quite a show!"

I soon recovered and got back to almost normal, and Freeman admitted it takes time to get as good at smoking as he was. But he added that I wasn't bad for a beginner, which made me feel a little better.

We cloud watched a while longer, jabbering about whatever popped into our heads, and lost all track of time. We never did get to the ponds that day, nor did we use the slingshots as the hour got late, and I had agreed to take care of the twins that afternoon while my mom was off doing something.

3

"I never got too good with a slingshot," Freeman told me, when his rock sailed about fifteen feet over the three brown beer bottles and vanished in the weeds. "Mainly 'cause I never had one."

"It takes a lot of practice. Probably like smoking," I explained. "You can use that one all you want though, 'cause it's mine. But I have to return this one tonight, before Timmy figures out it's missing."

We stood by one of the small ponds, shooting at bottles we'd found along the way and placed on a log for targets. Freeman's idea was to get good enough to use the slingshot for protection against JC, though I had doubts about how practical that was. For one thing, it seemed unlikely that a slingshot would slow JC down much if he were serious, especially if he had his buddies with him. Plus I imagined it would take Freeman another couple of years to be able to hit a beach ball right in front of his nose, bad as he was.

But I held my tongue and tried to encourage him since he seemed content, and at least he wasn't moping around worrying.

"You need to aim a bit lower," I advised him. "And don't hold back so long. That makes it wobbly."

"You mean like this?" He pulled the pouch loaded with a rock about the size of two marbles toward him .

"Be careful now, you're angled to the side a bit too much," I tried to warn him.

"Oh, son-of-a-bitch!" he moaned as the rock ricocheted off the handle, flew back and whacked him in the forehead.

He sat down and rubbed the sore spot for a while. "Seems like everyone's gettin' hit in the noggin these days," he groaned.

"That's what happens if you don't hold it straight." I felt my own bump and was pleased to see it was nearly gone. "You have to keep the elastics even. After a while you do it automatically."

"Seems like I gotta do a hundred things at once! Pull back just so far, keep the thingies even, watch the target, aim lower, don't shake, have a good rock. Hell, how am I gonna do all that if JC is chasin' after me and I'm crappin' in my pants at the same time?"

"It won't be easy. But that's exactly why you need more practice."

He got up begrudgingly and went at it a while longer. With a bit more practice he got so the rock went in the general direction of the bottles, and at least I felt more comfortable standing behind him. Then after a time it got so the rocks only missed by ten feet or so. I kept running around looking for ammunition to keep him in business, and it was beginning to wear me out.

"Let's get a big pile together and set them here. Then when they're gone you can stop for the day."

We did that, and I had to admit he got better, missing regularly by only two or three feet, though he never did hit a bottle. When he got done, I took five shots and smashed all three bottles.

"You're one little hot shit, ain't ya?"

"All it takes is a couple years of practice." I didn't mean to boast, but that was the truth.

"Maybe I'll just keep you around and I won't need to worry about JC no more."

"I'll be around. But you still need to learn to defend yourself. Just like I'd have to if he ever came after me." I felt very confident giving advice like that, and it was clear that Freeman needed not to depend on me completely.

We lay on the side of a hill overlooking the pond. Two mallards flew in and paddled around, sending ripples across the calm brown surface. We watched them while we discussed all manner of things, and somehow got to the topic of religion. I explained that my mom was not keen on the idea of me hanging out with non-Catholics, which was why I hadn't tried to make friends before. "Plus she gets really worked up when people don't go to church. I know she's nuts, but she says anyone who doesn't go must be a heathen."

"But we do go. On Christmas and Easter, and a few other times. My mom likes to go, but my dad's a security guard so he has to work weekends. And she won't go without him."

I was pleased to hear this. It would be good ammunition when my mom tried to discourage me from hanging out with Freeman again, as I was sure she would.

"But I hate the place," he added. "That guy up there hollerin' about hell and damnation, and how we need to think about others all the time. Plus the money they're always cryin' about. I'd rather be sleepin,' or readin' comics. Or takin' a good dump for that matter."

"I hate going to Saint Frances," I told him. "Those nuns are mean as slave drivers with hemorrhoids. They'll whack your knuckles with a yardstick if you just have the wrong book out. Which I often do, because of all the important things on my mind."

"Like Maggie?"

"Well, that's the main one," I confessed.

He smiled and shook his head. "Sounds a whole lot more important to me."

"Plus there's no end to religion, day in and day out. It makes you feel terrible about being alive. Everything in the world turns out to be sinful, especially if it's any fun."

"That's just about what the minister says too."

"It's like we're all going to hell or purgatory just for being born, according to the nuns. Except for a few people who can squeeze through the eye of a needle, which is how you get into heaven."

"You'd have to be awfully damn small."

"That's what I always thought."

I explained how hard it was to listen to the nuns rant and rave about sin and judgment day and purity and Satan and related topics, all day every day, it seemed like.

"I always wondered what you guys did in that joint."

"Then there's the time Sister Monica told us the world was going to end on February twenty-fifth, in a nuclear war, if we didn't say enough rosaries. She told us right before Thanksgiving and I got so depressed I could hardly eat my turkey. We prayed our rear ends off, four rosaries a day for three months. Plus on weekends, for kids like me who listened to her. Ruined my Christmas, too."

"Ain't a rosary one of them things that looks like a necklace?"

"A little bit."

"When I get me a car you gotta get me one, so I can hang it on the mirror."

I nodded, wondering what Sister Monica would think if she could hear this conversation. Then again, I didn't really care.

"So did all them rosaries get you out of math and stuff?"

"I wish. But she always found time for that junk too. On top of which we had to practice hiding under our desks twice a day, in case there was a nuclear war. It made no sense if the whole confounded building was going to melt like butter, the way she said it would."

"We do air-raid drills in Piney Wood, too. Twice a year. I don't mind though, 'cause you can see the girls' behinds across the aisle, and sometimes even their panties."

I thought of Maggie and all the guys gawking at her, and I wished I knew judo so I could beat the hell out of them, though I'd probably spare Freeman because I liked him. I was picturing all this when Freeman added, "Well, if there really is a nuclear war, you can kiss your own ass goodbye!"

He put his head between his legs and attempted to demonstrate, making me laugh so hard I nearly wet my pants.

"That place sounds crazy, Joey," he said after I recovered. "And that Monica must be a nutcase."

"True, but at least we got the war put off."

"Aw hogwash! That's a pile o' pig poop, Joey. There never was going to be one in the first place."

I wanted to ask how he could be so sure, but the certainty in his voice made me afraid to. I suddenly wondered if Sister Monica could have made that story up, just to get us to say all those rosaries. I didn't like what the nuns told us, but I had never seriously doubted them before. I lapsed into worried thought.

"So ya believe all that crap they teach ya, huh?" he asked after an uncomfortable pause.

I fidgeted and cleared my throat. I'd never thought of it as crap before. My stomach tightened and I felt defensive.

"It can't all be crap. Why would they lie to little kids?"

I looked to him for an answer, but all he did was shrug his shoulders. My stomach knotted tighter and I got gas pains too.

"And why would my mom make my dad fork over all that money to send me and Timmy there?"

Freeman just rolled his eyes and shook his head. I didn't really want to consider these things any further, but I had to ask one last question.

"There must be some truth to it, don't you think?"

"I'm just glad I wasn't born Catholic," was all he said as he tossed a rock aimlessly into the pond.

I had often wished I were Protestant, especially on Sundays so I wouldn't have to ruin the day with Mass. And Fridays so I could eat a lousy hot dog. But I wasn't about to tell Freeman that.

"Well, anyway," I explained, "the nuns said it's the truest religion out there. It goes back to when Christ turned the show over to Peter, who passed it along to the popes, who still have a hook-up to God somehow. We studied all about it. So I oughta know what I'm talking about. It's like a big family tree or something with God at the top, though I admit it's a little tricky to explain. You can't do much better than that."

He said nothing, just tossed another rock far out, like he didn't seem convinced. I watched as the ripples fanned out in widening circles.

"Mainly I guess I'd hate to be wrong and end up in hell," I pointed out. "On top of which I have to do what my parents say, and that's that."

Sunday came along and was a wasted day as usual with Mass and brunch in the morning and then reading the Sunday comics and loafing around in the afternoon. Timmy conned me into playing twenty-one and I made fifteen cents off him, but it was hardly worth all the time it took. "I really like playing with you, Joey," he said. "I wish you'd play with me more often." Then Patrick and Mary pestered me until I read a few stories from Grimm's Fairy Tales to shut them up. Thus the afternoon slipped by and disappeared like it usually does. One day I'm going to sit down and put my mind on it and figure out where the time goes, and I'm going to start with Sunday afternoons.

Monday I had to babysit while my mom visited my aunt, who was at the hospital having another baby. I took Patrick and Mary for a long walk downtown, while Timmy went off with Ryan. Of course I kept my eye out for JC, but I never saw a sign of him and don't know what I would have done if I did see him. We got home and played with blocks and Lincoln Logs, then Monopoly for an hour or so. But I quit when Mary got Boardwalk and Park Place and had no idea what she was doing. It occurred to me that I'd need to babysit for a few million years to buy real places like that. But then again, why would anyone ever want to buy such things?

Thus a couple of days went by before Freeman and I got back together. I found him playing solitaire at his kitchen table.

"Who's winning?"

"Not my sorry little butt. I can't even win when I cheat myself, with this confounded game. But take a look at this!"

He waved a two-dollar bill at me. He said he found it in his watch pocket while he was trying to find some matches. "I forgot all about this thing. My dad gave it to me when I turned fifteen last March."

"You ought to save it. It may be worth real money someday."

"It's worth real money today! Two dollars to be exact."

He flapped it in the air like wings of a bird, then suggested we buy a few new comics at Callaghan's Stationery Store, and of course I didn't resist.

When we got there a large red convertible was parked by the curb, freshly waxed and shining in the sun. It had clean white seats, whitewall tires, and a large pair of dice hanging from the mirror.

Freeman's eyes fell upon it. "Nice, nice car, Joey! That's the kind girls like, the kind we oughta have someday!"

He slapped the hood with his hat, as if to polish it more, then neither of us gave it a second thought. We walked to the large comic rack near the front window, and began inspecting the latest ones, *Prince Valiants* and *Veronicas*, mostly. We were so wrapped up in flipping pages that neither of us paid much attention when footsteps approached from the rear of the store.

But the footsteps stopped and a familiar voice interrupted our reading. "You still got 'em, huh?"

We looked up and there was JC not three feet away, with Tony Angeli, Hank Powers, and Billy Ferguson standing around him. They all wore leather jackets and white T-shirts. JC and Billy had sunglasses on, and Tony had a pair pushed above his head, his black hair oily and slicked back. We stared and said nothing while a wave of panic swept over me. I glanced to see if the clerk was watching, in case we needed him, but he was busy on the phone behind the counter with his back toward us.

"Your balls, I mean! You still got 'em, huh?" JC put his face in front of Freeman's. The area around his mouth was brown and yellow and a bit swollen, and he wasn't talking too well, though he sounded better than the last time I heard him. I figured he must have gotten the temporary teeth my mother said he'd be wearing for a while.

"Yea, I still got 'em," Freeman retorted boldly, a bit too boldly, I thought. "You got yours?"

The four hoodlums broke up laughing, like this was the funniest thing they ever heard. I felt a small relief that they thought this was actually funny. But it didn't last long.

"Yea, he's got his!" Tony inched up and stood taller. "And he's gonna keep his too! Unlike a couple of other guys around here!"

JC moved closer still, pushing his chest against Freeman's, though Freeman didn't budge. I wanted to scream for help, but nothing had really happened to scream about.

"Maybe I'll keep mine too," Freeman boasted, amazing me that he had the guts to say anything. I was cowering like a rabbit in my own skin and couldn't have uttered a word if I wanted to. I thought of stories I'd heard about JC and Tony carrying switchblades, and I envisioned them being pulled out right about now.

I imagine my eyes were bugging from their sockets too, because Tony suddenly wheeled and stepped in front of me. "Look at this little shit! He's scared out of his mind! Hey, are you a homo too?"

My throat went dry, my heart pounded fast, my armpits broke into a sweat; I imagined my hair standing up like it does in cartoons. But worst of all I suddenly had tremendous gas pains. I tried my best to control them through various contractions and movements of my stomach. But Tony's glare did me in. I let out a tremendous SBD, thanking God that it was so silent.

"You leave him alone or I'll kick your ass, Tony." Freeman seemed to grow bolder at the prospect of protecting me, which both pleased and worried me as the last of my gas passed out.

"Ooooh! Mr. Big Talk here," Tony turned back to Freeman and inched a little closer. "All you need is a baseball bat to feel tough. But I notice you don't have one now!"

Out of the corner of my eye I noticed JC looking me over, and I wondered for a second if maybe there was some remnant of feeling from our old friendship. But even if there was, I couldn't imagine it would change anything now—not after all the trouble he'd been in over the past few years, and certainly not with his friends standing there eager for action at our expense. On top of which I couldn't actually see his eyes behind his sunglasses. Perhaps he was merely trying to figure out who cut the cheese—right about then it was starting to take over something terrible. I thought I saw his nostrils wiggle, but I couldn't be sure.

"Let's leave these pussies for today," he said abruptly. "You know the plans we got for 'em, and we got places to go right now."

"Right," agreed Ferguson, who had said nothing till now. He stepped back two steps as he spoke, and so did Powers, who had also done nothing but watch and smile like an imbecile.

"All right," said Tony, sounding disappointed, but backing up a bit too. "But we will see you girls later! And I suggest you enjoy those while you can!" He pointed to Freeman's crotch and made a nasty smirk.

The four freaks strutted out, JC leading the pack. I was surprised when the clerk waved to them, but I was even more surprised when they piled into the red convertible in front of the store with JC in the driver's seat! The engine roared, the car jumped into reverse, and then lurched forward with tires squealing. Powers' hand shot up and flipped us off, while clouds of blue smoke puffed from the rear wheels.

"Jesus, he got that thing quick!" said Freeman.

The clerk, who was now off the phone, overheard us. "He gets whatever the hell he wants. Didn't you guys know that?"

"You know him?" Freeman asked, surprised as I was.

"He comes in here all the time; to buy cigarettes and look at girlie magazines mostly. And I gotta listen to the little twerp."

"So how did he get the car?" I asked, surprised I was able to talk again, and equally surprised at what I was hearing.

"Like I said. That kid gets whatever the hell he wants. He's spoiled rotten as far as I can tell. I heard him say his parents thought it would make him more responsible—and he was laughing when he said it." He mopped the counter with a dishrag as he spoke. "And I gather some kids bashed his teeth in so his folks felt sorry and were bigger idiots than usual."

He shook his head, like it was all a huge mistake. "At least he's got a job lined up.

That's a start." He rinsed the rag in a sink behind the counter.

It was incredible, yet there it was! JC with a car on the road, a menace to the world, one of his buddies already flipping us off. And talking of plans that appeared to involve the removal of my family jewels, along with Freeman's! My crotch tingled as the thought ran through my head.

"So did you hear how he got his license?" Freeman asked.

"Near as I can tell, he got a junior license a while back. Which means he can drive in the daytime if he stays in Nassau County." The clerk filled the coffee machine as he spoke.

"You say he's got a job lined up?" Freeman pressed for more information.

"In a concession down at Jones Beach. Can't imagine why the hell they'd hire a kid like that, but I guess they did. Four days a week. Which leaves three too many for himself. How do you kids know him anyway?"

Freeman filled in a few details, leaving out those of the last ball game. We learned that the clerk's name was Daniel Callaghan. He owned this store along with several others in nearby towns by the same name. He wore a gold ring and a gold necklace that went down into his shirt and I imagined had a cross on it, and he had one gold tooth, giving the appearance that he did all right with his businesses.

He was pleasant to us, but he didn't seem at all thrilled about having JC in his store so often.

"So what are ya gonna do? The kid needs help, and his parents don't have a clue. Maybe between the job and the car he'll come to his senses and stop being angry at the world."

I wanted to talk and talk about JC, but I wasn't sure what topics would be proper to discuss given that we hardly knew this guy, so I said nothing.

Walking home, Freeman heaped no end of praise upon my performance in front of JC. "It was the most perfectly timed gas ever to blow my way, Joey!" He slapped my back and carried on as if I'd saved his life. "Why, for all they knew, it could've been JC who did it! I even thought it was him, till I saw the way he looked at ya! Havin' you for a friend is better than carryin' a skunk around!"

"Thanks," I replied, since I couldn't think of what else to say. "But you know, the problem's hardly over. And to tell you the truth, I'm beginning to get worried now, Freddie. What the hell's JC talking about, a plan for both of us?"

"Well, we know the main plan, don't we?" He put one hand to his crotch. "So it's not real hard to figure he's plannin' the same for you."

"But why me now? It doesn't make sense!"

"I guess he decided he likes you too." Freeman grinned, obviously pleased with the increase in my concern.

"That's ridiculous! I didn't do a thing!"

"So what did I do?" Freeman asked. "Herman's the one who nailed him!"

"This whole thing's a pile of crap, Freddie! That guy doesn't deserve to live!"

I was angry at the unfairness of it and disturbed at being threatened when I was just an innocent bystander. I hoped JC would crash his car that very day.

"Well, I'm glad you're taking this thing a bit more serious, now. I don't feel so all alone anymore."

"Okay, I'm sorry I didn't see it before, but now I do! We gotta put our heads together and figure a plan of our own."

It didn't take long to conclude we had to build the fort as quickly as possible. Neither one of us had any desire to see JC or Tony again, and we deeply feared they'd seriously damage us one way or another, even if not exactly as the note described. We'd build the fort, therefore, and pretty much live in it for the rest of the summer, avoiding JC at all costs, going home only to eat and sleep and let our parents know we were still alive.

"And buy comics and scout for girls now and then," Freeman reminded me.

My biggest worry soon had to do with the lumber. Freeman could call it whatever he wanted, but to me it was stealing, a violation of the Seventh Commandment, a mortal sin. And I knew what that meant, after a year of listening to Sister Sylvester in fifth grade.

What it meant was this: Even if you stole the stub of a pencil from your neighbor, with scarcely any eraser left—for example, the one Tom Haley had stolen that very day from Trina O'Neal, who sat next to him—it turned your soul pitch black and made Satan happy as could be. And if you died before confession, that was it! You'd spend the rest of your days—"forever and ever," as we had to practice in cursive for twenty minutes—roasting in the hot place with every other thief and unforgiven sinner. So that after a while you'd wish you never laid eyes on that pencil, nor listened to Satan when he whispered for you to take it.

I reckoned if that's what happened for lifting a pencil stub, then hauling a load of lumber off would get me a choice spot down there. I pictured my soul glowing like iron under a welding torch, with no letup ever, and no water trough to get tossed into when it's over, since you're down there for all eternity.

Worse yet was knowing that Freeman didn't have the foggiest notion about any of this. I doubted he knew he had a soul, the way he talked and acted.

My head split to think about it, even though the solution was obvious, for anyone who ever went to Catholic school: We'd have to steal the lumber on a Friday night, so I could make confession on Saturday to get my soul cleaned up with the shortest possible delay. And, of course, pray fervently that I didn't die in the meantime.

But there were other complications, too.

"There's no way I'll be able to sneak out, Freddie. My parents' bedroom is at the base of the stairs, and they hear every move."

"So? We just sleep out in my backyard. I do it all the time."

"I don't know if that'll work either. No offense, but I can't see my mom letting me sleep out with you."

"Ya gotta ask, Joey. That's all there is to it."

So in addition to breaking the news about hanging out with Freeman, I'd have to ask about sleeping out. Common sense said it would never happen.

"Friday's the earliest we can go, if I can do it at all. I'll need some time just to work on my parents."

It was a good excuse to go on Friday, if I was going to do it. But what Freeman said next lightened things up considerably, and I felt much better.

"The first trip will just be to scope the joint out anyway. And maybe scarf up a few nails from the ground."

"You mean we won't have to steal anything?"

"Stop talkin' like that, will ya? It makes me feel like a criminal. All I'm sayin' is we don't even need to touch a board on the first night. Just go see where things are, get a bucket or two of nails, and check out how close they watch the place."

"I'll see what I can do."

The discussion with my parents went smoother than expected. To my surprise, my dad argued that I needed a friend, and that there didn't seem to be a lot of choices, even though he still wasn't crazy about the Freemans.

"There's no question that place is going to the dogs," he said, nodding toward the Freemans' house, sitting in his easy chair with the *Wall Street Journal* on his lap. I thought of the missing shingles, the peeling paint, the ratty front yard, Matt's endless junk collections, and I kept my mouth shut. "But kids are kids, honey, and Joseph needs someone to socialize with."

On the rare occasions that my dad takes a stand, my mom usually goes along. I was pleased this was no exception, though from the way her eyes never left her sewing, she didn't seem too happy about it. As for my sleeping out with Freeman, she was even less enthused.

"The devil could easily tempt two boys in a situation like that," she quickly pointed out.

"Aw, honey. They just want to sleep in a tent. There's no harm in that."

"Wherever the devil shows up, there's always harm. And two young boys in a tent, with no adult around? He should have stayed in scouts if he wanted to sleep out. That way there'd be an adult around to keep an eye on things."

"What things, honey?" My dad sounded almost angry, and I cheered inwardly for him.

My mom went silent and seemed to be sewing faster, as if that would help to relieve some tension. I listened with great interest to find out whatever she might have to say.

"You just never know for sure what kind of trouble! I just don't like the idea of two young boys sleeping out in a tent alone! Her raised voice combined with her squirming in the chair convinced me that would be the end of the discussion; it was not like my dad to continue a cause after words like that.

"But we agreed Joseph could quit scouts," he went on, to my amazement. "And I slept out all the time when I was a kid. Nothing ever happened to me."

Yay, dad! I thought, as a surge of pride came over me.

"But we don't even know Freddie that well! How do we know we can trust him? I'll need to think this over."

It was a bad omen, but further discussion led to an agreement that my mom would take the kids and me and Freddie to the beach. My dad convinced her that this would help her get to know Freeman better, and she could decide thereafter about my sleeping out. It was an unexpected outcome, but it made good sense and I wasn't about to complain.

"I suppose we can go tomorrow," my mom said reluctantly, after my dad reiterated his belief that I needed someone my age to play with, and the sooner the better. Her eyes remained on her sewing and she didn't look like a happy person, but she seemed resigned and even conceded in the end, "We haven't been to Jones Beach for a while."

Which is how Freeman got stuck in the front seat of our Mercury station wagon, headed to the beach like a prisoner between my mom and me. She had to be certain he wasn't the kind of kid who'd lead me straight to hell, although by now I realized this was a real possibility. However, I was far more concerned about the immediate outcome of this little trip since it would surely be a critical test and much rode upon on it—like whether I'd be able to build a fort that I could take Maggie Engles to, and whether I'd be allowed to hang out with Freeman and not go stark raving mad for the rest of the summer.

We got off to a bad start. The car was scarcely out of the driveway when my mom extracted the fact that Freeman's parents were Methodists who went to church "every now and then." And we were not much further when she learned that Freeman had been baptized but didn't think he had a godfather.

"You don't *think* you have a godfather?"

"Naw. We're not even Italian."

My mom's jaw tightened and she seemed to be paralyzed at the wheel, staring straight ahead. I poked my elbow into Freeman's ribs to let him know this answer was unsatisfactory.

"Well, maybe I do." He glanced my way and I nodded my head yes. "Is that one of them guys who pours water on your head when you get baptized?"

"No," my mom replied icily. "It's someone your parents pick to teach you about spiritual things, such as the Holy Ghost, in the event they aren't able to. It's generally a relative or a friend of the family."

I nudged Freeman again in an effort to get him to do better, realizing that none of my previous coaching about sounding intelligent was making much difference.

"Oh, yea!" he blurted out. "I'm pretty sure I got one of them. There's this one uncle who used to tell us ghost stories when we was younger!"

He sat smugly while my mom shot him a glance that told me Freeman had blown it before we even got to the beach. "And just what makes you think this particular uncle might be your godfather?" I thought I could see my mom's knuckles tighten on the steering wheel.

"Well, you know. That's how I learned about spirits and ghosts and junk like that."

My mom drove in silence for a while, as if there was not much more she wanted to know about Freddie. But she is not one to quit and after a while longer she asked, "So, how often do Methodists say their prayers?"

Freeman took a breath and I was already cringing before he said anything. However, loud screaming and laughter from the backseat cut him off, along with a colorful beach ball that sailed between his head and my mom's, before bouncing off the dash and landing in Freeman's lap.

"Nice catch." I patted the ball with one hand, while I readjusted the statue of the Sacred Heart on the dashboard, which was now looking out the windshield instead of blessing the passengers.

The car abruptly halted on the side of the road, then my mom chewed out Timmy and Ryan and gave a lecture on safety and what it takes to drive, and how you have to sit still and not disturb the driver. Then she made those two sit up front, so they could "practice acting like human beings," while Freeman and I rode in back with Mary and Patrick, quiet as angels and happy as devils to avoid the rest of the interrogation.

"Whew!" Freeman whispered. "She's a ballbuster, ain't she?"

I jabbed him with my elbow and spoke from the side of my mouth, "That's nothing, believe me!"

Near the water's edge, we rolled out beach towels, Army blanket, picnic basket, Kool-Aid jug, suntan lotion, and various religious books my mom was reading for the third or fourth time. Timmy and I raised the green and white striped umbrella and placed my mom's beach chair beneath it.

"Will you bury us now, Joey?" begged Timmy, before Freeman and I had a chance to disappear.

"No, let's build castles!" screamed Patrick.

"I wanna dig for sand crabs!" wailed Mary.

"Listen! Be quiet and I'll tell you what's going on!" I exploded. "Freddie and I are going in the surf, and you guys can do whatever you want!"

"That stinks, Joey!"

"Come on! Play with us!"

"You never play with us anymore!"

I couldn't tell who said what. They were all talking at once, making me want to get out of there even faster.

"It's okay, Joey. We can play with them first," Freeman piped up.

"Yea, yea!" Timmy, Ryan, and Patrick shouted, while Mary grabbed Freeman's hand.

"Let's get sand crabs!" she said. Freeman claimed he didn't know how, and Mary delighted in showing him. "Just dig holes when the waves go out, then scoop them up fast!"

They worked together, while Timmy, Ryan, Patrick, and I looked for clams. We put them all together in a bucket.

"These are the craziest things I ever saw!" Freeman observed as he poked his finger at a sand crab. "Ow! Damn!" he added, jerking his hand back.

"You said a nasty word!" Patrick informed him.

"It's okay. Daddy said the same thing when he hit himself with a hammer," Mary replied in defense of Freeman.

We all laughed, while Freeman shook his finger in the air.

"They just pinch a little," gloated Timmy.

"I gotta take some of those guys back for James," Freeman exclaimed, still fascinated.

"You can, but they won't live long in there," I replied, pointing to the green plastic pail. "And they'll stink to high heaven if you don't get rid of them real soon."

We got back to the blanket and left the bucket under the shade of the umbrella, where my mom appeared to be engrossed in her book, though I suspected she didn't miss much of what we were up to. I convinced the kids that they should collect seashells for James too, while Freeman and I went for a swim.

"Promise you'll bury us later?" Mary squeaked.

"Yea, yea. But only if you get going now!" I said to get rid of them.

"All right! He's gonna do it! Let's get shells!" responded Patrick.

"I'll get the most and Freddie will bury me first!" shouted Mary as the four kids headed down the shore.

"I think she likes me," Freeman observed.

"Maybe. But all I know is let's go before they're back!"

Splashing through the sudsy foam, I shouted to Freeman, "We need to get out past the breakers!" We were only knee deep, and I was anxious to body surf and have contests to see who'd get closest to shore.

"No!" he answered firmly, surprising me as much by his answer as his tone of voice.

His feet were suddenly stuck in the sand like anchors, and he shook his head vigorously.

"What d'ya mean, 'No'?"

"My mom never took me to the beach," he hollered, frozen in place, his baggy brown suit flapping in the breeze, and his lily-white skin nearly as bright as the beach sand. Only slowly did I realize that what he meant was he didn't know how to swim.

It had never dawned on me that someone his age couldn't swim. But I quickly made up my mind not to laugh at him. Instead, I showed him how easy it is to go past the breakers if you bounce off the bottom. But he shook his head and wanted no part of it.

"Even if I keep my head up, what if there are sharks out there?"

"There are," I shouted over the crash of a breaker, realizing my mistake as I said it.

"You're nuts!" he screamed through cupped hands.

"But they're only harmless little sand sharks."

"Sharks are sharks. And I hate sharks. They'll chew your legs off!"

"They're afraid of people. And they're too small to do that."

"They're not too small to bite some other things off! And they're already half frozen off!" He turned sideways against a large wave, hands in the air, fear in his voice.

"You'll hate yourself if you don't come out here. The waves will always take you back. There's nothing to be afraid of."

He had moved to waist depth without meaning to, and shouted, "I ain't goin' any farther. No matter what you say. So stop wastin' your breath."

He turned and moved toward shore, his head twisting back and forth, evidently in search of sand sharks. He had not gone ten feet when a large wave crashed over his back and collapsed into seething white foam into which he disappeared. He went under for several seconds before his upside down legs broke the surface and cartwheeled under again.

It was several more seconds before he stood up, coughing, sputtering and trying to catch his breath.

"I'm gettin' outta this stupid place!" he screamed, terror in his voice as he splashed back to the beach.

Thus I gave up my plans for body surfing and sat in the wet sand with Freeman, near the water's edge, making models of the fort. Our first several attempts were too high or too flat or looked ridiculous somehow, but one finally came out half decent. We pulled back and admired it: A low rectangular affair with a sloped roof, nestled among odd-looking bushes made from sand and seaweed, with a circular clearing in front. There was a refrigerator pit and a fireplace and something Freeman called a "beautiful outdoor picnic table for summer banquets," though it looked like a gnarly hunk of driftwood to me.

Rolling hills and valleys surrounded the place. A long curving path led to it from the nearest road, the path we planned to be traveling soon, with two beautiful girls clinging to our arms—Maggie with me and someone else with Freeman, though it was idle speculation as to who that someone might be.

We snuffed the whole thing before the kids got back so as not to give any secrets away. Creamy peanut butter sandwiches, red grapes, and Kool-Aid appeared and disappeared for lunch. We reassured the kids we'd bury them later, then excused ourselves and lit out toward the sand dunes. Freeman wanted to see the terns dive at our heads like kamikaze pilots, the way I said they would.

"They'll get right up to your face, then zoom away before you can touch them," I assured him.

"Fifty cents says I can touch one!"

"You're on! I could use fifty cents!"

A dozen or so terns rose up in circles as we approached their nesting grounds, then dropped like rockets through the air. They approached with great speed, almost vertically, as if to land in our faces, cawing loud warnings. They scared me as much as the first time I'd seen them, years ago. But I held my ground, knowing they wouldn't actually strike. It wasn't long before Freeman tried to whomp several with a stick in an effort to win his bet.

The birds kept bombing and Freeman knocked himself silly and was soon sweating profusely, in addition to swearing loudly. He jumped and danced and wheeled in circles but never touched a tern. His stick whizzed and lashed the air and did more tricks than a baton in a parade, but it missed by inches every time. The terns almost seemed to like it, as if pleased to have a sucker on the line.

I enjoyed the spectacle and smiled contentedly, especially when Freeman ran out of steam and laid on his sweaty back in the sand, panting and gasping like a dog.

I shoved my hand in his face and said, obnoxiously as I could, "Fifty cents, please!"

He laughed and vibrated in the sand and explained it was only a gentleman's bet because we never shook on it. This made me kick sand all over his sweaty body, where it stuck like sprinkles on ice cream. A grisly, sandy statue that looked like Freeman sat up, sputtering sand from its lips.

"You simpleton, Simpleton! Ya got me good, buddy!"

Before I knew what happened he tackled me and grabbed my ankles, then dragged me through the hot sand on my back. The brute had an iron grip and wouldn't let go despite my screaming and beating my hands in the air and kicking to get loose.

He hauled me like a sack of potatoes, enjoying it more the harder I struggled and screamed. But then he stopped and dropped me. He put his hand on my mouth for silence. "Sssh!"

"What the hell are … " I started to say, pushing his hand away. I squirmed in the sand and wiggled onto my stomach.

"Sssh!" he repeated, one finger on his lips, another pointing down a small valley between two sand dunes.

I floundered to my knees and looked where he was pointing. A couple sat on a blanket, a stone's throw down the valley. The guy's back was facing us, his arms and legs wrapped around the girl, who faced him; she did not look too much older than us. They had bathing suits on, and the guy wore a baseball hat and a large T-shirt. But even as we looked, the girl was slipping off the top of her white bikini, which she dropped in the sand. Then she held up her small round breasts to show them off, as if they were small cantaloupes!

Freeman beamed and gave me two thumbs-up, then motioned to move behind a sand dune. We dropped to hands and knees and crawled quickly to the top of the dune from where our bug-eyed heads poked through the stringy weeds.

The guy leaned forward more and began rubbing his hands in circles on the girl's back, while he kissed her face over and over, creating a tremendous longing in me to do the same.

Her hands began stroking his neck and scratching his back, and I felt great envy.

How on earth do you get a female to do that, I wondered? I needed desperately to find out. I wanted so badly to do the same thing with Maggie someday in the very near future.

To my amazement, the girl lay on her back and slipped the white bikini bottom from her tan shapely legs. The guy helped out, somewhat clumsily, then dropped that skimpy little bottom in the sand next to the skimpy little top. And there she lay, naked as a tadpole, even though the guy blocked much of the view.

Freeman shook two fists in the air and whispered, "Yes!"

A throbbing pressure filled my swimsuit and I wondered if you could rip your suit that way. At the same time a little voice spoke in my head. "You shouldn't even be here, should you?" I knew it was my guardian angel, and I really ought to listen up.

But another voice answered right away, the one that always makes good sense and tries to trick me. "Of course you ought to be here! It's the best thing you've seen in your life, and it's a good chance to learn a few things! Besides, you can always go to confession." And I knew right away whose voice that was.

I was trying to sort these thoughts out when the girl reached up and slid the guy's green nylon suit to his knees. I wondered if my eyes might pop out of my head from straining so hard. But then, as if to spare my eyes, the guy pulled a second blanket on top of them, like a sheet. It was a profound disappointment. All we could see were various protrusions of the blanket, which squirmed and wiggled and moved jerkily about.

But it did not take long before those lumps and bumps began heaving and twisting and contorting wildly, as if there was a full-blown circus underneath.

"Oh, that feels so good!" came muffled cries from below. "Oh baby, it feels so good!"

Freeman whispered excitedly, "They're doin' it, Joey! They're doin' it!"

I had a hankering to run down and rip the blanket off and see what was going on, but I did not think that would make me popular, nor be too healthy for me personally. I had an overwhelming urge to be there, taking the guy's place and having one of those crazy lumps be me.

At the same time a sense of guilt and shame came over me and I felt unclean and sinful. "I told you not to watch," admonished a voice in my head.

I glanced over and saw Freeman rocking to the movement, enjoying the show without any such reservations. I turned away embarrassed, but also envious of someone who never worried about his soul. "He knows what he's doing, huh?" sneered the other voice in my head.

"Oh, yes!" came screams from the girl, followed by more hurried movements of the blanket. "Come to mamma! Oh yes!"

I wondered if watching something like this could make a person go insane; it seemed like a distinct possibility.

By and by the thrashing bodies slowed down, and after a time, they stopped. The bumps separated and the larger one sat up. The guy took off his hat and T-shirt and set them on the edge of the blanket, then for the first time turned in such a way that we could see his face.

And behold! In the three seconds it took to do this, we received the shock of our lives: The guy we had been watching, envying, and dying to replace was none other than JC!

He dived back under the blanket, but our world was already upside down. Every ounce of excitement vanished, as if we'd been doused by a bucket of cold water. We slipped away in silence and moved over the hot sand to the water where we sat in the cool foam of the surf.

The tingly white suds felt good, but the image of JC and the girl filled my head making me numb inside. And I had no doubt it was the same for Freeman.

Currents and foam tossed our bodies about for a long while, like spineless jellyfish.

Seagulls glided and cawed overhead, while saltwater splashed over us. It was as if nothing existed in the universe but Freeman and me and the memory of what we'd seen.

"Still worried about sand sharks?" I asked after a time.

"I wish one would swallow me up and put me out of my misery, this very second! All I can think about is that hairy ape back there—I can't believe it was him."

"Callaghan told us he worked at a concession down here. I forgot all about that. Must be that one by the parking lot."

"And this is how he spends his lunch hour?" Freeman asked in disbelief.

"I guess it's a nice dessert."

"How'd a guy like him ever get a girl like that? She could've been last year's prom queen. I'd give my left nut to know what she sees in him."

"You may be giving both of them and not finding anything out," I reminded him.

"Yours too!" he reminded me ruthlessly, without a care for how I felt.

We drifted aimlessly and meditated on JC and his girl a while longer before hiking back along the shore. Upon returning, we buried the kids in the sand with nothing but their fool little heads sticking out.

They loved it and so did my mom, and Freeman especially appeared to enjoy himself. I hoped our small display of kindness would help my mom think better of Freeman, at least enough to allow me to sleep out with him.

"So did you boys enjoy your hike?" she asked as we were putting finishing touches around Patrick's neck.

"Oh yea," I said. "I showed Freddie the terns, and we walked through the dunes a bit."

"See anything interesting?"

"Naw, just a few older kids."

"Boys or girls?" It was so like my mom, prying under every stone, sniffing for goods, looking for trouble.

"Oh, some of each. You know. A guy and a girl." I pretended to be engrossed in my work on Ryan's neck.

"And what were they doing?" She sounded even more suspicious now.

"Oh, just lying on a blanket." I continued pushing sand about Ryan's neck, and I felt like burying his head.

"Lying on a blanket?" She spoke a bit sarcastically, and her stare seemed to be scorching the side of my head.

"You know. Sunbathing or something."

"Or something?" She asked as if one of us was a fool, and it wasn't her.

"Um, I think they was sleepin', Mrs. Simpson," chimed in Freeman. "I mean we didn't disturb them or nothin'."

We continued pushing sand and neither of us looked up.

"Anything," she corrected.

"Yea, you know," I said. "People go back there all the time and sunbathe in the peace and quiet."

The way she looked at me I felt like she might be reading my mind, which contained nothing but a picture of JC banging away at that screaming girl. I imagined she was checking my ears out too, so I relaxed as much as I could and kept pushing sand.

She went silent for a few excruciating minutes. Then, "I really am glad you two are getting along so well. And I did like how you carried things down here and helped us get set up."

Oh, but I was thrilled! My mom does not render such compliments easily, and it was clear that she must have taken a liking to Freeman, in spite of his not being Catholic.

Burying the kids must have done it, I thought. She could see that he had a kind heart going for him, if not much else. She went back to her reading, and I gave the nod to Freeman.

There was a good chance that he had passed the test, even if he wasn't the most perfect example my mom might hope to find as a friend for her son.

4

Friday dinner was salad and spaghetti with no meatballs, which is something like a bike with no wheels, or a bow with no arrows, but a typical Friday meal nonetheless. Even so, it was the things on my mind that troubled me most. Thinking of JC in the dunes caused a bulge in my pants a few times every hour, in addition to tremendous jealousy and guilt.

And a knot of panic permanently gripped my chest, due to worry about our trip to Stoneridge later that night. I felt jumpy as a kangaroo on hot coals.

"Are you all right, Joseph?" my mom inquired after she'd asked me to pass the salt and I somehow hadn't even heard her.

"Yea, I'm okay. I must have been thinking about something. Sorry."

"Girls?" chimed in Timmy, grinning like an imbecile.

I must have turned ten shades of red, because everyone looked at me, then broke up laughing. My face and ears felt as hot as peppers, and I could suddenly think of nothing but that girl in the dunes. It was as if my whole family was reading my mind. I was so flustered and embarrassed I felt like killing everyone then and there, in one happy little family home murder.

But I kept my mouth shut and simmered inside, reminding myself that they really couldn't see what was going on in my head. Timmy started singing. "Joey's got a girlfriend, Joey's got a girlfriend, Joey's …"

And the twins didn't waste a second joining in. "Joey's got a girlfriend, Joey's got a girlfriend … "

"Be quiet now!" my dad interrupted, returning to his food and forcing the smile from his own face. I thought I heard my mom swallow a laugh, but I was too upset to tell for sure.

I shot daggers at Timmy, vowing to myself that I'd deal with him later.

"May I be excused early, please? I need to get my sleeping bag and things ready."

"Where's he going?" cried Patrick.

"I'm not going anywhere. I'm just sleeping in Freddie's backyard."

"Why can't I go?" wailed Timmy.

"You're not going anywhere, young man," my dad assured him. "Except to bed early if you keep it up!"

I was greatly pleased with my dad's attitude, though I found my-self turning to Timmy nonetheless and sticking my tongue out, since I know how much he hates this. He gave a look of hate back, but what did I care?

"You may be excused, Joseph," my mom offered. "But you had better be on your very best behavior this evening!"

"Oh, I will. You have absolutely nothing to worry about!"

"And please take that bucket of shells and crabs to Freddie's to-night! It's already starting to stink."

Not only had Freeman convinced my mom he was an okay kid, but he also convinced Matt to set up his army tent for us beside their garage. He and Matt were tightening the ropes on it as I arrived.

"That's perfect!" I exclaimed as I crawled in on my hands and knees, trying to ignore the tomcat odor.

"Maybe, but it's not worth a turd when it rains," Matt informed me. "Plus it turns into an oven in the sun. But it was free, so I'm not complainin'."

"It stinks to high heaven," added Freeman.

"Yea, well, this will help air it out a bit," replied Matt. "And getting you out of the bedroom will give me some peace and quiet."

"Thanks, Matt," I said, trying to keep the peace. "I appreciate that."

"I'm glad to see someone using the thing." He turned and head-ed to the house.

"Especially Joey," he added, over his shoulder.

That made me like him all the more, even though Freeman flipped him off behind his back. As for the stench, Freeman said it was "purely natural," and he was sure we'd get used to it. Which proved to be true, because in a short while I forgot all about it.

Dusk came around nine thirty and we both claimed to be pleased, but in fact I suffered from a nasty outburst of stomach butterflies. Our plan was to take off after Freeman's dad went to work, which would be quarter to twelve, because he worked the midnight shift. So we played twenty-one in the dim glow of Freeman's flashlight, till the batteries quit and he couldn't knock them on again.

We laid in the dark and told jokes, but the only new ones were two of Freeman's.

"What do you call a blonde with an average IQ?"

"I give up."

"Highly gifted!"

He laughed and slapped his sleeping bag, then told the second one.

"What do you call a blonde with an above average IQ?"

"What?"

"A golden retriever!"

He guffawed and slapped his bag all the harder, but when he was done I pointed out that he was a blonde himself, in addition to which Maggie was blonde; and on top of that we wouldn't mind having two blondes that very moment.

"Aw screw it, Joey. It's just a damn joke. You're way too serious about things."

It was a terrible thing to say, but I knew it was true. I blamed it all on the lousy nuns, though I suspected my mom had something to do with it too.

Not long after, we heard noises through the kitchen window. Freeman's dad was bumping around, swearing at some pots and pans, which he evidently had knocked off the counter. Freeman claimed that meant he was fixing something to eat and almost ready to leave.

"So we oughta be ready, too," he claimed excitedly, "because our loafin' time's up, and we'll soon be off into the murky night!" My butterflies cut up like gangbusters, giving me a throbbing wooziness and a desire to be back in my own bed.

"Ain't you excited, Joey?" He shook me by the shoulders, like I was a kid on Christmas morning. I nodded numbly in the faint light from the kitchen window. Freeman's dad started the car.

"It's eleven forty-five!" Freeman said.

My glow-in-the-dark watch verified that was so as I heard the car back down the driveway.

"Let's go!" Freeman exclaimed, his head out the door, his rear end in my face.

"Maybe we should wait till after one o'clock." I wanted to buy more time. "To be sure everyone's asleep."

"Don't be crazy! No one'll see us slip out now, even if they are awake. That's why we were sleepin' out in the first place. Remember?"

A large pressure pushed on my abdomen. It was like a thousand cocoons had hatched at once, and were making a tortured flight through my intestines.

"Oh, shit!" I sat straight up. "I gotta go!"

"That's what I been tryin' to tell ya, Joey! We both gotta go!"

"No! I mean I gotta take a dump!"

"Aw Jeez, Joey! Can't ya hold it?"

"No!"

"Then ya better dig a hole behind the garage." He motioned, like I might have forgotten where it was. "'Cause if ya go in the house you'll wake my mom up."

"What about toilet paper?" I protested. "I gotta have some, especially for this one!"

"Use leaves; we can't risk goin' in now!"

I hate leaves. They're always too itchy and too thin, and your hand usually gets skunked anyway. But he was right. I could have kicked myself for not thinking of it sooner.

I walked gently to avoid an early outburst, grabbed a few peach tree leaves, and squatted behind the garage. There came a hot, wet blast, and I nearly died from my own fumes.

The leaves proved next to useless. I rubbed my used hand in the dirt, then tried to drag my ass across the grass, like a dog, but it felt no more helpful than the leaves. I was glad no one was around to watch.

Then I spied a crusty old newspaper lying by the garage, so I grabbed that and made do. I kicked dirt over the whole mess and tried to forget about it, but it wasn't easy because I never got all the stink off.

"Let's go," I said, keeping as large a distance from Freeman as I could without being too obvious.

And so we slipped into the night on what was to be the first surveillance run, silent as fleas on a dog's behind.

We held to the shadows, moving fox-like past streetlights, ready to jump in dark places if need be. Freeman said any cars most likely were cops, since normal people were all in bed. "So if ya see headlights jump behind the nearest bush or whatever," he insisted.

We jumped three times but it was just regular cars. Folks going to work, like Freeman's dad, I imagined. I grew tired of it after the third jump, when we landed in wet grass and got nailed by a rotating sprinkler. I tried to clean my hand in the grass as I complained to Freeman about the needless jumping.

"We gotta do it anyway," he said resolutely, "to be on the safe side."

Close to Stoneridge we plopped to rest by a small fence. We'd barely sat down when a cop car rounded the corner, nearly on top of us! There was no time to think, let alone jump. With his inside light on we could see his face, so close was he. I was glad we were wearing blue jeans and dark T-shirts, as Freeman had suggested. We stayed put and he drove by.

We snuck up to the development along the railroad tracks. My butterflies were gone, but high-powered jumping beans seemed to have replaced them. Which was worse, because I couldn't tell an ordinary fart from the real McCoy. Plus I had to whizz like a racehorse.

"Hold up! I can't go on like this."

I watered a small tree near the edge of the tracks, while Freeman got the other side.

Then we moved amongst the houses to scout for boards. I was grateful it was a dark night.

We circled one house and looked on the side of another, but no boards were to be found.

"Damn!" exclaimed Freeman. "I wonder where they put the things?"

"Maybe they used 'em all." I was already considering that we might use logs and branches instead, and I wondered if this wasn't a sign that we ought to.

"They gotta be somewhere! You go that a-way." He pointed like a drill sergeant at eight or nine houses to the north. "And I'll head that a-way." He pointed south. "Then meet here and tell me what ya seen, and I'll do the same."

Goose bumps covered me from head to toe and I didn't like it, not one bit. In addition to my fear of getting caught, I was deathly afraid of the dark, at least in strange places like that. I wanted to tell Freeman, but before I could think of how to say it he was around the corner of a house and there I was all alone. I looked around dumbly and stood in place for a long while, hands in my pockets, wondering what to do.

"I am a fish out of water," I said aloud, hoping it might comfort me, "and I'm not even sure what kind." But it only made me realize the frightful truth of the situation. I was weak and scared and miserable, and the night was so still and dreamlike.

Then I thought, "What if I am dreaming?"

I kicked a rock, and I heard it and felt it and saw the thing move a few inches, so I knew it wasn't a dream. I looked at the moon. It was a thin sliver above the scraggly black trees across the tracks, like in ghost stories. Shivers crawled up and down my spine. I tried to whistle, but no sound came out. There was nothing left to do, so I reminded myself that, no matter what happened, Maggie was worth it all, and I began inching in the direction Freeman had said.

I tried to walk like a mouse on tippy-toes, but the crunchy rocks made me sound like a wounded elephant. My heart pounded like a drum. I found myself sweating and breathing hard without doing any work.

I passed like a ghost across two lots, looking furtively between the houses and all over the ground as I went. Not one board appeared, save what was already built into the houses. I wondered if Freeman would consider using those, then realized I'd better not mention it, since he probably would.

I circled two more houses with no better luck. I made up my mind to peek in one of those spooky, dark windows, since I had to find boards somewhere. But there was no easy way to look in with the windows up so high. I snuck past one more eerie, morgue-like house, examining the ground as I went, till I came upon one window that was lower than the others, about three feet off the ground. I forced myself toward it, slow as a snail, then peeked in. I squinted and let my eyes adjust, and behold: There were boards scattered all around inside! And three neat piles of boards along the walls, too.

My heart beat louder, and I wished I'd never seen it. I figured the workers must take the boards into the house they're working on, then leave them there so they'll be ready the next day.

I breathed deep and asked myself, "What are you, Joseph Simpson, a man or a mouse?" But it was a stupid question, so I ignored the answer.

I began to climb in the window, hoping to get a better idea how much lumber was there to report back to Freeman. I was as nervous and ready to collapse as if a nun had asked me a history question. I wiggled both legs inside, then worked myself through backward, like an animal backing into a hole. I felt about with my toes till they found the floor. I squeezed through and stood up, shaking like a Christmas tree ornament.

I waited for my eyes to adjust, gazing into the blackness. Then, out of nowhere, two powerful hands grabbed me, and a voice shouted in my ear, "Whatchya find, Joey?"

I leapt back through the window headfirst, like I'd been shot from a cannon. I hit the ground, scraping my hands and arms, then bounced up and started to run. Only then did it sink in who this was. I stopped and listened and heard Freeman laughing and hooting hysterically in the window.

"You pathetic piece of pig shit!" I hollered. "Are you trying to give me a heart attack?!"

From the black hole came strange alternating sounds, like gasping and choked-off breathing and shuffling around. It didn't take long to realize Freeman was howling with laughter and rolling on the floor, and gasping for air at the same time.

My arms were cut and I was banged up something terrible, in addition to which all this excitement had resulted in a genuine Hershey squirt—and I thought I smelled bad before. Lord! It was humiliating. I squinted in the window.

"What the hell is wrong with you?"

He didn't hear me, he was still laughing and snorting so hard. I climbed in and grabbed him by the shirt.

"You ugly, worthless ape! What's wrong with you?"

"Oh, you should've seen yourself!" he gleamed. "I've never saw anything so funny! That was great!" He slapped his legs.

"If you ever, ever do that again, I'm going to cut yours off before JC does!"

"Aw, don't be such a party pooper, Joey! Now we know we can get through that window real fast if we have to."

He slapped his hand on a wall several times, merrily ignoring me. It flashed through my mind that there was more than one meaning to the term "party pooper," and I could scarcely deny that I was one.

"Say, don't this look like a good place to start, Joey, with all this wood here?"

He swept his arms around the room, oblivious to my misery, so pleased was he with the wood and the joy of watching me sail out the window. My ailments mattered nothing to him. I counted to ten, then counted backward, trying to calm down.

"Oh, that was great, Joey! I wish you coulda seen it," he snorted and held his stomach, making strange noises as he tried without success to contain his laughter. Then he stood more erect and acted serious.

"Okay, let's get down to business. Let's get these here piles first." Laugh, laugh. "They're longer than we need, but two-by-sixes are what we want for the frame, and we can cut 'em later." Laugh, snicker, laugh.

"Wait a minute! Wait a dang minute, Mr. Funny Boy!" I exclaimed as it dawned on me what he was proposing. "What are you talking about, anyway?"

"What I'm sayin' is we'll do one trip now, then get the rest after we ditch that one down the tracks, near the Westwoods." He put his arm over my shoulder to calm me down.

"Now just get outside there and I'll pass 'em through the … Oh God, that was hilarious!" He withdrew his arm and lapsed into spasms of laughter.

"No, Freddie! You said we came to check the place out. And maybe get nails. You didn't say a thing about getting boards."

"But we came and we found, good buddy! We hit the jackpot. Pure gold. Don't ya see? It's time for phase two!" he laughed as he spoke, unable to control himself.

"I didn't prepare myself for this. You tricked me, Freddie!"

"I wasn't tryin' to! But here we are. And here are the boards, and so what are we waitin' for? It ain't gonna get much better."

"I'm not ready to steal any lumber!" I threw my arms up and paced in a circle.

He got serious, finally, and sat on top of the boards by the wall. He paused, as if to be sure he'd say things right.

"Look. You don't need to do nothin,' 'cept load me up. Okay? I'll haul the bastards myself. You just brush up our footprints, then tag along in case I need a hand. All I'm really askin' is that ya talk to me if I get lonely. You can handle that, can't ya?"

I asked myself what I had to lose. I wouldn't be stealing anything if he carried the boards. And it didn't look like we'd ever get caught. I glanced at the lumber and thought of it framing the fort, and then of the finished fort, and then of Maggie and me in the candlelight.

"All right. But you better not ask me to carry anything, or I'll say no. You think you can handle that?"

"Of course! Said the big strong horse!"

"I'm not joking."

"Me either! I hate jokers!" he snortled through his nose.

I slipped out the window, still pained by hurt feelings and a battered body, not to mention disgusted with my own stench, which amazingly Freeman didn't seem to notice.

Freeman cheerfully fed the boards out, one by stolen one, whistling his head off—"whistle while you work, whistle while you work." I stacked them on the ground, till we had a pile of eight.

"Enough!" I shouted into window. "And stop whistling, will you?"

"Just a couple more, Joey. And I can't stop whistlin'—it makes me feel good!"

"All these'll break your back!"

"Don't be such a worrywart. It's bad for your health."

He whistled and passed two more out, then came through himself. He walked to the pile and bent over beside it. "Stack 'em on my back, Jumper!"

I stacked five of the monsters in a wobbly arrangement on his back, while he stooped like a hunchback. He reached up to secure them with his hands, in the most awkward way, while the low end nearly dragged on the ground.

"You're right," he said hoarsely. "This is all I can take!"

"We better put the others back so no one sees them," I said.

"Naw, leave 'em," he spoke in short grunts from under the boards. "The workers'll think they left 'em out by mistake."

I knew I wasn't going to put them back by myself. "All right then! Let's go!" I swatted his protruding ass with my hat. "Giddyap, horsie!"

"I feel like a horse," he moaned.

The boards started inching turtle-like toward the tracks. "Don't forget to brush our footprints now. Use a branch from that tree we watered. I gotta move. These suckers weigh a ton!"

The boards continued off in slow motion, and I was thankful it was not me underneath them. I wondered if I could be considered a real thief under the circumstances—all I'd done was arrange some boards on a friend's back. Just the same, I feared my soul had turned black and was probably shriveled as a prune, all ready for roasting in the hot place.

Freeman had started down the tracks by the time I cut a branch for a broom. I brushed furiously, as I didn't want to be left behind. The branch scratched loudly on the rocky ground, and I doubted it did much good, assuming I was even brushing in the right place. I was about to chuck it and get out when an eerie chill came over me—I felt positive someone or something was watching me.

I froze and didn't move a muscle, hoping whatever it was would disappear. I turned my eyes to the left, then to the right, then back and forth several times to see what I could without moving. There was nothing. Yet I felt certain that a pair of eyes was staring at me.

I turned my head ever so slowly to the left, and there, a short way behind me, stood a huge black dog, nearly as tall as my waist. His big white eyes were fixed on me just as I had imagined!

I turned my body slowly and there we stood, staring at each other in the faint moonlight, me wondering what on earth to do. If I could have leapt to the rooftop I would have, and I wished I could've, and I thought maybe I should give it a try.

No sooner did I think that then the dog began barking and yapping and carrying on like an army of dogs, not moving from his spot. I worried that the whole neighborhood near the edge of Stoneridge would be out in their pajamas to see what the ruckus was, and find me standing there by the remaining boards.

I needed to shut the beast up quickly and at all costs. I began walking toward him with my hand out, whispering loudly, scared out of my mind that he was going to attack.

"Here boy! Good dog!"

He backed up and barked louder, making enough noise to raise the dead.

"I have to get out of here!" I said to myself. "But how am I going to shut this beast up and get away?" He went on barking, with no letup.

"Okay, you need to tame him down somehow." I kept talking to myself. "You can't run, or he's likely to take a chomp out of your leg, and maybe your behind too."

I forced myself closer, using every ounce of courage I had, my hand extended.

"Good dog; here boy," I repeated nervously. "Good dog; here boy."

I closed in, scared to death he'd wolf my hand in one chomp, leaving a bloody stub to explain to my mom. But I got right next to him, and thereupon he stopped barking and sniffed my hand, the way dogs do. I stood quietly and petted his thick, bony head. To my amazement, he wagged his tail and acted friendly! I couldn't believe it!

"What could possibly make him so friendly, just like that?" I wondered.

Then I recalled where my hand had been, not so long ago.

He soon tired of my hand and developed a keen interest in the seat of my pants, no doubt as a result of my various recent difficulties, and the goods now packed inside there.

The dog's behavior was a severe embarrassment, even with no one watching. But I was determined to let him get it out of his system. Sniff, sniff, sniff; sniff, sniff, sniff. He nudged his nose in good several times, and it was all I could do to hold still and not run like a madman toward Freeman, even though I didn't know what Freeman could do anyway.

Sniff, sniff, sniff; sniff, sniff, sniff.

He raised his head high and appeared to be contemplating that thin sliver of moon, as if the richness of the setting filled him with intense delight and was almost unbearable. He took several more sniffs, then seemed satisfied that he'd gotten his fill. He shook his head as if to give that dog's stamp of approval. I kneeled and petted his head once more.

"What do we do now, doggie?" I asked, like he might answer me. I saw that he was the very kind of dog I had wanted when I was a little kid, but that my parents would never let me have: a black Lab, the sort that was supposed to make friends so easily, just like he did.

Freeman was long gone and I didn't know whether to take the thing with me or try to make him stay. I was relieved he wasn't barking, and it didn't seem like he was going to hurt me.

Pet, pet, pet; pet, pet, pet. I continued telling him how good he was, trying to assure that he'd stay shut up, wishing at the same time I could somehow make him disappear.

"What am I going to do with the blasted thing?" I wondered.

I finally commanded him to "sit," which he did, while I began walking slowly away.

But within seconds he was up and after me, wagging his tail at the delight of having someone to follow, particularly a kid as ripe as me. I considered ditching my underwear in hopes that might entertain him while I escaped, but the thought of taking off my sneakers and pants with that beast watching, combined with the chance of a night guard coming by, left me no choice but to take him. So I trotted after Freeman along the base of the railroad tracks, with the black monster jogging beside me, encouraged by what he obviously considered the finest of aromas.

I deeply feared getting a foot stuck in the tracks and having a train grind me into chopped liver under those cold steel wheels. My mom had scared me about that since I was a little kid. Plus in such an event I would never make it to confession. I contemplated such a scene as I traveled toward Freeman, working myself into a frenzy of guilt and worry.

Then again, I didn't really think there'd be any trains at this time of night, and I was not on the tracks anyway.

When I caught Freeman he was hiking along the middle of the ties, trying to whistle; he had not an ounce of fear, but the weight of the boards was beating him down. He spoke without looking up. "Grab ahold of them boards and lift up a bit! If this load was any heavier I'd be squished like a bug!"

I really didn't want to go up on the middle of the tracks. I told God I was only trying to help my friend, as in the do-good-to-others idea; and all right, maybe he was up to no good, but it wasn't his fault—he thought everything fun was good! So there was no excuse for God not to help me out while I was helping Freeman.

I made up a short prayer: "Please do not let my foot get stuck in the tracks, no matter what! And forgive me if I am actually breaking the Seventh Commandment. I don't mean to, or want to, or even think it's a good idea. I only want to make a fort with my wacky friend—that idiot there on the tracks. You can see that, can't you?"

I got behind and hoisted up the ends of the hot cargo, to ease the pressure on Freeman's back. Why, it's like lending a hand to Jesus, I thought, on his way up Cavalry.

With a few small differences. For example, the terrain was flatter and Freeman was a thief, rather than a Savior. Which meant we had something to look forward to at the end, besides crucifixion. It almost sounded like a good thing.

"Much better!" Freeman grunted. "Why, I could've taken more boards this way!"

"What am I supposed to do now? Keep holding these things and trot along behind you?"

"Sounds good to me," Freeman replied, just before noticing the dog, which had suddenly decided to walk beside him. "Hey! What's this dog doin' here?"

I explained his appearance from nowhere and how I couldn't get rid of him, as I danced along, trying not to slip or break an ankle or get a foot stuck.

"I'll be damned!" Freeman gasped. "Looks like we got us a friend, Joey!"

I was pleased he liked the dog, though I had no idea what we'd do with him.

"We gotta name him!" Freeman came to a stop. "Plus I gotta rest."

He set the boards across the rails, then took the top board and laid it across separately, a few feet away. He motioned for me to sit on the big pile, while he sat on the single board, in such a way that we could face each other.

"By damn he's a big one! He could take your hand off in a single bite."

The dog wagged his tail and looked lovingly at Freeman, or maybe hungrily.

"He's a giant all right. It's the biggest Lab I ever saw."

"Why he could amputate a whole limb quicker than a doctor!"

"A lot quicker, I'd say."

"Why, that's it, Joey! We'll call him Doctor Dog!"

And so we met Doctor Dog, or rather Doctor Dog met us, and joined our party for the evening. We promptly called him "Doc" for short, and as happily as he responded, I wondered if that might actually be his name.

Freeman explained that the main problem was how the boards dug into his back and that we should have taken a towel or a couple of rags to cushion them. Then his eyes lit on my T-shirt.

"Why don't you just give me your shirt?"

The air was warm and I didn't need it, yet I didn't want it soaked with whatever juices might ooze from his back. But I had no good excuse, and he needed it more than I did, so I took the thing off and handed it over.

"Try not to sweat too hard, okay?"

He offered me a cigarette and I didn't hesitate. I needed to calm my nerves and to cover my stink, which I was amazed he hadn't noticed.

We were getting ready to move again when Doc sat up and looked south, apparently intent on a new scent.

"What's he thinking about now?" I said.

"Prob'ly a skunk. They're all over this place."

"I don't smell one though."

"Dogs smell a hundred times better than us—ya knew that didn't ya?"

"I know all about how dogs smell. They especially like bad smells. But I'd still like to know what's on his mind."

Doc kept sitting and didn't budge, and I feared there might be people ahead. I imagined I saw a faint flash of light on the trees, like someone blinked a flashlight on and off. No sooner did this happen than Freeman said, "By damn, Joey! I think a train may be coming!"

"No—that can't be! Not at this time of night!"

"Well, there's somethin' comin'! And I don't suppose it's a little red wagon."

"Then let's get the hell out of here!"

"We gotta take the boards! They'll derail the train if it hits 'em like this!"

"Oh, shit!"

The lights now shined around the bend, maybe a football field away, while the engine vibrated the night air. A deep rumbling came through the rails.

"Let's get your pile first!" Freeman shouted. "Grab that end now!"

We snapped to action as the train lights bore upon us, and the sound grew deafening.

Freeman grabbed one end and ran backward down the sloped gravel.

"Watch the mud puddle!" I hollered, seeing a pool of water behind Freeman, where he was about to step. But it was too late. He slipped in the mud and threw his hands in the air. The boards splashed into the puddle, and Freeman landed on his back.

"Aw, shit!" he screamed, sprawling out beside the boards. I was glad at least they didn't fall on top of him. I dropped my end and dove like a football player, landing next to him.

"Hurry!" he shouted. "Get that last board before the train does!"

He was half sitting, trying to catch his balance. Doc came over and watched with great amusement, wagging his tail. The intense light cast eerie shadows on one side of everything, including Freeman and Doc. The remaining two-by-six shone like a luminescent fixture across the tracks, ready to derail the train.

A piercing whistle split the air and I nearly jumped out of my skin. The engine bore down right where we'd been sitting, its whistle escalating and bright light growing brighter.

"Screw the board! Get cover!" screamed Freeman.

I shot farther back in leaps and bounds, flew horizontal and slid to a stop in the weeds. Freeman landed a foot away. We turned to watch. The massive engine was not fifty feet from the board. I realized then it was an engine with no cars, probably going to pick up cars for a morning run. The monstrous machine crashed down on the board, splintering it into countless pieces, most of which flew up vertically at some fantastic speed, before arching back and gliding over the roof, as if in slow motion.

But we did not hear the crack of the board, so loud was the noise from the engine. In the shadows beneath the train, splinters of wood zigzagged up and down in lightning fashion, moving forward with the wheels of the train, quite like I had imagined happening to myself. The whole event took seconds or less, yet it seemed like several minutes.

"Damnation!" Freeman rubbed his head after the engine had departed as quickly as it came.

We examined the pieces. White splinters lay everywhere, and I didn't see one section longer than about six inches. Freeman picked up two pieces slightly longer than the others.

"Think we can glue 'em?"

"Jesus! That could've been us!" was all I could say, petting Doc's back for comfort.

We brushed ourselves off with my T-shirt, which had miraculously stayed put in the middle of the tracks. We had no enthusiasm for moving the remaining boards any farther that night, so we lugged them into some bushes beside the tracks and covered them up with leaves and dirt.

We slid in silence through the shadows toward home, Doc running to and fro beside us, dashing up front, darting back and sniffing at everything in sight. And, of course, coming to sniff my behind now and then, like home base, or some central point for comparison. I was glad Freeman seemed too tired to notice.

But by and by Freeman said, "I smell somethin' funny around here. Though I can't be positive if it's my imagination or not."

He raised his nose and appeared to be sniffing around, trying to locate the source of the problem. "Don't you smell it, Joey? It's like there's a pile of fresh shit nearby."

"I can't smell a thing."

"It's almost like it's followin' us. You really don't smell nothin'?"

"Nope."

"Oh, man, it's a rank one. Can't you smell it?"

I pretended to be whiffing at the air, then shook my head negative.

"Not even a little?"

"No, not really."

He stared at me like I was not being honest, like surely I had to smell something.

"Well, maybe a little." I acted like I just got a whiff of it. "Hey, I'll betchya it's Doc! I'll bet he rolled in something or other!"

"God, it's disgusting."

"Stupid dog," I replied. "Now I see why my parents never wanted me to have one. For once I can see they might have been right."

"I ain't sure it's him though." Freeman stopped, called Doc over, held him close and sniffed all around. "It don't smell like him, Joey."

"Well, it has to be. What else can it be?"

"I don't know." He looked at me pensively. "It couldn't be one of us, could it?"

"Not unless it's you."

"Nope. It ain't me. I'm sure of that."

"Well, blast it! Then it has to be that stupid dog, like I said."

"Unless it ain't."

"You're not pointing a finger at me, are you?"

"I ain't pointin' no finger. All I'm sayin' is that there's a powerful stink around here, and it don't appear to be no Doctor Dog. And I know for a fact it ain't me."

"What do you want to do about it? Stick your nose up my crack? I can't smell it anyway."

"I thought you just said you could."

"Well, I can't really. I only said that so you wouldn't feel so stupid yourself."

"Oh," he replied with a smirk, looking satisfied that he had solved the mystery. "Then it must be my imagination."

"Must be," I said, disgusted with myself and at the same time mad at Freeman since it was his fault in the first place. I wanted to pound his head a few hundred times, and if I wasn't afraid of losing my only friend I probably would've.

But soon thereafter he dug two crumpled cigarettes from his back pocket and silently passed one to me, like a peace offering. His raspy lighter lit us up and we sat down on the curb, all set for a much-deserved rest. The smell of the smoke created a comfortable feeling in me, and I believed I could understand why people liked cigarettes so much. I inhaled a bit and was relieved that at least for the moment I could not smell myself. I gazed across the street in the dim light and contemplated the stillness of the leaves there and how quiet the night was, disturbed only by the ghost-like clouds of smoke we exhaled now and then.

But the peace and silence did not last long. It could not have been more than five minutes before two headlights abruptly shot out from a side street ahead of us, turned rapidly in our direction, and in another moment glared upon us! As they did, I noticed an unlit globe light on top of the vehicle.

"Run!" we shrieked together. We jumped up, wheeled around, and leaped over the low picket fence behind us, landing in tomatoes, chrysanthemums, and pansies, smells I knew from my mom's garden, and I can't recall what happened to the cigarettes.

Doc poked his snout through the slats and whined at us, but it was too late to worry about him. Through the fence we could see the cop car come to a stop, directly in front of us. We stared for about two seconds, whereupon the dome light began flashing red and blue and a floodlight burst upon us like sunshine, nearly blinding me.

"Go!" squealed Freeman as he bounded off and vanished around the side of the house. I couldn't see a thing and hesitated a moment for my eyes to adjust. They had barely done so when I lit out like a rocket toward the other side of the house. But no sooner did I start up than I realized both my feet were entangled in a chain that I hadn't seen due to the blinding light.

I found myself decked out on my face and hands across a concrete patio. And I soon noticed the chain was hooked up to a German shepherd—who at that very moment began growling! I crawled on my hands and knees faster than I ever thought possible, scraping and grinding like a deranged animal across the concrete, lit up in that dazzling police light like the main attraction in a circus.

I stumbled to my feet and took off like a champion, in spite of my blindness and fear.

At the very moment I thought I was free and clear, that huge shepherd sank his teeth into my pants! The dreadful tug was on the inside of my left leg, down near the ankle. He missed the flesh but I stumbled again, and my heart sank with me.

Yet at the same time I was mad. I yanked with the stuck leg and kicked the dog's thick skull with the other foot, hard as I could. There was a flashing of fur and a dog yelping and rapid movement of my legs, and in one quick blur I was on my feet again. The dog had a hunk of my pants in his mouth, but I didn't care; he was whining and acting stunned, and it was all the time I needed.

In two more seconds I crossed the yard and jumped the picket fence on the other side, like a hurdle in a track meet. Unfortunately, I hooked my pants atop one of the prongs; the crotch ripped as I flopped down the other side like a rag doll, where I landed in another garden, my face mushed firmly in the soft, moist earth.

"Stop and come out with your hands up!" came a deep voice on a loudspeaker. And so help me if I didn't pee my pants clear down to my knees, the first time since I was a little kid. The warmth spread slowly and actually felt good, though I was not inclined to enjoy it.

I thought about what the cop said for however long it took to take the whizz: maybe I should have done what he said, but with all the commotion and the dog barking and my blindness and other problems I couldn't think clearly. I dragged myself up and sailed through the rest of the garden, squishing what felt like several mushy tomatoes beneath my feet.

I was almost around the corner of that second house when a porch light burst on beside me. The porch door flew open in front of me and some pot-bellied guy with a hairy chest stepped out, pulling his bathrobe together.

"Hey, you!" he shouted.

But I was not in the mood for chitchat. I flew past, so close I thought I felt the warmth of his belly, then down the side of his house, out to the next street, then into another yard; I leapt one more fence, in a single bound—a chain-link fence nearly chest high—and damn-me-to-hell if another dog didn't start barking madly!

But it was only a noisy poodle. Still, I was obliged to scramble back over the fence, charge around it, and race down the next driveway, that loathsome poodle working his vocal cords like they probably never worked before.

I flew past the garage and into a backyard, where I disappeared in a patch of rhododendrons, cracking off a few of the branches, though not on purpose; and soon enough I tumbled into another backyard with lots of trees around it, where all was quiet, finally.

I was terrified and filled with anxiety and other discouraging emotions, not to mention that I smelled like a cesspool and was covered with cuts and scratches. I wanted to break down and bawl like a baby, yet I knew I had to lay low and stay quiet at all costs.

I crept to a basement window well, in the blackest shadows underneath a large picnic deck. I dropped into the nearly invisible hole there, intending to hibernate for however long it took for everything to blow over.

I was twisted and mangled as a pretzel, trapped in the stuffiness of my own foul air, but it seemed like a safe spot to hide and rest for a while. I breathed deep and tried to think happy thoughts, but it was impossible. I told God I was ever so thankful that he hadn't let that cop shoot me dead. I swore I'd never steal again in my entire life if he'd just let me out of there alive, that one time, so I could make it to confession. I shook like a rabbit, and couldn't remember being so scared.

I prayed an Act of Contrition, ten Hail Marys and ten Our Fathers. I wanted to do more, like the Apostle's Creed and those other oddballs we do at Saint Frances, but I couldn't remember all the words. So I repeated the Act of Contrition, slowly and thoughtfully to show how much I meant it, really truly meant it. For I knew if I died that night it was most likely all over as to whether I'd be playing the harp, or getting served up at the Big Forever Barbecue, sizzling away with all the other crooks and sinners.

My head was tucked in my knees, and I was reviewing these things over and over, whereupon I fell asleep. I dreamt I was lying on a chaise lounge alongside a kidney-shaped pool filled with cool blue water. Small waves crashed gently over the edge and turned into sudsy ocean foam, which made soft noises and swirled underneath me. I was getting a nice tan, lying on my stomach, my head turned toward the pool.

Then along came Maggie from behind! I could see her without looking. She was dressed in that very same white bikini that JC's girlfriend had been wearing and was positively stunning, bursting with loveliness and happiness at seeing me there. She stole up quietly, leaned over, and began licking my ear; I felt limp and warm and satisfied, and I laid there enjoying the licking of her warm tongue, which soon turned into a wet, hot slobbering that felt better yet. It was one of the most pleasant dreams I'd ever had, and I wanted it to go on forever.

But presently it seemed my ear was turning into a damp sponge, and I woke up. I thought, "Aaah, what a wonderful dream! I only wish I could have one every night!"

Then my heart stopped and my brain stopped and I turned into an icicle; I knew I was wide-awake and stuffed in someone's window well, yet the warm, wet slobbering continued!

I was losing my mind!

I was afraid to move, but I slowly looked up in fear and dread—there stood Doctor Dog, licking my ear, slobbering all over it! I laughed and smiled and hugged him and even cried a little, then asked, "Where's Freeman?"

Of course he didn't answer, but I knew it was time to head out before he barked or made noises that would give me away. Plus the thin grayness of morning had arrived, and people would be up soon. We left quickly and slunk home in the shadows and finally made it to the safety of Freeman's backyard, which was quiet and still as a graveyard.

Sore and wretched, I crawled in the tent where I was greeted by the comfort of Freeman's voice. "Where ya been, pokey wokey? I was startin' to think ya got caught."

"I dang near did! And I thought you did, too. How'd you escape?"

"Run like a bandit with my pants afire, mainly. Then bolted up a tree and hid in the branches. Thin mothers too, and I almost fell out twice. That blasted cop drove back and forth a few hundred times right under me, beamin' his light into the bushes and all over the place, everywhere but up that flimsy tree. I thought sure he'd spot me!

"Next thing I knew some clown stepped out on his front porch in his bathrobe with his belly hangin' out. Then he cut a big old fart and went back in. Made me glad I was up in the tree, too. The lights went out and the cop stopped going by.

"I waited awhile—quite a long while, really—then climbed down. I called all over for ya, but had to give up 'cause that German shepherd barked every time I shouted. I figured you'd get back sometime, after that cop took off."

"I didn't hear you call," I said in an accusing tone.

"You must have been far away, or else ya got potatoes in your ears."

I told my story, then showed the tear in my pant leg and the hole in my crotch. I thought he'd show great interest and sympathy, maybe even be jealous; I hoped he would, but I guess he was as tired as me, because all he said was, "Looks like good air conditioning, Joey."

At least he didn't mention the stench again, whose source in that small tent was more evident than before.

"What do you think will happen with Doc?" I asked.

"He's got no collar, so we can keep him. That's the law. We just need permission from my folks, which shouldn't be no problem."

"What about dog food?"

Doc snored away and moved his paws as if in a dream, chasing something or someone—me, I imagined.

"Matt once said he can get all the free food he wants behind Willey's Hamburgers. He sometimes eats there himself." Freeman added that we could probably build a doghouse with boards from Matt's junk pile. My watch said five fifteen when we laid back down on the sleeping bags, in that soup of many aromas enclosed and enhanced by Matt's small tent. Doc was smashed between us, like he slept that way every night. It's the one time in my life that I think I fell asleep before my eyes actually closed.

Rays of sunshine streamed through pencil-sized holes in the tent canvas, and waves of heat rolled off the walls. Flies whirled and zinged around the place, attracted and driven crazy by the smells, but there was no sign of Freeman or Doc. In pain, I remembered I had to get to confession, and had better not get killed beforehand. I popped out of the tent, but there was no Freeman and no Doc.

"What the heck?" I thought.

Sounds of barking led me to the front yard, where I sat on the steps and watched Freeman and Doc play, along with James who ran around excitedly. Freeman was holding a stick in the air, making Doc jump. He kept jumping too, hopping on his hind legs like they were pogo sticks. James laughed and screamed with delight as Freeman kept the stick just out of reach.

"C'mon, let him have it!" cried James after a while.

"He's gotta work for a livin'! Like everyone else."

"Don't be a jerk, Freddie," I said. "Let him have the thing. You wouldn't like me doing that to you."

"I ain't that dumb, though."

"Give 'im the stick!" James and I said together.

Freeman handed it over. Doc chomped on it, then dropped it at Freeman's feet. I suddenly felt less pity for the dog. Freeman grabbed the stick again and bounced Doc to the side of a tree, Doc whining and crying all over again, now scratching the tree trunk to get the stick.

"Look! He's learnin' to climb a tree!"

James clapped and laughed in ecstasy, which made Freeman move the stick higher.

Doc cried more and kept scratching, but it was all I could take. I needed to go home, clean up, and get more sleep.

"Good luck!" I said, leaving them to their games. "See you tomorrow afternoon."

I couldn't wait to rip off my clothes, hop in the tub, leap into bed and then snore away till confession time. I thought my mom was visiting friends and I knew my dad was at work for the morning, so I looked forward to doing these things without interruption.

But there was my mom, in the middle of the kitchen, flour on her apron and arms across her chest. My head was down and I nearly plowed into her.

"Have a good night, Joseph?"

"Oh, yea. Just great!" I feared my stench would knock her for a loop, but she didn't appear to notice.

"Did you get enough sleep?"

"Oh, sure. As much as you'd expect anyway."

"That's an interesting dog Freddie's got in his front yard." She must have been looking out the window. I wondered how long she'd been watching.

"He's a big one isn't he?"

"Where did Freddie get him?"

"Oh, he followed us home last evening. From near Stoneridge. He has no collar either, so Freddie says we can keep him. If his mom lets him."

"Why were you near Stoneridge?"

"Well, we planned to pick up nails the workers drop. Though we really didn't find too many." She looked me over as if this were highly suspicious and certainly not on her list of acceptable activities.

"You know, so they don't rust and go to waste. Which they would otherwise. And you know how the nuns are about not wasting things!" I thought of how the nuns made us use pencils till there was almost nothing left, how they went into a tantrum if you threw a piece of half-used paper in the garbage, and how the books they gave us were probably a hundred years old or so. Anything tied to the nuns in a positive light might help.

But my mom didn't seem interested, and it appeared that I was speaking to a heart of stone. "Plus Timmy and me cooked hot dogs there once, before they built any houses. It's interesting to see the place now." I tried my best to smile and look cheerful.

She examined my ears and ignored my babbling. I thought I was saying more than necessary, so I shut up.

"Timmy and I," she corrected coolly, her gaze on my ears.

"Timmy and I once cooked hot dogs there. That's correct."

"That's all?"

"Marshmallows too."

"I mean is that all you did there last night?"

Her suspicious tone made me desperately want to keep the lid on. "Well, we walked around and looked at new houses. It's real interesting how they build them these days."

I wondered how I might escape before the stench zapped her. I was amazed it hadn't hit yet.

"When you're with Freddie Freeman, I want you to be sure you behave yourself!"

"Oh, I try! I really do try!" Then without thinking, I added, "Freddie's a good kid, even if his family is a bit different. And they do go to church … on Christmas and Easter and when his Dad isn't working on weekends."

"You sound so like your father! But I guess that shouldn't surprise me." There was displeasure in her voice, and she shook her head as if dealing with the two of us was more than she could handle. "Please be sure your room is cleaned today, Joseph. And don't forget to vacuum your floor—thoroughly, and not like last time!"

"I'll get it right," I assured her.

I started away, elated she hadn't smelled me or asked more questions. Then I recalled that she had complained recently about her hay fever and her sinuses were probably stuffed. I was by the kitchen door when her voice sank into the back of my neck.

"What happened to your arms, Joseph? They're scratched and bloody on back."

I turned as if she held a gun on me and acted surprised as possible.

"Oh, that?" I squeaked in a high, faint voice. "I took a bad fall. A stumble, actually."

"How did you fall?"

"Jeez, Mom." My voice lowered, most embarrassingly. "Do all moms ask questions like you?"

"They should."

"Well." I rolled my arms around; till then I hadn't looked in the light. Purple bruises, caked blood, and smudges of dirt blended together, from my elbows to my wrists. Much worse than I thought. "I took a spill and landed in some dirt real hard."

"You tripped?"

"I was moving too fast and I landed in a patch of rocky dirt."

"You weren't running away from something … or someone … were you?"

"No. Of course not!"

I was flying out a window, Mom! Because Freeman scared the holy bejoly out of me. Warmth rose in my ears.

"Is that a tear in your pants?"

Her eyes went to my lower leg. I supposed the only reason she hadn't spotted the airy opening in my crotch was because I had my legs pinched together. I looked down like I'd never seen the missing ankle piece before. The German shepherd hole was large as two hands, with ragged edges.

"I'm not exactly sure how that got there." My voice lowered. True I wasn't exactly sure, even if I was pretty sure. I recalled the flash of fur and my foot clobbering the dog's head. "It must have been from when I fell." In front of the shepherd. In the blinding light. Because a cop was chasing me. But you didn't ask those details, thank goodness!

Her eyes narrowed and bored down like dentist drills. "Is that a scratch on your face, too?"

"Probably, Mom. I brushed my face when I landed." The other time, when I dived away from the train—but you didn't ask that either! I focused my eyes about where I imagined her navel was.

"Come here a minute, Joseph."

My ears felt ready to flame. Christ!

"Why, Mom?"

"Just come over here."

I knew it; she smelled me! Like a little kid! Like a skunk! God, it was humiliating!

"You didn't wet your pants, did you?"

"Why are you asking that, Mom?" High voice.

"It smells as if you wet your pants, Joseph. Did you?"

I reached to feel them, as if I had no idea what she was talking about. I kept my head down and patted my crotch to check for dampness.

"You know, they are a tad dampish."

"A 'tad dampish,' Joseph?"

"Look, its embarrassing Mom. Real embarrassing. I was playing with Doctor—I mean that dog of Freddie's—and he got all excited. The next thing I knew my pants were all wet. But he's just a pup, Mom! And he's gotta learn to control himself better." My voice was shooting up and down like a yo-yo.

"You think that monster's a puppy?"

"Well, you know, mentally, I mean."

"And I suppose you just happened to roll by accident in a dog dropping, too?"

"How could you tell?" I asked, keeping my head down. My ear temperature rose a hundred degrees; it was the final straw!

"Do you know your ears are as red as Satan's spear, Joseph?"

I did know! I raised my head slowly, drawing a deep breath as I met her beady, icicle-gray eyes. My ears sizzled but I asked, as calmly as I could, "Wouldn't you be embarrassed if this sort of thing happened to you, Mom?"

She paused and moved back. "Well … I dare say I would! But I would never play with a disgusting animal like that! Nor would I recommend that you do it again!"

She shuddered, perhaps at the thought of me rolling around with Doc. I didn't know if she had seen the crotch rip. If she had, she must have decided that she'd had enough and her nerves could take no more. Her eyes probed mine intensely.

"Are you lying to me, Joseph Simpson?"

Was I lying? Had I lied? I couldn't see it, though the truth couldn't get much thinner without disappearing altogether. Yet there I was, cut and battered, stinking unbearably, ears lit up, and the rest of my summer riding on the answer. I did the only thing left. I stretched my story one teensy bit more.

"You know me, Mom! I'm as honest as Thomas Jefferson!"

"You mean George Washington?"

"Oh, right," I squeaked, shaking my head. Damn—I always get those two mixed up.

"Honest George, Honest Joey," I corrected myself.

"Well, Mr. Honest Joseph, I want that room cleaned by this afternoon!" She moved back a step, seemingly repulsed by the sight and stench of her own son. Not that I blamed her one bit.

"Don't you worry! It will be cleaner than it's ever been! I'm just tired right now, and I think I need a bath and a nap. If I may be excused."

"You had better be more careful, Joseph! I worry about you." She stood with her hands on her hips, examining her son-with-many-stories.

"Oh, Mom," I squeaked, vanishing down the hall like a sickly ghost. "Just don't you worry about Joseph Simpson!"

5

A dozen or so people stood in line ahead of me. The confessional signs indicated two priests were in, Fathers Sedrick and Hannafin. I always chose Hannafin. He's older and kinder and less of an idiot, and has more faith in everything working out, including sins committed by kids. But mainly I like him because he doesn't play twenty questions, and gives just five Hail Marys for penance, no matter what. This takes maybe fifty seconds and always makes the week affordable.

So I got in Hannafin's line, happy to see lots of people ahead of me. More people speeds the priests up and makes them less concerned with embarrassing details. I soon knelt in the darkness, waiting for the screen to open. I wondered what Freeman was up to—probably snoring away and having a girlie dream, that good-for-nothing bum!

Mumbles and jumbles came from the other side, but I couldn't make out any words. But soon enough my screen flew open, and in the dim light was the outline of a new face, not Hannafin's like the name outside indicated. This guy looked younger and taller with longer hair and a large nose.

He slouched to listen better. A sinking feeling came over me as I recalled that Hannafin was on a trip to Italy or Ireland or one of those Catholic joints to visit his family, according to my mom. But I couldn't back out. I'd have to forge ahead and hope this visiting priest wasn't as bad as Sedrick.

"Bless me, Father, for I have sinned. It's been a week since my last confession. Father, I cursed and swore about twenty times; I had obscene thoughts about fifty-five times; I lost my temper four times; I beat on my brother three; I smoked five times but I didn't inhale much; I stole once and I masturbated."

It was my usual spiel with a few variations, such as stealing and smoking, which I mumbled softly near the end to the best of my abil-

94

ity, in hopes they'd slip by without the need for humiliating explanations.

"How many times did you abuse yourself, son?"

"Beg your pardon, Father?" I didn't think I said anything about "abusing myself." I was sure I hadn't. In fact, it was a new vocabulary word used that way. I had no idea what he meant.

"How many times did you abuse yourself, son?"

"I'm sorry, Father. I never said I abused myself." I resolved to look that one up when I got home—it sounded like an interesting idea.

"How many times did you masturbate, son?" His voice rose and seemed unnecessarily accusatory. My ears warmed up and I got an instant bad feeling in my gut.

"I ... I ... I'm not exactly sure, Father."

"Every day? Once a day? Twice a day?" He spoke louder, definitely accusatory. I worried that people outside could hear him. Dollars to doughnuts the person in the next confessional could. I felt like dying.

"Yes, Father," I squeaked.

"Which?"

"Which what, Father?"

"Which number of times a day, son?"

"Oh. That. Maybe one and a half."

"One and a half?" He spoke like I must be an imbecile, and his voice raised another notch.

"On average, Father. You know." My ears were ready to burst, along with the rest of my head.

"What do you think about when you do that, son?"

"Not much, Father."

"Whom do you think about when you do that, son?"

"I don't ... I don't know her name." I barely whispered.

"Excuse me, son? I can hardly hear you. Please speak louder!"

"I don't know her name, Father."

"You don't know her name?" His voice boomed and reverberated, loud enough for people in the church to hear, along with anyone in the neighborhood who had good hearing, it seemed to me.

"It's ... it's a lady in a picture I saw once. Its ... its part of the obscene thoughts," I squeaked like a mouse, ready to cry. How I wished

Hannafin were in! He only said God didn't like that sort of thing and such ideas aren't good for developing minds. You'd get your Hail Mary's, be done in a minute, and your soul was back to normal. This nut was too much! And of all the times I could've gotten him, why now?

"Tell me about these obscene thoughts, son."

"They're mainly about that picture my friend showed me. Three years ago in my basement." My lips moved and I hoped he heard me; I wasn't about to repeat it. He leaned closer, flattening his ear to the screen. "You still remember such a picture?" His voice shook the walls like a cannon.

"A little bit, Father." A lot less than I wanted to, anyway.

"You know that's a serious sin? The solitary sin, the sin of self-abuse?" The walls seemed to amplify the sound, in a way I never noticed before.

"Yes, Father." My lips were stiff and parched, my throat was dry.

"When you feel these urges you need to pray extra hard and think of the Virgin Mary. You do know how to pray, don't you?"

"Yes, Father. I go to Catholic school."

There was a long pause, like he had to do his religious calculations all over again—like there was something really wrong with me now! I, who with a Catholic school background, ought to know better!

"I'm sure that going to Catholic school will help with your journey and create a reward for you in the hereafter, son. But if you die with a mortal sin, you'll be throwing all that away, casting your soul and your upbringing to the eternal flames of perdition!"

"That's why I'm here, Father. I'd like to get my soul cleaned up a bit."

"Where did you get the cigarettes?"

Oh Dear Jesus! This guy was something else!

"My best friend, Father." My only friend, too.

"Where did he get them?"

"I'm not positive. Maybe his dad's dresser." Probably his dad's dresser. That's where he usually gets them.

"Do you plan to stop doing that?"

"No, Father."

"Excuse me?"

"I said 'No,' Father."

"You don't plan to stop smoking?"

"Oh. I thought you asked if I was going to keep doing that. Yes, I plan to stop, Father." Someday. I felt confident Freeman would be caught sooner or later, then I'd have to stop.

"Was taking cigarettes the stealing that you mentioned?"

"No, Father." I mumbled and coughed a little, wishing I could learn to lie, wondering if God wasn't already punishing me.

"What was it you stole, if not cigarettes?"

"A few boards, Father. From a new house."

"What did you do that for?"

"My friend and I are doing some building. And we can't afford it. So I guess Satan suggested we do it that way, Father."

Another pause, followed by a deep breath, like I was the largest fish he'd ever caught on a confessional line. I wondered if this was one of those homo priests I heard rumors about, who liked to do funny things with kids like me. I tried to banish the thought.

"I believe that's correct, son. I don't think you or your friend would get ideas like that yourselves. Satan is a terrible influence. And the road to hell is certainly paved with good intentions."

I wondered if he cared that other people were waiting. Was I going to have to stay here all night?

"How much do you think these boards were worth?"

Jezum! "I, uh, I don't know, Father. Maybe what I make in six months." Or fifteen years. I had no idea. What was I, a lumber salesman?

"Stealing is a very, very serious sin. More than anything else you told me."

"Yes, Father." What the hell do you think I came here for?

"Do you think you'll do it again?"

"No, Father." Then again, how could I be sure? What do I look like now—a prophet?

"I believe God wants to forgive you, son, though you've hurt Him deeply. For your penance, say fourteen rosaries, two each day for the next week. "If you do that instead of abuse yourself you'll be much happier. It's a good habit, one that could save you a lot of trouble. And I think you should give the boards back too, but I'll leave that up to you."

Two rosaries a day for seven days? I'd never heard of such a ridiculous penance! Not since the days when they burned people at the stake!

"Okay, son?"

"Yes, Father."

"Don't sound so unhappy—you should be glad that's all you have for penance."

"I'm very glad, Father." I lied to appease him and I didn't care, and for once my ears didn't even get hot.

"Anything else I should know, son?"

"No, Father. But … "

"Yes?" he asked, with a ring of enthusiasm.

"If I die before seven days are up, will I go to hell for stealing?"

"No, son; it wouldn't mean that. God wouldn't send you to hell for stealing a few boards. If you stole a car, maybe, but I'm sure it has to be at least a hundred dollars for Him to consider that drastic option."

Well, goddamn! You're shittin' me, dad! I wanted to shout, but I controlled myself and held my thoughts under a bushel of happiness while he proceeded with the Latin mumbo-jumbo. I suddenly wanted to hug and kiss this guy!

So those old fart nuns had fed me hogwash all those years! I should have known, especially when Sister Sylvester said you could go to hell over a pencil stub with Trina O'Neal's cooties on it! I wondered about poor Tom Haley. And I wondered what other lies we'd been fed.

But one thing they had said was right: You do feel better after confession! I floated out of that dark box with more penance than ever before, yet I felt like angels must feel. I rode my bike down the middle of Jefferson Avenue, racing a few honking cars, whistling to myself. I even weaved in and out of the dotted yellow lines, like they were a bicycle slalom course. So … I could continue my activities with Freeman, and didn't have to worry about a blackened soul anymore!

"You should go to that visiting priest who's filling in for Father Hannafin," I advised Timmy before he left with my mom and the twins for confession. "He's really cool."

"Why's that?"

"He's so easygoing. Doesn't ask a lot of questions or poke his nose in your business. And he'll only give a few Hail Marys, if you haven't been too bad."

I felt like a snake, and I knew it was one more lie to confess next week. But I was a happy snake, and it's good to feel that way every now and then.

"All right! Thanks for the tip!" Timmy replied with what almost sounded like brotherly love.

James opened the door when I knocked. "Thanks for all them crabs, Joey! I really like 'em!" he burst out with enthusiasm.

"Did you hold them in your hand?"

"Yea! They tickled me!" He laughed like I'd given him a million dollars. I was pleased to see him so happy.

"Where are they now?"

He reached in the pocket of his shorts, fumbled around, and pulled one out.

"This is my best one!" He beamed.

"Um … I think maybe you should put him back with the others."

"Why, Joey?"

"Well, um … they get lonely if they're all by themselves."

"Aw. All right." He held the crab up and whispered something to it that I couldn't hear.

"And you need to keep them outside, so they don't start smelling," I added.

"I know. Freddie made me put them by the garage."

"Where is that guy, anyway?"

"He's gettin' stuff from Matt for the doghouse. Out back."

He led me to the backyard where Freeman and Matt were discussing a pile of boards that lay between them.

"You sure you know what you're doing now?" asked Matt.

"I know exactly what I'm doin'. I'm makin' a doghouse."

"You still haven't showed me a plan, though."

"I told ya, it's all in my head!" He pointed with two hands to the sides of his head.

"And I still say you ought to put it on paper," retorted Matt with an air of authority and disappointment.

"Just gimme the hammer, will ya?" Freeman sounded impatient, eager to begin.

Matt handed the hammer over, shaking his head. "Watch him real close, Joey. He might be dangerous."

Matt laughed and continued shaking his head as he walked away. It appeared to me he was being unnecessarily negative.

But we didn't waste time worrying about him. Freeman and I measured and hammered and banged and sawed, while James looked on cheerfully, passing boards and nails and telling me now and then I was doing a "really, really good job."

Doc slept peacefully under the peach tree, wagging a tail at flies occasionally, oblivious to the new home being built for him.

An hour or so had passed and a large boxy structure was beginning to take shape. I had a feeling of accomplishment and usefulness, even though several things didn't seem quite right. For example, a great many cracks could be seen in the walls and roof, and pretty much wherever two boards came together.

"I wanted the cracks, actually," explained Freeman after I pointed them out, "because dogs need good ventilation to stay healthy." I was considering why he hadn't mentioned cracks from the start when he added, "Especially this guy, Joey—his farts are almost as bad as yours!"

James and Freeman laughed like this was a big funny joke, and I would have laughed too, except I was worried that it might be true.

We examined the final product and it became apparent that all the walls were lopsided and the edges crooked. Large nails poked in and out, some of them spiked up and down like daggers in the roof. Plus the contraption weighed half a ton. We lugged the thing behind the garage nonetheless, then dragged Doc over to check it out, eager to see his reaction.

I don't know what anyone expected but Doc just stood and looked at what was supposed to be the door. He started to whine and make noises, like he wanted nothing to do with our work of art. We had to push and roll him like a sack of potatoes to get him inside. Then James kneeled in front so he couldn't get out.

"He'll adjust and learn to like it when he realizes it's his new home," I said, trying to be optimistic.

"Maybe we should nail a door up, until he gets the idea," Freeman suggested. Doc howled and cried and sounded like a tortured being, and it became obvious he was not going to quit until we let him out.

James couldn't take it anymore. "This thing's junk, you guys! He hates it! I do too!"

Doc howled as if in agreement.

"He's right, Freddie. We can't make him live in there. How would you like to be locked up in a place like that? Especially with all those nails jabbing into you." Freeman wasn't happy, but he had to admit we were right. So we let Doc out and he ran around and around the yard, jumping and barking and chasing shadows and thin air. Freeman hung his shoulders and looked despondent.

"What's going on, guys?" It was Matt, who had come back to examine the doghouse.

We watched in silence while he checked it out, leaning on one side to see how heavy it was, and how wobbly, which was quite a bit. He touched a few of the nails sticking up, kicked one side, then stuck a finger in a few of the cracks.

"Nice job, James," he said, ignoring Freeman. "You want me to make a real one for you now?"

"Yea, yea! Doc does too! Make it soon, Matt, okay?" Matt turned to Freeman and snickered. "You shoulda helped him, Freddie."

"Very funny, Matt. I'd like to see you do better."

"What you need is a plan, guys. Whenever you build something you got to have a plan. That's number one."

He spoke without sarcasm, and acted like at least we might learn a lesson from the effort. Then he pulled a paper from his shirt pocket, which had a picture of a nice-looking doghouse with numbers and writing all over it and arrows pointing here and there.

"Like this," he said.

Then he put himself to work, giving orders to James to get him the hammer, go find a pry bar, lay the boards he was taking apart in a neat pile, and so on, and it soon became obvious that Freeman and I were better off reading comics.

My mom stood before me that evening as I emerged from the bathroom, towel around me, still dripping from a bath.

"We need to have a little chat, Joseph."

I immediately had visions of questions about Stoneridge. Or complaints about Freeman. My ears warmed up before she began. It's terrible to have a guilty conscience, particularly right after you've already taken care of things in confession.

"Your father and I have discussed this Freddie Freeman situation," she began. The way she said "situation"—as if she was dealing with a disease or some kind of problem with the Russians—made me cringe and fear the worst.

"I agree with your father that you need a friend. But I'm very concerned about your soul, Joseph—and I worry about all the temptations you may be subjected to. Still, I was impressed with how well you boys behaved at the beach."

I breathed a sigh of relief, and tried to imagine what she could possibly say next.

After all, we had already slept out together.

"So I was wondering if you'd be willing to babysit Timmy and the twins tomorrow, while I do some volunteer visits for church? I thought perhaps you and Freddie could take them and James to the park for a few hours and keep an eye on them?"

So, we were to be a joint babysitting service! Well, that would alter our plans, since we had already agreed to explore the Westwoods for a fort site—it was the next logical step, even though I still had serious doubts about getting enough lumber. But what the heck? If it meant my mom would feel better about Freeman, I was all for it.

"Sure. Those kids seem to like Freddie, you know?"

"I did notice that. And that's why I think you two might do a good job babysitting together."

And so the next morning we all started walking downtown to the wooded park north of the stores. The kids were excited, except for James because he didn't like having to leave Doc home.

"But it's a nice doghouse Matt made." I tried to console him. "He'll be just fine in there."

"I want him to come!" James cried.

"They don't allow dogs at the park," Freeman said. "So stop crying and act your age."

Freeman was as pleased to hear my mom's thoughts as I had been. But as we walked along I now worried about red convertibles, which I kept looking for, wondering when we were going to bump into JC next.

To my surprise, James and Timmy got along well, and together they pushed the twins on the swings. Freeman and I sat on a bench by the maple trees, discussing the fort, when a voice hailed from behind us.

"I thought that was you, Joseph Simpson! How is your summer going?" At first I did not recognize the girl with a white baseball hat, white knee-length shorts, sneakers and high socks, and a light blue, tucked-in T-shirt. Nor did the long brown, wavy hair ring a bell. Shiny black binoculars hanging from a strap on the girl's neck further confused me. It was her voice that finally registered, in a delayed sort of reaction.

"Annabelle! Hi. It's going well. How's yours?"

"Good so far. My parents got me these binoculars, and I've taken up bird watching. But right now I'm studying those squirrels over there."

She pointed to two squirrels scampering about the base of an oak tree, not far away.

"They've had their second litter and I'm watching to see how long before the babies become independent. It's part of a report for my biology class." She turned to Freeman.

"Your friend looks familiar, Joseph."

"This is my neighbor, Freddie Freeman."

Freeman readjusted his baseball hat. "You look a bit familiar too."

"I used to go to Piney Wood, before my parents sent me to Virgin Mary Academy. That's probably where I saw you."

"I do remember you! You were a few grades behind and you wore pigtails! I think you've changed a little."

"Thank you; I would hope so."

Freeman snapped his fingers. "Annabelle Finnegan, isn't it?"

"Close. But it's Annabelle Flannigan, actually."

"Do you like the academy?"

"Oh, yes! The nuns make us work real hard and we do lots of interesting reports. Like this one on squirrels. I learn so much more! Public school was way too easy!" I looked at the ground and said nothing.

"Joey here likes Catholic school, too." Freeman pointed his thumb in my direction. I kept my focus on the ground and nodded my head slightly. "But I think I'll stick with public school myself," he added.

"Isn't that the twins and Timmy over there?" She pointed to the swings.

"Yea. And Freddie's brother, James."

"So you're babysitting. That ought to keep you out of trouble." She laughed and I flinched, thinking back to a day she and I spent in the junkyard, three years ago.

"Well, it's nice to see you, Joseph." I looked up and she was smiling at me, blue eyes sparkling and her hair longer and browner than I remembered it.

"And you, too." She turned to Freeman again.

"Good luck with the squirrels," Freeman said.

"Why thanks!" she replied as she turned and strolled off toward the trees.

"Moses on a merry-go-round!" I said the second I thought she was out of earshot. "That girl's gone through some changes!"

"I guess. She's sproutin' a nice set of knockers there, ain't she?"

Right then Timmy came storming over, looking terribly upset, like we'd done something wrong.

"You guys were talking to that girl and not watching! James pushed too hard and made Mary fall off! Look!"

We glanced where he pointed and there was Mary, face down in the hard dirt, not moving. Before I even got up, Freeman was off and running and by the time I was halfway there he was picking her up.

"You'll be fine, now," he said soothingly. "It's just a little scratch."

He sat her on his knee and wiped her face with his shirttail, one arm around her back.

"I'm sure James didn't mean it. Sometimes he plays a bit rough, but he's just trying to have a little fun."

Patrick and Timmy looked on quietly, and James hung his head.

"Say you're sorry, James."

"I didn't mean it!" he wailed.

"We know you didn't, but you still have to say you're sorry."

"Sorry!" he shouted, unhappy and depressed with the whole situation.

Mary calmed down and put her arm around Freeman.

"You saved me. I love you," I heard her whisper.

Freeman set her on the swing and pushed her gently for a while, then things returned to normal. He told James he needed to be more careful, and we went back to the bench.

"Now where were we, before we were so rudely interrupted?"

"Annabelle's boobs, I think." Freeman stuck a weed in his mouth and promptly began chomping.

"Yea, I think she may be your answer, Freddie."

"My answer to what?"

"To who you can bring to the fort. What else?"

"But she's just a young one, Joey. And she's Catholic, so I'd never be able to expect much."

"First of all, she's not that young anymore. As you may have noticed." I looked to see his reaction.

"All right. You got that point. She is kinda cute. How old is she now?"

"A year younger than me. So thirteen."

He mulled that over for a minute, then said, "She's still Catholic though. So what's the difference?"

"She's not that good of a Catholic, is my point number two."

"I'm all ears, Joey." I reflected that that probably wasn't something he ought to say around other kids, but I bit my tongue. As if responding to my thought, he pulled out his ears till they looked like sideways pancakes. I laughed and continued.

"Well, three years ago she stayed at my house for a day so my mom could babysit her. You know, all these church moms like to help each other out."

"Yea?" Freeman turned to face me on the bench.

"So she and I talked and made some plans that I promised I'd never tell anyone about. The only one I told so far is Timmy. 'Cause I had to tell someone."

"Go on."

I was pleased to have such good attention.

"Well, we went to the junkyard by ourselves one Saturday." I paused for effect, and noticed that talking slower seemed to encourage his curiosity.

"Yea, yea, yea?" He tugged on my T-shirt as if that would make me talk faster.

"So we played this little game I came up with, see? And in order to play she had to take her clothes off."

His weed wagged faster and he nodded his head with great interest, but I took a moment to retie my sneaker.

"So get to the main idea, will ya?" he pleaded.

"Hold your ding-dong. I'm trying to get to it, and if you'll be quiet and listen, maybe I'll be able to."

I gazed at the sky as if lost in pleasant memories, which I was.

"So what happened, for cryin' out loud?!" He swatted the back of my head.

"Oh, yea. Well, we played photographer, see?"

"You had a camera?"

"Yep. The Brownie that my Uncle Timothy gave me."

"And?"

"Well, I took my clothes off too, to be fair about it. Even though I was the photographer and she was the nudie model."

"You was both naked?"

"We kept our socks and sneakers on, on account of all the crap around there."

"Nothin' else?"

"Correct," I said, lapsing into another daydream.

"So keep talkin', dang it!"

"So. I was the photographer who needed all these angles and different lighting conditions, and of course all the different poses. See?" I paused to be sure he was still with me.

"Are ya tryin' to make me die of suspense, Joey?"

"So I had her sit on the car roofs and the hoods, and in the backseats and on the bumpers and all over the place, with her legs here and there and everywhere, so there wasn't much I didn't get a good shot of."

"I thought ya was a good Catholic!" he said in astonishment.

"Well, I did confess it," I confessed. "And I imagine she did too. But that's not my point."

"So ya still have all them pictures?"

"That's the sad part," I informed him. "I never could afford to get film for the thing." I watched as he slumped in disappointment; then he leaned back and put his arms over the bench as he tried to digest all this.

"It's a cryin' shame ya didn't use film, Joey! A cryin' shame!"

"Well, it's history now."

"And ya never did it again?"

"I was afraid we'd get caught, so I never asked. She was younger then—fourth grade is getting down there, you know? And I was only in fifth."

I was sure Freeman was trying to picture it all, but he wasn't connecting the dots like I wanted him to.

"Don't you get it?" I said finally.

"Get what? You're a goofball for not havin' film?"

"No! You're a goofball if you don't get it."

He pondered that, and I thought I could tell when his lightbulb finally lit.

"So ya really think ya could get her to come to the fort?"

"I don't promise anything. I imagine she's a lot more bashful these days. But she's always been friendly to me—as you probably noticed—and she only lives a few blocks away. If you behave yourself, I might be willing to ask—though she might say no and hate my guts forever. On top of which we need to build the confounded thing first."

"You're a genius, buddy! Albert Einstein in disguise! Even without the dang film!"

Freeman exclaimed as he slapped me on the back, and I could see no basis for argument.

"Well, you boys look like you have a lot to talk about." It was Annabelle again, who had snuck up from behind! I flushed red while Freeman slid his hat to one side and sat quiet as a stone. "Sorry if I interrupted," she said, looking from one of us to the other.

"Oh, no. N-No," stammered Freeman. "Joey here was just tellin' me about … " he put his hand to his mouth and faked several coughs, "about Mary!" He pointed to the swings. "He thinks maybe she has a crush on me."

"Oh, that's so cute! I'll bet she does! It's very nice of you guys to take care of them. Most boys your age are only interes … " she looked down, like her enthusiasm might have taken her in the wrong direction. "Well," she said and looked up quickly, "you two have a real good summer! Perhaps I'll see you again."

She spoke cheerfully and flipped up the brim of my hat. Then she waltzed off, binoculars swinging from her neck, hands in the pockets of her shorts.

"Did she hear us?" I asked when she was gone, as I redid my hat.

"I hope not. I don't think so."

"I don't know, Freddie. Maybe I won't be able to ask her after all. She's not the same person anymore."

"Too late! Ya gotta do it now, as soon as we get that fort done. Which we will, real, real soon!"

We set out on bikes to find a fort site in the Westwoods, early on a weekday morning. Freeman said we'd ride about halfway, then ditch the bikes in the junkyard and proceed on foot. Thus we rode our bikes past JC's house. As we approached, I noticed freshly planted grass in front, bordered by a white string fence, with red triangle flags hanging down. A shiny new sign with bold letters said "New Grass! Please Keep off!"

No sooner had I read the sign than Freeman shot off the sidewalk through the seeded area, not slowing down in the slightest. One pedal hooked on the string and yanked up the green metal stakes while his tires cut a huge arc through the soft earth. He bounced back over the sidewalk and into the street, dragging stakes, string, and flags. The stakes rattled like cans behind a wedding car till the whole colorful mass came unhooked and dropped in the road.

"It's what I think of him!" Freeman grinned diabolically.

"Damn, Freddie! If anyone saw that and it gets back to my mom, it's all over!"

"Saw what?" he blurted. "I didn't see nothin'!"

I pedaled faster and tried to act like I'd never seen this guy before. It was a terrible habit he had, acting first and thinking later, but I knew of no cure.

As we turned the corner, the front door of the house flew open and JC stepped out and looked around. I didn't think he saw who we were, but I couldn't be sure, and I resolved to keep my mouth shut and act like the incident never happened.

We laid our bikes under an old flatbed trailer at the junkyard, then walked toward the Westwoods. We halted by Cranberry Boulevard, the new highway under construction, which now divided Westwoods from the Piney Hill Development.

"This place used to be nothin' but fields and pine forests," Freeman said. "With lots of sheep grazin' in the fields."

"I know." I thought of the many times Timmy and I had hiked here and seeing it laid to waste created a bad feeling in my chest. I felt anger toward the workers, about fifteen of them who milled about with shovels and rakes or tinkered on various earthmoving equipment. The road looked five times wider than necessary, and several of my favorite spots were now replaced with rocky, debris-strewn earth. As we drew closer, Freeman motioned for us to go sit on a mound of dirt and bulldozed trees, with branches and roots jutting out, so we could watch what was going on. I didn't want to, but Freeman seemed intent.

"Check out the size of that Cat!" Freeman motioned to the huge bulldozer traveling back and forth, pushing rocks, logs, dirt, and anything in the way into piles like the one we sat on. "I can't imagine that mother slowin' down for nothing!"

The monster bulldozer clanged back and forth, spewing smoke from two upright exhaust pipes. The large muscular driver had broad shoulders, blue jeans held up by red suspenders, no shirt, and a dark hairy chest. He wore an engineer-looking hat, and a chunky stub of cigar hung from his mouth. After we'd watched for several minutes, the dozer appeared to be coming our way and the driver looking toward us. I thought I was imagining it, until the machine lurched to a stop and the driver leaped to the ground, muscles rippling as he landed.

The machine idled loudly as he pointed our way. "Hey! Co'mere a minute!" Butterflies lifted off in my stomach, though I wasn't sure why. We turned to see if he might be talking to someone else, but there was no one else, so we left our packs and walked over. The large dark nipples on his hairy chest loomed in my vision, and for some reason my eyes kept returning to them. He was Freeman's height, with short curly black hair and wraparound sunglasses. Now that we were closer I could see the words on his hat, Diesel Power. A tattoo of a beautiful lady in a bikini covered his right bicep.

He looked like a person you did not want to mess with or say the wrong thing to. His skin shone with sweat, his hands rested on his hips like my mom's when she's about to chew me out.

We stopped a few arm's lengths in front of him, and I could smell his aftershave lotion, or else deodorant. He had a mighty air about him and examined us like flies on a dog turd that had no business being there. I imagined him mushing us together with his bare hands, if he got the urge.

"You kids come here much?" His gruff voice reminded me of that German shepherd, when I tripped on the leash.

"No, sir. Scarcely ever," replied Freeman calmly. "Why?"

"You been here in the last three days?"

"No."

He eyed us up and down as if we might be escaped convicts, and I got the feeling that maybe I was one and didn't know it.

"You sure you haven't been around here lately?"

"No, sir," said Freeman calmly. "Why do you ask?"

"You don't ask me questions, all right? You just give me answers. Okay, kid?"

"Yes, sir."

"You know where Stoneridge is?"

"Stoneridge? What's that?"

"Didn't I just say don't ask me questions?"

"Sorry, sir."

"You don't know where Stoneridge is?"

"No, sir."

He walked in a slow circle around us, examining us like stuffed animals, though I had no idea what his interest was.

"You don't know where Stoneridge is?" he repeated as he finished his inspection. Could this guy be deaf? I wondered. Or was it maybe a memory loss?

"No, sir," said Freeman again, cool as a cucumber, at least on the outside. "Why do you ask?"

"I thought I said don't ask me any … " he stopped and glared at Freeman as if he forgot what he was going to say. Then he stepped forward and put his nose not two inches from Freeman's. When he continued speaking, I could see drops of saliva, illuminated by sunlight from behind, landing on Freeman's face.

"You a wise guy or somethin'?"

"No, sir. My teachers say I'm not very bright."

Muscle Man took that in and shut up for a second. Then he sprayed out another sentence, "You know anything about some kids was over here two nights ago?"

"No, sir."

"What about you?" he said, turning toward me.

I shook my head negative and released a silent fart.

He looked back and forth at both of us a few times, as if trying to decide if we were lying. Something about the guy made me most uncomfortable; it seemed like he was out to get somebody and we happened to be the ones to cross his path.

"Either of you know any kids who might've dicked with our equipment the other night?" He swept his hand in the direction of the steamroller, his bulldozer and a smaller one, along with a backhoe parked between them.

"No, sir," replied Freeman.

"And you don't know where Stoneridge is?" he repeated for the fourth time.

"No, sir," said Freeman once again.

"The cops mentioned they got problems there too—some punks stole a batch of lumber and damn near derailed a train about a week ago."

Goose bumps washed over me, my ears overheated, and my balls got tight. I tried to calm down and give off that cool normal look. But it didn't feel like I accomplished it. He waited like we were supposed to answer but neither of us did. I was thankful he was focused on Freeman.

"Well, I don't suppose that matters to you kids. Where you goin' anyway?"

"See some friends on the other side of the woods," responded Freeman. Muscle Man squinted as if that might help him see us better.

"Well, I guess you kids are all right," he announced finally. His hands went to his sides and he appeared to relax a bit. "We had trouble with someone firing up our equipment the other night and ridin' around in the dozer. And we think it's a couple of punks your age."

"Couldn't be us," said Freeman. "We wouldn't even know how."

"And you haven't been over to Stoneridge, huh?"

"We haven't been over that a-way since before the new houses got started," Freeman said.

"I thought you said you didn't know where Stoneridge is?"

"Well I … " Freeman shifted his position and looked at the guy's shoes. "I forgot until you mentioned it."

Muscle Man stared at Freeman and time seemed to stop as he weighed him up once more. It was a while before he spoke again. I tried hard to guess what he was thinking, but couldn't.

"We're offering fifty bucks to anyone who helps us find whoever's been here, and I hear they got a similar offer over at Stoneridge. Plus tighter security. Those little bastards are gonna pay for this crap. Ya see anyone, ya let me know. Okay?"

"We'll keep our eyes peeled, sir. We could sure use fifty bucks," Freeman said.

An uncomfortable pause followed, as if no one knew what to say next. The guy turned to me. "Don't you talk, kid?"

I shook my head negative again, pleased that at least I wasn't giving off more gas. He grimaced like I was the strangest kid he'd ever seen, then turned back to Freeman.

"I hope you help us catch them punks. Here's my card. You gimme a call if you find anything out!" He held out what looked like a white business card toward Freeman.

"You bet we will, sir," Freeman promised, reaching for it from the guy's grimy hand.

"Yea, thanks!" I blurted out. The guy shot me a glance like I was a nutcase.

My eyes skimmed the card as Freeman took it:

Evergreen Construction Co.
A Decade of Paving the Earth
Mario Giovanni and Sons

On the bottom was small print that appeared to be an address and phone number.

"My name's Mario," he said gruffly. "Same as the old man's."

We returned to our packs where I whispered, "Let's split!"

"No … that'll make us look suspicious. We gotta sit and look cool. For ten minutes or so."

So we sat and waited. My legs itched to bolt but I forced myself to sit.

"You think they could get our fingerprints if they examined those boards we stashed?"

"It's possible."

Jesus, Mary and Joseph! I thought.

"Wouldn't they need our fingerprints first, to match them up?"

"If they took us to the station, they'd get 'em quick enough."

Oh God! I thought. The end is around the corner! What on earth am I hanging out with Freeman for? I must be nuts! I'd be better off staring at the walls in my room. Not only am I headed to hell, I am going to jail first! I gotta find another friend!

"Want a cigarette?" Freeman poked a filter in my direction.

"Right here where that guy can see us?"

He lit that one for himself then held another toward me. My hand reached out and took it, and there we sat on the rubble heap, huffing and puffing and wheezing on occasion, me stewing in my own thoughts. By the time we snuffed the butts out I had recovered from my anxiety attack, and I concluded once again that cigarettes really can help a guy relax, if you just focus on the smoke and forget whatever else is on your mind, and of course your lungs.

We disappeared into Westwoods, hoping to find a rise in the land, or maybe a tree, from which to survey the place and narrow down locations for the fort. But it was slow going from the start.

A thick tangle of gnarly oak trees impeded every movement and discouraged us severely. I imagined that dense scrub oak was the reason Westwoods had been left alone, by kids or anyone else. Only by following close behind Freeman, as he plodded and crashed like a brontosaur through the brutal undergrowth, was I able to move at all.

After considerable effort we spotted a lone evergreen tree that stood above the surrounding vegetation. It rose from the base of a small hill, which appeared to be the source of its water. We worked our way to it and climbed up, me first, since I was lighter and could go higher. Gooey black sap gummed my hands and clothes in no time, and dropped on Freeman's head.

"Confound it, Joey! Can't ya be more careful?"

"I am being careful! You shouldn't be so close behind."

He muttered some obscenities I couldn't make out, but we soon got near the top and had a grand view of the area.

Cranberry Boulevard lay to the east, where the road crew looked like ants toiling in the sun. Two hills, wide, rounded, domelike affairs, like most nuns' boobs from the side, I thought, loomed in the west under the carpet of scrub oak. On top of one hill was a cluster of trees, all taller than the one we were in. I imagined we'd get a better view from there; the trees were high up to start with, and closer to the middle of Westwoods. But they were perhaps a quarter mile off, and a jungle of oak laid between them and us.

"Think they're worth going to?" asked sap-covered Freeman.

"They'd be better for checking things out. Plus they might be a good place for the fort."

"But all that scrub oak! It'd be a nightmare to get to."

"True, but that's exactly what will keep unwanted visitors out, once we get the place built."

"Damn, Joey! Why'd you have to say that?"

So we scraped back down and forged ahead. We fought and beat at snaggly limbs, inching our way along. But we soon realized it was a terrible, ferocious war. Brittle, twisted twigs scraped and lashed wherever flesh was exposed and picked at our clothes with a vengeance. Branches scratched our heads and blocked our way at every step, in addition to nearly poking our eyes out. One branch tore a big hole in Freeman's shirt, then rasped across his shoulder, leaving a huge red welt. I grew discouraged and ready to quit, even though Freeman was the one breaking trail.

"I don't see how we'll ever get girls through here, let alone lumber and tools to build the thing. This stuff is denser than a monkey's pubie hairs!"

"What do you know about a monkey's pubie hairs?"

"Jesus, Freddie! All I know is they can't be this bad. Unless they're made off steel wool or something."

"Don't be a crybaby, Joey. It beats the hell out of baseball, don't it?" He snapped a dead branch that hung between us, as if for emphasis. "Besides, we'll be safe from JC and his goons when the work is done."

"Aw hell, Freddie." He was right and I knew it, and I saw no alternative but to forge ahead.

"Smoke?" He fished about in his shirt pocket. I was getting less and less happy about my new habit, and I promised myself I would quit soon, but this situation seemed to scream out for it.

We lit up in a place scarcely big enough for a sardine, branches dusting our heads, twigs stabbing into our backs and sides, and leaves tickling my neck. Plus I didn't dare turn my head in either direction, lest I get jabbed in the ear.

"We gotta go slower on the butts, Joey. My dad's gettin' suspicious. I heard him this mornin' talkin' to Matt about a pack that was on his dresser—these very ones we're doin' now."

I acted upset, though I wasn't. This might help my resolution along, and there was no doubt I was starting to inhale. On top of which I worried I might get nailed by my folks—I was already brushing my teeth three or four times a day, a suspect activity in anyone's book. It occurred to me that we were maybe halfway to the destination—not even the destination, but merely a lookout point—and we were whipped and tattered something terrible. I had real doubts about getting to the trees, let alone whacking a trail and hauling lumber in. I was sure Freeman had doubts too, but neither of us mentioned them—how could we cross the fort off our list of things to do, when it was the only thing on our list?

Still, it was a whale of a discouragement sitting in that oak thicket, even if we believed we could find a spot and clear a trail. So we did the only thing two people in such a situation can do. We tried to trick ourselves and pretend the project was doable. We boasted about being tougher than a few trees, and how we ought to be able to do it, in spite of the obvious.

"Just remember one thing, Joey: Now how's that go again? Oh yea … when the going gets tough, the toughest ones get the hell outta there."

"That doesn't sound quite right."

"Of course it's right. It's ancient wisdom, but it applies to times like this."

"Well then, maybe we should get the hell out."

He thought and scratched his head. "Well, it's somethin' like that. I can't remember exactly how it goes."

"How about this one." I knew it sounded more positive than I felt, but what was to lose? "Quitters never win, and winners never quit." It was the only thing I remembered from fourth grade, though I had no idea why.

Freeman mulled that over and took his last puff, then proclaimed in a cloud of smoke, "Hang it! I ain't no quitter! And I ain't gonna let no lousy scrub oak stop me, either!"

I was amazed at the effect those words had. It was far more than they ever had on me. Even Sister Alphonses, who taught it to us, would have been proud. Freeman jumped up and said he'd find a location for the fort, and he'd whack a path to it, even if it took the next two weeks. "I'll use my bare hands if I have to!" he proclaimed.

"That's great," I replied, marveling at the change in him. "I'm real anxious to try that path too."

We blazed ahead with fire in us, in Freeman anyway, bushwhacking toward the west. Bit by bit we grew accustomed to the cuts and scratches, and to that untamed jungle snapping and sticking and jabbing and a hundred other things it did to obstruct us.

Sweat soaked my clothes, dribbled in my eyes, and stung my scratches. My undies rode high between my cheeks. But Freeman kept thrashing on, pushing back branch after endless branch, cracking some, bending some, letting some snap back and swat me in the face or the chest and a couple of times where it hurt the most. I was dirty, sore, sap-covered, and tired, and reasonably confident the whole thing was a waste of time. I reminded myself that if we ever succeeded and I could get Maggie to come visit, it would all be worth it. This recharged my batteries, in spite of everything else, and then I didn't care how long it took, or what kind of pain we had to endure. But presently there came a complaint from Freeman.

"Maybe I am a quitter, Joey." He dropped to the ground and laid on his back.

"Aw, you just need a little break." I thought of Maggie's beautiful face and curls and realized I couldn't let him quit now.

"Maybe you was right the first time. We ain't gonna get no girls into this wasteland."

"We won't know till we try. Besides, what else can we do?" I reminded him.

He went to light up but the last four cigarettes were too soggy to be of use so we laid there and gazed at the oak leaves.

"Let's do this," I said, checking my watch. "We've been almost an hour so far. We gotta be close. Just give it fifteen more minutes. Then we'll call it quits if we haven't got there. I just know it's right close, and we can't bail yet."

"Hell, it seems like we've been goin' for a year now."

"Trust me! I have a good sense of direction and a good feel for distance. I always have, and I know what I'm talking about."

He agreed without enthusiasm, I suspected because he was too tired to disagree. But I didn't need enthusiasm; I only needed a little more work so certain was I that we were almost there.

"Look!" I stood and craned my neck. "You can see one of the big lookout trees right now!"

And sure enough you could! It was not far off, and it was a perfect goal for Freeman. So he arose and continued the battle, thrashing, whacking, crashing, inching forward, mad and determined to get to where he was going, to shut me up if nothing else. I thought if some tree angered him too much he might just yank it out by the roots and fling it overhead, though that never happened.

It wasn't much longer till we got to that lookout tree, which I was certain would give a bird's-eye view and help us find the ideal spot.

"This tree looks familiar, don't it Joey?" Freeman inquired as we got closer.

"Naw, it can't be familiar. We've never been here before."

"But I thought there was a bunch of trees, and I don't recall goin' up no hill."

"Well, we must have gone up the hill without noticing it. And those other trees must be around here somewhere." I looked around but saw none.

"Hang it, Joey! This is familiar! It's the same damn tree we started out from!"

"It can't be!"

But it was! We had bushwhacked in a huge circle, arriving at the very spot we started from! I'd read about this sort of thing in a Boy Scout book, but I never believed it really happened.

Of course, we were discouraged, and Freeman said he wouldn't even mind killing me.

"Five or six times, if I could figure out how!" he exclaimed.

"If I had a gun you wouldn't need to," I assured him. "I'd do it first!"

But we got over our disappointment by and by, and there was an unexpected reward for our persistence. Freeman insisted we climb that lone evergreen tree one more time and take a last look around.

"What else can we do?" he reminded me.

I had serious doubts but also no argument, so up we went again, gathering more sap on our clothes, snapping branches, scraping rough bark, and swearing at each other. But we finally reached the top and to my utter astonishment, not fifty feet from where we had started, if you looked in the right direction, namely down instead of out, was a nice little clearing covered with soft grass and a sprinkling of red, yellow, and blue flowers; the scrub oak receded to a circle about the size of a house, forming what just might be the perfect place for our fort! It was incredibly similar to what I had originally imagined.

We clambered back down and stepped into that clearing, then looked at each other without uttering a word; we flung ourselves to the ground and rolled about in the grass, laughing as if we'd found an oasis in the Sahara, our bodies shaking like lawn mower engines. I imagined we were delirious from all the work and the sweat, not to mention the countless scratches and the dark gloom of failure, but it didn't matter—we were the happiest kids on earth, and if there was a problem in the world that moment on that sunny afternoon, we were the last two people to give a hoot!

Our problems were solved, and the future was a bright sunshiny day. Save for one minor detail, namely that Freeman lost his marbles and turned into a lunatic.

"We're home, Joey! We're home at last!" he whooped prior to leaping onto his hands and doing a cartwheel that I didn't know he was capable of. Then he dropped to his hands and knees and hopped about like a wounded frog. "We're home, Joey! We're home at last!" he croaked from somewhere deep in his throat, appearing all the more like a frog.

Back to his feet he leaped, then he lifted me off the ground with a powerful bear hug, causing me to exhale; he swung me in circles then dropped me down in a heap while he danced in circles like an Indian, hollering and twirling about, exclaiming he'd never been so happy.

Next he broke into a song: "This is where our fort will be! This is where our fort's gonna be! Don't you love me baby?!" He glanced over to see if I was watching, then spun like a top in the other direction. "This is where our fort will be! This is where our fort will be! And you're gonna love me baby!"

He held his crotch and waved one hand in the air, cowboy style. "This is where our fort's gonna be, and I'm gonna make me a baby!"

"Stop being a nutcase, Freddie. I'm glad you're happy, but get a grip, will you?"

He gripped his crotch with both hands, grinning stupidly, then raised his arms in a "V," and spoke sweetly, cocking his head to the side. "Aw, Joey! I'm gonna name my baby 'Joey'!"

"Yea? What if it's a girl?"

He looked up to the left and tugged his ear, pondering. "Well, then, I'll call her … Joella!"

"What if it's twins?"

"Why then … Joey and Joella! Of course!" He gleamed.

"Gee, thanks. That's mighty thoughtful of you. I just hope they come out normal."

When he finally calmed down he pointed to the west part of the clearing. "The fort will go there, facing east for morning light, tucked back into the trees for camouflage."

"Then the firepit can go here." I pointed to the spot right where we stood. "And the kitchen table there." I indicated a spot several feet south of the firepit.

"Refrigerator hole!" Freeman stomped his foot a few yards to the north.

He walked around for a minute thinking, then said, "Benches there, opposite the fort; food tripod on the north."

120

"Woodpile on the south, back in those trees. Damn Freddie, I can see it already!"

"This is so fine, I wish we had a bottle of wine! It's the nicest place I've ever seen! And Maggie and Annabelle are gonna love it! Just imagine that!"

6

Having found a location for the fort and agreeing that we needed to ponder the lumber situation more thoroughly, we determined the next step was a nail run, as we'd talked about originally. This would be less risky than another lumber run, and would give us a chance to learn if anyone was guarding Stoneridge at night, which might be the case after what Muscle Man Giovanni had said. But even a nail run was nerve racking to me now.

"It's creepy, Freddie. We got JC and his goons after us, and now Mario and the guys at Stoneridge; and my mom's always after me. Plus I have to live with the nuns all year, whacking on my knuckles and screaming till it hurts my eardrums. You'd think I was a criminal or something, yet all I want is to be a normal kid."

"Just think about the nails. That other crap'll drive ya crazy. It's what I do. Except JC sometimes, which I know I shouldn't. But we gotta have them nails, ya know?"

Of course it wasn't that simple, and it wasn't long before more complications arose.

The first one came as a note wedged in the picket fence around Freeman's yard. We found it as we walked into his driveway that very evening, on a large hunk of Cheerio box cardboard, addressed to "Freeman & Joy."

It looked like the same red crayon as the first note: You guys fuckt my lawn and the same will happin to you! Sune!

"I didn't touch his lawn!" I said, feeling unfairly picked on and wrongly involved.

"Me either!" joined Freeman.

"What do you call what you did then?" I had feared his little stunt would come to haunt us, but I didn't think so soon.

"I hit a bump on the sidewalk and went out of control." He smiled sheepishly, but I didn't have much sympathy. Then again, I thought, what did it really matter? If JC was going to cut our balls off how much worse could it get?

"Who the hell cares anyway?" Freeman said as if reading my mind. "Besides, if he's gonna do somethin' he oughta do it soon, because he won't even find us once our fort is built!"

He tore the cardboard into little pieces and put them in the garbage. After some debate, it was decided the nail run should be between seven thirty and nine in the evening. Though I was still anxious and jumpy about Stoneridge, I was pleased we weren't going to steal any lumber and I wouldn't need to get permission to sleep out, since we'd be back before dark.

"The workers'll be gone by then. So we should be able get nails by the bucketful," Freeman declared as he squirted gobs of oil on his bike chain. "And, of course, we can check out the lumber situation better in the light."

"What about the 'tighter security' that Mario guy talked about? I still have the jeebers about that. I'm as worried about getting nailed as I am about getting nails, if you get what I'm saying."

"He was blowin' it out his behind, Joey. He wanted to scare us to keep us away from the place."

"How can you be so sure?"

"Easy." He stopped oiling his chain and moved to oil mine. "They're not gonna waste money on a security cop for a few lousy boards."

I held the bike, and he pedaled the wheel as he oiled the chain and gears. "Plus I could hear it in his voice, Joey. The guy was full of baloney, take my word."

I thought Freeman might be full of baloney, and I imagined we'd find out soon enough. But what was the worst that could happen, I asked myself, if we got caught merely picking up abandoned nails? It made me feel better, if not fully at ease.

"Oil makes the world go round!" Freeman grinned through an oil-smudged mouth as he stood up, the slimy can in his blackened hand. "And the more you put on, the smoother she spins!"

He aimed the spout down his pants, pretending to squirt the rest in there. "Remind me to pump 'er up real good, too!" He laughed and shot two squirts at the ceiling, which fell short and landed on the concrete floor. "Let's go, slippery dippery!"

We laid our bikes on a crunchy mound of blue gravel, on the outer edge of Stoneridge. Acres of dirt, weeds, rocks, scrap lumber, and construction equipment sprawled before us. Scattered trees stood in odd locations, most of them with bark that was badly scraped. Concrete foundations appeared here and there, along with excavations and house frames in different states of construction. A battered bulldozer and several beat-up dump trucks were parked as though the drivers had had too much to drink. Overall, the place had the look of a battlefield. But there was no sign of life or anyone watching.

"This used to be a real nice forest with beautiful ponds," Freeman said. "There were zillions of birds and animals here too."

"I came here with Timmy a lot of times. One day we cooked hot dogs about where that house is now." I pointed to a wooden skeleton with plywood sheets tacked to its sides, and a triangular framework for the roof above.

"I never saw so many birds as used to live here, especially by the marsh," observed Freeman.

My heart sank as I pieced all this together. "Looks like they filled that in too." I recalled that the marsh had been near the center of the place.

It's difficult to explain the change; the place was so chopped up and devastated. It was as if someone had splashed dark ink on a beautiful painting, then kicked it and kicked it till there was nothing left. The picture would never be replaced, and no one would ever see it again. My heart felt pained and there was a stone in my stomach as I looked over Stoneridge Estates.

"I was here when they filled up the marsh," Freeman said in a sort of delayed reaction. "I watched 'em do it. They came with dump truck after dump truck for half a day."

A thick cloud of despair came over me and the only consolation was that there seemed to be more lumber than last time, and many piles that we hadn't seen on the night of our first visit.

Three kids appeared on trikes on the sidewalk across the street, which a new sign proclaimed to be "Marshy Woods Lane." The kids looked about five or six, with crew cuts and nothing but shorts on, out for an evening cruise. The biggest one pointed to us while the others looked on.

"Teenagers!" he announced.

He spoke the word with disdain, as if we must be inherently evil and up to no good since we were teenagers. At first I wanted to kick his behind, but then I recalled thinking the same thing when I was younger, and ... well, maybe he did have a point.

We waved and they drove off and we soon forgot about them. The shadows were growing longer and we had our work cut out. Freeman said we were lucky the days were so long and that we were only a week past the longest day, June twenty-first. "Which is the only worthwhile thing I learned in school last year," he added.

"That's more than I learned," I told him. "And it's solid proof that public school beats Catholic school."

"Yea, but it still seems like a terrible long time to learn one teeny-weeny little fact."

"At least you're getting smarter, Freddie. That's the main thing. And it beats the hell out of practicing cursive till my fingers are ready to fall off, then saying rosaries all afternoon."

"You really do that every day?"

"It definitely seems like it."

We started scouting for nails and making mental notes of the piles of lumber laying about. We were soon plunking the nails in three empty paint buckets, busy as ants at a picnic. There were nails galore, size sixes mostly, but with a few other numbers mixed in. We merrily gathered them up and assumed we could use them all.

"Ya feel better now, Joey?"

"Pretty much. This is hard to beat, anyway." I happily clinked nails into the buckets, which were filling up rapidly.

As we crawled around in the rocks and weeds it became apparent there was an abundance of lumber too, though the best boards were stacked in neat, bundled piles, waiting to be used by the workmen. I got a knot in my belly every time I pictured us hiking off with it in the middle of the night "just letting them give it to us," as Freeman had said.

"This is terrific, Joey! It looks like we're gonna get the best lumber they have to offer."

"I still think we ought to get it from the scrap piles. Look … there's piles over there, ready for burning!"

"What girl in her right mind is gonna come to a place made from junk like that?"

"How would they even know where it came from when the thing's all done? Besides, if we use scraps it won't flag down attention and make us risk getting caught for stealing."

"Don't be such a sissy, Joey. No girl's gonna respect that, either."

"Well, I still don't see how we're going to haul enough of the big pieces all the way to Westwoods. You nearly broke your back last time."

"If you'd've held up the ends from the start, I could have carried twice as many boards. I thought I already told ya that."

"You did. And my parents told me all about Santa Claus too."

He laughed. "I may as well talk to this bucket here, Joey. At least it wouldn't talk back."

We crept along the foundation of a nearly done house, topping off the last bucket with nails when I thought I heard tires grinding over rocks on the road. Looking up I glimpsed a blue-orange flash of color in the slanting rays of the sun, about ten lots away. I froze as the car disappeared behind a house. It reappeared and there was a blue-orange cop car headed our way.

"A cop!" I hissed.

"Behind the house! Quick! And stay down, Joey!"

We scrambled on all fours, arms and legs moving like pistons, through rocks, nails, weeds, and scraps of lumber, behinds waddling in the air, fear in our hearts. Freeman promptly knocked over two of the buckets we'd spent the last half hour filling; I scooted through the nails, knocking the noisy cans and scratching my hands something fierce.

I glanced back but couldn't see the cop due to a dirt hill in the way. As I did my head bumped Freeman's behind and knocked him flat. My momentum caused me to land on top of him and he wiggled beneath me like a huge ugly night crawler. It was a terribly uncomfortable feeling, yet worse for him as he floundered in the rocks and dirt.

Somehow we disentangled and got going with my face not three inches from his rear end. Which is when he let go with a dinosaur-sized ripper that I feared might scorch my eyeballs. The noise was amazing, but the stench about killed me—it was the kind that clings to your nose hairs for that long-term horrifying effect. He laughed his hyena laugh till I swatted his behind with a one-by-six and brought him back to his senses. I wondered if fumes this deadly could cause permanent damage to my lungs, or even my brain, and I feared they might. Freeman stifled his laugh but shook with glee as he crawled along. We crept to the corner of the house then looked back to see where the cop was. I hoped our movement had not given us away, though it may have since the cop was now parking across the street. We darted behind the house and leaned on the foundation to catch our breath. I was frightened half to death and fairly certain that we'd be caught and hauled in for fingerprinting.

"Think he knows we're here?" I gasped.

"No. But we'd best lay low. Let's scoonch down to the basement and make sure he never finds out."

We scurried through a rectangular opening that looked like a basement doorway, where I wanted to sit down and not move a muscle. But Freeman resolved to spy out a small window in front of the place. The opening was up high so he grabbed a metal bucket from a corner, turned it upside down, and stepped on top. He slowly poked his head into the opening.

"Aw hell! He's gettin' out!"

A car door slammed.

"He's lookin' around, but he's still on the other side of the street. I think he's tryin' to figure what to do next."

"Let's get out the back way before he comes over," I whispered.

"Naw. I don't think he really will. He's walkin' toward the kids on the trikes. We're gonna be okay." He motioned for me to remain silent.

"He's gettin' closer to the kids … Oh hell! Our bikes are over there too!" He paused, keeping me in suspense.

"He's right by the kids. Dang! I think he sees our bikes too."

"Let's blast out back, Freddie!"

"It's okay, it's okay … Quiet down, will ya? He's just talkin' to the kids."

"Let's bolt! We can cross the tracks and hide in the woods." I was pacing in circles.

"No; he ain't gonna come over here."

"I don't want to take chances!"

"Quiet, Joey! I want to see what … " His sentence trailed off as he kept looking out.

"Uh-oh … the kids are pointin' over here."

Freeman went silent and froze like a Popsicle.

"Damn … he's lookin' this way."

"Let's go!"

"One more second … Oh, hang me, Joey!"

He leaped down and grabbed my shoulders, a terrified look in his eyes. "Christ!

He's startin' to walk over here!"

I danced a jig to hold back a whiz while I tried to figure out what to do next. There was no way to escape with the cop headed over. He'd see us out back and no doubt chase after us. And our bikes were by his car.

Frantic, we searched for a place to hide. Freeman pointed to the darkest section of wall, near the opening we'd just come through. We shot over like bullets, squatted with our arms wrapped around our knees, and tried to blend into the concrete; we looked to each other in disbelief.

"Maybe we should just walk out front and act like normal kids," I whispered.

"No! We gotta stay put. If we go out now he's gonna ask a thousand questions about what we're doing here and who we are and everything else. We gotta hope he don't see us. That's all we can do."

"What if he does see us?"

"Then we need to bolt for the bikes somehow; run right past him if you have to."

I whizzed a few drops and wanted to let loose with a geyser. We sat perfectly still for what seemed like forever while the cop's footsteps came closer. And closer. We scarcely breathed. His footsteps echoed in the empty basement. Freeman pointed to the small opening he'd just been looking out. Two blue pant legs stood there, with shiny black shoes pointed right toward us. I suddenly had to take a crap real bad too.

We sat still as the dead. I bit my arm. A cigarette lighter rasped and clicked, and a deep breath went in and out. I could picture the cop inhaling and looking around, trying to figure out what to do.

All was silent for what seemed like eternity. Then the cop walked to the side of the house where we'd been crawling around. He stopped about where the nails were. There was the kick of a bucket and a tinkling of nails. The cop continued around till he was by the opening we'd just come through; his footsteps halted, and I could almost hear him listening.

My mental chalkboard flashed big white letters: Oh hell! It's all over now!

More movement from the cop. His cigarette smoke hit my nostrils, and I was sure he was looking in the basement. I didn't know how dark the basement appeared to him, but my eyes had adjusted and it seemed like broad daylight to me. I wanted to let loose with my bladder, a god-awful scream, and a blast of hot mush and race right past the guy and pedal home like a madman.

I squeezed my eyes shut and bit my arm harder. I thought of a lesson I'd gotten once on "delayed gratification"—something about the longer you wait and put off getting things, the happier you'll be in the long run. Sister Boneventure said it was a good way to get to heaven, and the only way, really. It sounded like a terrible idea then, and it seemed next to impossible now.

Seconds ticked by, each one stretching out like five minutes. Finally the cop shuffled about and began walking toward the front of the house. I thanked God and opened my eyes a wee little slit and looked at Freeman. He winked, like the whole thing was no big deal.

Before the cop had time to get back, Freeman tiptoed to the window and put one foot on the bucket to step up and look out again.

I saw it coming but there was nothing I could do. His foot was near the edge of the bucket when he put his weight on it. That metal can flipped out with a crash and a bang and a series of loud rattles, all with deafening echoes off those concrete walls. Freeman slammed to the floor and landed on his side in a way that made me grimace. He rolled about in pain and cursed and swore at that spinning bucket, like it was bucket's fault. And like there was no cop standing right out front to hear the commotion and come back on the fly.

I prayed a quickie to St. Jude that the cop might have a sudden loss of hearing, which he evidently did since he didn't come back. Freeman got ahold of himself, but proceeded to give the final proof that he really was insane: he got up, brushed some dirt off, fetched the bucket, and stepped up again. He looked out and didn't say a word.

A light year or two went by before a car door opened and slammed shut. The motor cranked and started. I said "Thanks" to St. Jude, who I was certain had pulled a few strings on that one. There was no other way that cop couldn't have heard all the racket.

"It's safe and the coast is clear, Joey!"

"Hang your safe and the coast is clear! That's the closest I ever want to come to getting caught!"

"Aw, you worry too much, Joey woey. You'll be old before your time." But then he stepped off the bucket and said a bit more seriously, "You s'pose that guy comes every night?"

"Who knows? And who cares? All I know is it's time to split!"

"Why? It's safe now. He's gone like the wind." He waved his hands as if to indicate a little breeze had blown by. "Let's get them nails and scout for boards."

"Right now?"

"Of course. When did you think?"

"Are you nuts?"

"No. You?"

"Dang it, Freddie! We nearly got caught and hauled off not five minutes ago! What do you think will happen if that cop comes back?"

"Well … " he paused to consider, then threw his hands out like a preacher. "Why would he come back? He thinks there's no one here now."

He beamed a set of crooked teeth, full of confidence and certainty, in addition to pure stupidity. "We gotta get them nails. That's all there is to it."

"I'm leaving." I started walking toward the opening.

"That wouldn't be right. But I'll get 'em myself if you're gonna wimp out." He pouted and looked away.

"I'm not wimping out."

"What do you call it then?"

"Let's discuss this tomorrow," I pleaded. "I don't feel so great. I got gas pains or a bellyache or something. Besides, I told my dad I'd be home before dark."

He walked in several circles, mumbling to himself, hands behind his back; then he stopped and flung his arms up again. "You sure you're not wimpin' out?" He squinted in my eyes like a doctor, tapped my temples with his knuckles and shook his head like I'd lost my mind. I suspected this was a good example of peer pressure, which I learned about in fifth grade. It felt like peer pressure, and I knew I wasn't the one who was crazy.

"It was only a cop, Joey! One little old cop, who came by at a bad time. And now he's gone. How're we ever gonna build a fort if you're gonna act like a wimp? Besides, you want some excitement in your life, don't you?"

No! Not anymore I didn't. I'd be happy with a scaled-down version of the fort, made from logs and branches or sticks and mud. Or a stack of weeds. Or a pile of leaves, for that matter. But it made no sense to be there yakking about it when we could be headed home.

"I am not wimping out! Let's just get out and think about all this crap tomorrow!"

He shook his head in dismay, like my refusal was the biggest disappointment he'd ever experienced. "At least we gotta get them nails scooped up and put in a safe place. We gotta do that much, Joey."

I could see that doing what he said would be quicker than arguing, unhappy though I was about it. Thus we collected the scattered nails in the twilight, carted the three buckets across the tracks, and tucked them all in a dense patch of sticker bushes beneath a grove of locust trees. We laid mounds of leaves and dirt on top, then jumped on our bikes for home.

I was a bundle of raw nerves when I stepped into the living room that evening. There sat my father, reading the paper in his easy chair; my mother, sewing in her chair. My mind was a jumble, and the hour was late. I wanted to bypass all small talk and jump into bed.

"Have a nice evening, Joseph?" My mom went on sewing and didn't look up.

"Oh, it was great." I kept walking, in hopes they'd ignore me.

"Where were you?"

"Oh, you know … here, there, and everywhere." I had to stop so as not to look too suspicious, even though I was almost out the other side of the room.

"And where exactly is here, there, and everywhere?" My mom looked up and our eyes met.

"Well, it's a bit hard to say, exactly. We rode our bikes around, you know?"

"You haven't done that for quite awhile." Up went her eyebrows.

"But that's because I've had no one to do it with."

"Aw, honey, leave him alone," said my dad from beneath his *Wall Street Journal*. "The kid's thirteen and he needs a little freedom."

"Fourteen," she corrected him.

"Whatever. Just so long as he doesn't start smoking or drinking or stealing." He kept on reading for a moment, then said, "Or having female problems!" He laughed at his own joke, if you could call it that, put his paper down and winked at me. "You know what I mean, don't you Joseph?"

"Uh, yea. I think so."

"You are behaving yourself, aren't you?"

"Uh, yea. Of course, I mean." My ears seemed to be flaming, and I was thankful there was dim lighting where I stood.

"See, honey? We don't need to hound him to death."

My mom breathed a sigh of resignation and went back to her sewing. "I suppose you're right, dear."

"You guys have a good night. Don't forget your prayers," I joked, then turned to leave.

"Oh, Joseph. I almost forgot!" said my mom. "There's a letter on your bed. Timmy said it was in the mailbox today. It looks a little interesting." I thought she chuckled as she said it, but I couldn't be sure, and I slipped away before she had time to say anything else.

Interruption number two came in the form of Timmy when I entered our bedroom. He was sitting on a chair by the window.

"Hi, Joey. Wanna try my megaphone?"

He had a large cone-shaped affair made of cardboard, which he moved from his mouth and held to his ear, aimed at me.

"Naw."

"Don't talk so loud. It hurts my ear."

"I know how they work."

"But this one's larger and I messed around with the shape so it works really good. You can pick up sound from anywhere. And I mean anywhere! You should try it."

"Another time. I'm tired, and mom said you found a letter for me."

"Right there." He pointed to my bed, and went to lay on his bed. Resting neatly on my pillow, sure enough, was an envelope. Upon it were the words "Joseph Simpson," in the spot where the address is supposed to go.

Oh, hell! I thought, imagining another note from JC. But then I realized the writing was neat and orderly, though all the letters were in lowercase. It was in pencil, with no sign of a lunatic having written it. I nearly ripped the letter as I tore open the envelope. There was a poem on small, lined notepaper:

joseph simpson how i love you,
joseph simpson yes i do,
your gentle eyes they really send me,
and your words, how they thrill me!
your voice so soft,
takes me aloft,
for weeks on end.
do you remember
our time together?
oh so sweet!
why don't we meet,
and try once more?
all my love,

your one and only

Oh, my God! I thought. Annabelle Flannigan actually wants me! This kind of thing had never happened before, so of course I had no idea what to do. Annabelle was a nice girl, obviously not the skinny little thing she used to be. But she didn't hold a flame next to Maggie, and I certainly didn't love her. She was a friend I could say hello to and chitchat with on occasion; in fact, she was about the only girl I could chitchat with. She'd be good for Freeman—actually anybody would be good for him—but I wanted no part of the deal.

"So who's it from?"

"A girl."

"Annabelle, huh? I figured out that was her today. And I remember what you told me."

"Forget about what I told you, okay? That was a long time ago. And it doesn't say who it's from. It's not signed and it could be anybody."

"Can I read it?"

"No!"

A long pause. "You're turning into a bastard, Joey." He spoke in a deep voice through the megaphone, and I had to laugh, it sounded so authoritative and ridiculous.

I shook my head and turned out the light. "It's private, Timmy. When you get to be my age, you need a little privacy. You can understand that, can't you?"

"I just want to read it."

"Good night, Timmy."

"Just tell me what it says in your own words."

"Good night, Timmy."

"Do you like it?"

"Good night, Timmy!"

Images of Maggie filled my head, and I thought about how much I loved her and longed to see her. Why, oh why, couldn't the note be from her?

I reconsidered why we were building the fort, and I had a sudden vision of conquering my fears and going back to Stoneridge the very next night, scarfing up half a ton of lumber, and getting on with the building. Oh how I longed to be with that girl! I wondered what Freeman would say when he saw the note. I knew he'd be happy, but I didn't know just how happy. I tossed and turned as these thoughts went round and round, and I did not sleep much.

"Hot damn, Joey!" Freeman appeared filled with joy as he handed me the note back. "This is the girl for me!"

"It's a nice poem, but it doesn't have your name in it," I pointed out.

"Who cares? Your friend is my friend, lover boy! Your love is my love! And she's gonna be the first guest to our fort!"

"What fort?"

"The one we're gonna build real soon! Real, real soon!"

"But how can you possibly fall in love, when you've only seen her once?"

He looked at me funny, like I ought to answer that myself. I considered, then cleared my throat.

"Well, what I mean is, how can you be so sure she's the right one?"

He kept looking funny at me.

"Well, what I really mean is … um … I guess what I mean is, what are you going to do about it? The note is addressed to me."

"I'm not gonna do much of anything. You already said you'd ask her to come to the fort for me. You just get her there, and I'll worry about what to do when the time comes."

"I don't know, Freddie. All the changes she's been through, it's like she's a different person these days. I can't really imagine her doing what she did at the junkyard."

The truth is I feared there was a chance she might, now that I had read the note, strange as the whole thing seemed.

"You leave the hard part to me, okay? I'm older and wiser. More of a stud too." He smiled and patted me on the head. "You just get her to the fort. Ya can do that, can't ya?"

"Well, I … "

"Never mind. Just let's get the fort built, then I'll teach ya about the rest of it."

I considered what I knew he had in mind, and it didn't seem right, even though I realized it wasn't much different from what I'd already done with Annabelle. Still, she was older now and things were obviously different.

"Would you really use her just for sex?"

"'Course, Joey! What do you think girls are for?"

It sounded terrible, and I didn't like it. I thought of the lecture we'd gotten once at St. Frances, from a visiting priest, who told us everything we needed to know about sex. The boys had piled into the gym while the girls went off with the visiting nun.

"It's like this," the priest had admonished us as he held two paper clips high in front of us, the bottom clip suspended from the top one. "The top half represents your soul, which is the most important, the eternal part. The bottom part is your body, which you need to leave behind in order to enter the kingdom of heaven.

"And the bottom half is also the dirty half, the filthy half, the part that makes you want to have sex. It is that which holds you back and can actually drag you down to hell. And so it's a continual battle between the two, and in the end only one half can ever win. So what you need to do is leave the bottom part behind. Like this!"

He angrily tore the bottom paper clip off, then flung it back onto the stage somewhere where I heard it clink, clearly establishing that sex is bad and can lead you directly to the hot spot.

Still, I wasn't anxious to kill Freeman's enthusiasm. If his perverse ideas would give him a boost and help get the fort done, who was I to complain? Besides, I couldn't really imagine Annabelle coming to the fort to pose for either of us, in spite of whatever her note was supposed to mean. If and when we did get the fort built.

But all that was in the future, and the most important thing at the moment was seeing Freeman so fired up, no matter what the reason. One way or another we had to get the fort done; once that was accomplished, I knew I'd be in touch with Maggie, to give her a personal invitation to come see our handiwork—but of course Maggie was a whole different story, and that story was based on pure love and had little to do with what Freeman seemed to have in mind.

7

It took a long time to make the trail through what amounted to about half a football field of insufferable jungle. And it wasn't so much that we made a trail as that we bushwhacked back and forth through the dense oak, over and over, complaining and whining and trying to figure out what to do about a trail. In the process we developed a familiar passage, wherein some of the main obstacles, such as dead logs and offending branches were pushed back, broken off, or tossed into the surrounding forest, usually by Freeman. By and by, near the end of the second day, we realized that perhaps we'd made a trail after all.

"Actually, it's more like the equator," I pointed out. "Kind of an imaginary line that doesn't really exist, but people pretend it's there anyway."

"I don't know if we can even pretend it's there," Freeman replied as he tried in vain to budge a protruding rock that we'd both stubbed our toes on several times.

Still, it was a way to the fort site, and it was the only way, so it would have to do.

"At least it will keep JC away," I noted. "He'll never find us here."

"True, but there ain't no girls gonna come down this damn thing either. 'Specially at night. I only hope we can find it again ourselves, Joey."

"Don't worry. It'll get better the more we use it. Especially if we drag lumber down it a couple of hundred times. That's how trails get started, you know?"

The next day Freeman got the bright idea to borrow Matt's bow saw, army shovel, and a pair of pruning shears from his endless supply of salvaged junk.

"Won't he be mad if he finds out we're using all this?" I asked as Freeman rattled and rummaged through the pile of metal in the corner of the garage.

"Prob'ly. But how's he gonna find out?"

"Why don't we ask him just in case?"

"Then we'll have to tell him what we want it for. And we can't tell no one about the fort, not even Matt."

Back in the scrub oak we added killer amounts of elbow grease and sweat and swear words, and by late afternoon you could almost say we had a real trail instead of an imaginary one, though it was probably the skinniest, snakiest, most well hid trail in the entire world.

Then we got on with the campsite and made noticeable progress by sunset of the next day due largely to the borrowed tools. Freeman dug a round firepit and lined it with rocks, and also what I took to be a rectangular refrigerator, which was placed strategically in relation to the fort. I pruned and bow-sawed an opening for the fort itself, about the size of a large car and a half. Freeman cut branches for a table, stacked firewood, and made a tripod in a shaded area for hanging food.

"What about a latrine?" I asked, realizing belatedly my need to take a ferocious dump.

"Right there." Freeman pointed to what I had thought was the refrigerator.

"That's the latrine?"

"What's wrong with that?"

"It's gonna stink out the fort, that's what!"

"Not if you bury the stuff like you're s'posed to."

"You can't have a latrine right next to the fort; that's unsanitary. Not to mention embarrassing!"

"If I get up in the middle of the night, ya think I'm gonna care how sanitary it is?"

"If you go back to bed and smell it, you sure will! Besides, I don't want to wake up and hear you making funny noises out here. Especially if the wind is blowing my way."

"Then dig another one," he said, laying on his back. "I'm all wore out." So I slipped into the woods and made do with a twisted sheath of grass, the way the Indians did, resolving to bring toilet paper and dig a proper hole the next time out.

As the sun set we discussed what few site preparations still needed doing, then made plans for another lumber run, late some dark and moonless night. I was too exhausted to argue about scraps versus new boards, and there wasn't much more I could say anyway. We got home around dark, and I jumped promptly into bed, where I slept like a baby, dreaming of good things to come.

In the morning we tore apart another of Matt's junk piles in the garage, looking for rakes to finish up the fort site.

"I know he's got two of 'em around here somewhere," Freeman spoke into the tangled mass of metal, "the springy kind and that jobbie that's like a comb. We need 'em both."

James and Doc, who by now were inseparable, barged in right then. "Matt's looking for you guys!" James exclaimed. "And my crabs died too!" Tears filled his eyes, but we'd known this time would come sooner or later.

"I'll get you some new ones next time I go to the beach," I told him.

"Really?"

"If you're good. But they all die, and you can't really do much about it."

"Where'd ya put 'em?" inquired Freeman.

"Behind the garage. Matt helped me bury them."

Just then Matt burst in, not looking pleased to see us. "You guys took my tools without asking, didn't you?"

"We just borrowed them for a couple of days," Freeman answered.

"I told you to ask, didn't I?"

"I, uhh … " Freeman glanced at me, but I had nothing to offer. "I guess we forgot," he said.

"You didn't forget, Freddie! And this doesn't make me happy, ya know? I said you could use about anything, but you gotta ask first."

"Can we use your rakes?"

"You were going to take them too?" His blood pressure seemed to be rising.

"I'm sorry," I piped up, hoping to ease the tension. "It's my fault. I told Freddie we didn't have time to tell you. I didn't realize how important it was." For some reason my ears didn't even turn red, and I was very pleased with myself.

"Freddie knew! We've been through this a hundred times."

"Um … about those rakes?" asked Freeman boldly, as if nothing was amiss.

Matt shook his head, like he had one big idiot for a brother. I imagined he was trying hard to be civil mainly because he didn't want me to see him lose his temper. "What were you planning to do with them, anyway?"

Freeman looked at me and I looked at him. I shrugged, indicating the decision was up to him. I couldn't see what difference it made if Matt knew about the fort. Keeping it secret had been Freeman's idea from the start.

"I guess we're gonna have to tell you, Matt. But you gotta promise not to tell no one! And you gotta let us use the rakes too."

Matt agreed reluctantly, sat on a large spool of metal wire and listened to Freeman tell of our plans for the fort, along with a few of our recent adventures. He left out some of the more interesting items, such as the lumber on the tracks, the scene in the dunes, and our plans for Annabelle, but it was enough to whet Matt's interest.

"Damn!" exclaimed Matt, evidently jealous when Freeman was done and apparently over his anger. "Am I ever going to get to see this thing?"

"Well, like I said, it ain't even built yet." Freeman patted Doc's head as he spoke.

"I got one idea that may help you right off!" Matt came back.

"Yea? What?"

He pulled a pencil from behind his ear, turned on the light-bulb hanging from the wire above, grabbed a board to lean on, and sketched out some curvy U-shaped lines on the back of an old receipt.

"What the hell is it?" asked Freeman.

"You put that sucker on your neck. See? One on each of you. I can make it from canvas. Then you slip the boards in these slits and you can carry a whole batch of lumber without killin' yourselves."

"You're a genius!" I informed him, not considering that this contraption would push us toward taking the serious new lumber, rather than scraps. He smiled and lifted his hands like it was nothing.

"I'd still like to see the fort site, guys."

Freeman looked at me, as if the answer depended on what I said. I really didn't care if he saw it, any more than I cared if he knew about it; but I suddenly had the bright idea that this might be a good chance to see Matt's new invention, which I had wondered about several times.

"Well, I guess that would be okay," I said with reluctance. "But I wonder if we could see that new invention of yours—that thing that goes underwater?"

"Freddie told you about that?" He shot a glance at Freeman, angry all over again, and stood up like he was going to punch Freeman in the nose.

"Well, he said you were working on some real amazing project, but that's about all he told me." I spoke quickly before Freeman had a chance to open his mouth.

"I told you not to tell anyone!" Matt confronted Freeman.

"I didn't tell him about it. I don't even know about it anyway. All I said was that you were working on some underwater thingie."

Matt turned back to me. "That's all he told you?"

"He said that's all he knew."

Matt nodded, as if that answer satisfied him. Then he sat back down on the spool of wire and rocked back and forth with his arms folded and his eyes closed, in a way that I supposed made him think better.

"All right," he announced solemnly after a long silent pause. "I'll show you the main idea, but only after you guys show me the fort." His eyes went from Freeman to me in search of an answer.

Freeman rubbed his chin and acted like he was considering this proposal carefully, then turned to me for approval. I nodded. "So it's a deal," he replied to Matt. "But ya gotta promise not to tell a soul, and if ya do, we'll beat the crap out of ya!" He looked back at me.

"Huh, Joey?"

I shook my head slightly, utterly unable to imagine either of us beating the crap out of Freeman's own brother, yet pleased that we would get to see Matt's latest invention. The next day we all headed to the fort site to let Matt see firsthand what the rakes were for. Freeman and I walked together, each with a rake on our shoulders, while

Matt and James followed behind, James tugging Doc on a leash. Matt informed us that his newfangled "board lifters" would be ready in another day or two.

"But it's not as easy as I thought. I'm afraid the canvas'll rip, so I'm lookin' at makin' 'em outta rope. And I have to find a way to make sure the rope doesn't dig in and cut your necks off."

"That would be nice," Freeman replied.

We were nearly to the junkyard trail, with Doc darting in and out between us, when the loud blast of a car horn split the quiet of the morning, causing us all to jump. A second later, JC's red convertible roared past on the other side of the street. I couldn't tell how many were in the car, but two or three middle fingers extended upward while various shouts and screams filled the air, though I couldn't discern what was said. Doc jumped onto the road, barking and pulling James behind him.

"Jackass!" retorted Freeman. "I'd like to put this rake where the sun don't shine on that guy!" He held his rake vertically, in place of his middle finger.

"What a flock of bimbos!" Matt shook his fist in the direction of the car.

The vehicle vanished as quickly as it came, and we continued walking.

"I told you the guy's nuts." Freeman put the rake back on his shoulder. James said nothing, but he looked disconcerted and pulled Doc farther onto the shoulder. It was hard to tell if James was walking Doc, or Doc was walking him.

We continued a short distance, when the convertible burst back around the bend, on our side of the street, traveling faster than before. JC was driving and Hank Powers stood on the passenger side, pointing to us over the windshield. The horn blared and the car veered onto the shoulder, heading right toward us.

"Jump!" shouted Matt as he leapt toward James who was already well into the shoulder, pushing him farther to safety. Freeman and I leaped together while the car shot back into the street, not ten feet away. It happened in a matter of seconds, and no one got hurt, but my heart was pumping furiously. Doc barked, and we all stood shaking.

"Butthead!" called Freeman after the car. "Ya nearly killed us!"

"I can't believe this clown!" exclaimed Matt, who I thought was now in a better position to understand our fears.

"He scared my doggie!" wailed James as he knelt and hugged Doc.

"So now do you see what I mean?" Freeman asked amidst the settling road dust.

I thought he was talking to Matt but I soon realized he was talking to me.

"I always said JC was an idiot. What are you talking about?"

"About Maggie! Right there in the front seat!"

"I didn't see Maggie. I saw Hank Powers standing in front, and it looked like two people in back."

"I swear that was her in the passenger seat when they drove by the first time."

"You're nuts! Maggie would never go around with JC!" I looked to Matt. "Did you see a blonde up front the first time by?"

"I can't say. I was tryin' to get the license plate since I didn't know whose car it was. And the second time I was getting James out of the way."

I looked at James. "What did you see, James?"

"I saw a scary red car! With some guy pointin' at me!"

"It was Maggie, take my word," exclaimed Freeman. "You gotta find a different one to chase after, I'm tellin' ya, Joey!"

I didn't believe him; it wasn't possible. The thought crossed my mind that Freeman might be jealous but I promptly ruled against it. He was too good a friend for that. Surely it was the whole disturbing incident and nearly getting run over that made him think so crazy. And that was understandable so I dropped it and we continued on.

Matt loved our fort site, but he immediately began to reel off ways to improve the place, starting with a bigger clearing for the fort.

"It should be three or four times as large," he declared, "and three stories high. And you want a lookout platform on top so you can see all around and be ready if any enemies come."

"But we want grass on top," protested Freeman. "So planes can't see it. Besides which we're tryin' to stay hidden from view and your idea will attract enemies, along with everyone else."

"That's why you need to fortify the thing—so no one can break in. Like a castle. And you need to put booby traps all around the place, to ward off the intruders."

"And I s'pose you want us to build a moat too?" Freeman mocked.

Matt stood straight, looked around, and scratched his head, as if considering it.

"Well, I don't think you need a moat. Mainly 'cause there's not enough water around here. But I'd like to see your master plan. You've got one of them, right?"

"Of course we do, but I'd be afraid for you to see it."

And so it went, Matt offering one crazy idea after another, Freeman shooting them down while James and I collected acorns, which he was fascinated with. I didn't think James knew what anyone was talking about in regard to the fort since there was nothing to actually see.

"How many do you have now?" I asked him after we had collected several handfuls.

"A million and three!" he exclaimed gleefully, and it was obvious he was having more fun than all the rest of us put together.

Matt and James took off eventually, leaving Freeman and me to rake the place up and make it look more civilized.

"That's just like him. One harebrained idea after another and not one ounce of common sense. No wonder he ain't got no girlfriend, Joey! And I doubt he'll ever get one, either."

"Yea, but he means well. I like that. And if he makes the board lifters, what do we care?"

"Humph." Freeman shrugged his shoulders and kept on raking.

"By the way, did you really make a plan?"

"'Course I did."

"Where is it?"

"In my head."

"Maybe we should put it on paper, the way he did with the doghouse."

"Naw. But I learned from that one, believe me. I got this all figured out right here," he tapped his head three times. "Based on that model we did at the beach. Besides I can't draw too good in three dimensions anyway."

"Maybe we should try."

"Don't need to, Joey. I can see the whole thing just perfect. Paper always screws me up anyway."

"You sure about that?"

"I'm sure I'm sure!"

Sunday morning rolled around and my parents took the kids and me to the eight o'clock Mass. We left early, as always, so my dad could park near the doors and be one of the first cars out of the parking lot. We shuffled in quietly and took a pew three rows from the altar, so my mom could be closer to God she once said, though I suspected it was so all us kids would have fewer distractions.

Father Sedrick appeared and began the Mass. Everything proceeded as smoothly and boring as usual, with half the congregation going to sleep, the other half lapsing into daydreams. What else can you do with all that mumbo-jumbo that only dead Romans understand? He came to the sermon, the one part that's in English, and we learned again about the prodigal son, who pops up every year around the same time only to make the same mistakes and get the same treatment.

"So you see, my friends," Sedrick droned on, "the concept of forgiveness is very high on God's list. He is not only willing to forgive, but also eager to forgive us! That is the true meaning of the parable of the prodigal son."

Blah, blah, blah, he continued, causing my eyelids to get heavy and my head to roll. Blah, blah, blah, until the end, when he pounded the pulpit and hollered something that woke me up, though I can't remember what.

Only after communion did I wake up completely and feel truly infused with God's power and greatness. But it had nothing to do with inspiration from Sedrick. I had received communion and come back to my pew where I knelt in the aisle, my head bowed, thanking Jesus for entering my soul once more despite all the crazy things happening to it. No sooner had I done that than a pretty young girl with a shapely body knelt down at the altar, not fifteen feet in front of me. And behold! As I raised my eyes slightly higher I saw those same springy blond curls that I'd seen at the grocery store in April!

I swallowed the host in a gulp and nearly choked. Could this be my true love? My heart pounded like ten hammers at once. Mea maxima culpa! I said to myself.

The girl rose and turned. Yes! It was Maggie! She was wearing a white summer dress with a square neckline that clung tightly and slightly revealed the top of her lovely breasts, while her smooth curvy legs protruded below and moved toward me, graceful as a cat. I raised my eyes, and behold! Her lovely green eyes were smiling down at me!

My face flushed like the surface of the sun but I managed to return a smile, and as I did she winked at me! She brushed past, not two inches away. The trailing scent of her perfume practically caused me to die in my seat. I was too stunned to turn around and too shy. But it didn't matter. The image of her smiling at me was burned forever into my brain, like a brand on a calf, and it seemed like the very thought of it would be enough to bring me eternal happiness!

I heard nothing during the rest of the Mass, and Timmy had to poke me in the ribs several times when it was over to wake me from my daydreams and get me moving. I sat in the car gazing out the window, saying her name over and over to myself, like Helen Keller. " … that cute girl?" asked my mom, seemingly out of the blue.

"Maggie," I said aloud.

"Maggie?" She turned in her seat.

"What?" I asked, realizing belatedly I had spoken aloud.

"I asked if you noticed that cute girl JC brought with him to church?"

"I didn't even see JC! I was talking to myself just now. Sorry."

"About a girl?" chimed in Timmy, knocking my leg with his knee.

"I was just thinking of some lady on TV when you asked, Mom. I didn't even see JC."

"He left in his nice new car with her," she said. "I do hope all these new things in his life help him start behaving better."

Timmy whispered, "Maggie, Maggie, Baggie, Faggie," all the while grinning like a moron. I flipped him a birdie on my leg, which shut him up though he kept on grinning.

I hadn't the foggiest notion about JC, and I couldn't have cared less. All I knew was that Maggie smiled at me, and I knew exactly what that meant—I was right all along and Freeman was wrong, dead wrong.

We were back at the fort site, me raking, Freeman scribbling numbers on an envelope after finally agreeing that we ought to figure how many square feet of boards we'd need. "If we don't have a plan that's the least we can do," I had insisted last time we discussed it.

Now I broke out the good news, like a kid on Christmas morning, eager to share it with him. I was a ball of fire and happiness as I relayed my story.

"It was the most fantastic thing, I tell you! She smiled at me like we were already married!"

"I wouldn't get so worked up," he replied coolly when I was done. "Just one smile don't mean nothin'." He went on scribbling.

That cut me deep and I wanted to bonk his head with my rake handle. But now I was certain he was jealous. And who could blame him, really? So I simply refused to waste my breath arguing. There had been so much in that smile. I had no doubt the memory of it would last all my life, even if nothing else ever happened.

But I also knew something would happen, and it would happen soon. I was going to overcome my fears and look her up. I would memorize a hundred things to talk about, or a thousand if that's what it took. I was determined; I would show her I was the one!

"My guess is she didn't even recognize ya," Freeman said eventually after I had continued raking in silence. He spoke without looking up, as if the whole thing didn't really matter, like he knew more about Maggie than I'd ever know. "She prob'ly smiled just 'cause ya was some guy sittin' in her line of sight. That's the way she is."

"Yea? Then how come she winked at me too?"

"Humph," he grunted as he continued working on his calculations.

I held my tongue, determined to say no more to a jealous person, and put all my energy into raking twigs and dead grass and whatever came along with it. After all, isn't it basically a compliment when someone is jealous of you?

"Six hundred square feet," he concluded eventually, like there was nothing more to say about Maggie. "That's a shitload of boards, winky dinky! I hope Matt's gizmo is all he says it'll be, or we'll be haulin' boards till we're little old men."

Later that evening, we laid on the hammocks in Freeman's garage and discussed the fact that the site was ready for building. "So it's time for another lumber run," he spoke matter-of-factly, "just as soon as Matt gets them board lifters up to speed."

This produced intestinal cramps and a throbbing headache in me, though now it was from fear of getting caught—stealing itself was no longer the issue since I knew my share of the goods would never be over a hundred dollars. And I could find no reason to complain when Freeman brought up the next topic.

"So what we need in the meantime is a day or two of relaxation, to get us properly rested up for the job."

"I need all the relaxation I can get. And the longer we take, the better."

I would not have complained if he said we were going to rest up for the remainder of the summer, or the next five years.

Day one of relaxation found us at the ponds. Freeman claimed he needed more practice with the slingshot, even though I suspected he realized by then that a slingshot wasn't going to do a whole lot against JC and his pals. But practice sounded like fun and surely less stressful than anything we had been doing.

It soon became apparent that Freeman must have practiced. He had improved considerably, to the point where he actually broke a bottle on the tenth or so try.

"I been playin' with it in my backyard a bit." He smiled proudly.

"Not bad," I praised him. "If nothing else, you might scare JC to death."

"I scared the hell out of Matt just the other night—damn rock bounced off a tree and hit him in the ass!"

I grinned and shook my head. "Just be careful, or next thing you know some adult will be taking it away from you. Besides which, we need Matt on our side."

We roamed along the trail on the edge of the Big Pond where green and brown frogs splashed through the weeds as our footsteps disturbed their peace and quiet. Freeman tried to hit a large bullfrog once when it poked its head up. He missed by a long shot, but I wasn't disappointed.

"You'll feel like warmed-over poop if you hit one," I informed him, thinking of the two I killed when I first got my slingshot.

"I feel like warmed-over poop cause I can't hit one. Besides, I'll just pretend it's JC if I do."

Squirrels twittered in the trees nearby but Freeman didn't seem to hear them, and I didn't point them out. Three brown ducks flew over the middle of the pond in a wide V, as if to land; but they saw us and went up again, quacking loudly over the treetops. Freeman fired a rock, but missed by about half a mile.

"Bad, bad, bad," he muttered to himself.

We arrived at the marsh on the north end of the pond and stopped to decide which way to go. Freeman wanted to climb the largest hill in the area, to check out the Westwoods from another vantage point. "So we have a better idea where the hell our mansion is," he said. But to reach the hill we had to get past the marsh.

Six large logs stretched end to end, from our side of the marsh to the other side, half floating, half stuck in the muck. They'd been there for ages, dragged in by someone to make a walkway across. The marsh sprawled away on either side of us, with the trail going around the east edge, so the bridge could save time, at least in theory.

But the many times we tried neither Timmy nor I had ever stayed on top of the logs all the way. We always ended up slipping off and slogging through the shallow water and the stinky, thick ooze on the bottom. Last time was two summers ago. I was older and more coordinated now, I hoped, but I was still glad I had old sneakers on.

"Ever made it all the way across, Freddie?"

"Lots of times."

"Without getting wet?"

"Like I said, lots of times."

"Well great!" I played along. "Then you go first and show me how!"

"Naw. It wouldn't be fair." He tugged his ear and shuffled his feet, trapped by his own boasting.

"Of course it'd be fair. I never did get across. But maybe I will if you show me how."

"Let me tell you how."

"You gotta show me. That's how I learn best."

He sat down and chewed on a long weed, like we had plenty of time to kill. "Now listen up ... "

"Let's face it," I stopped him. "You're more coordinated. Look how good you did at the ball game, protecting Herman. I'm just positive you can do better. Besides, if we ever pick up girls this is one good way to impress them. I'll bet Annabelle would really love to see you walk across."

"For cryin' out loud! It'd be easier to go first than keep listenin' to you."

I felt a warm inner glow when he flicked his weed into the water, where it floated in a circle and then sank under. He adjusted his belt, held the slingshot in two hands, as though that might somehow help him balance, then stepped gently onto the first log.

In another moment he was slipping and dancing and shaking around like a drunken ballerina, clutching the slingshot in one hand, his arms pumping up and down and every which way as he tried to hang onto thin air. I grinned broadly, contented as ten cows in a grassy meadow.

He continued on like that across the first two logs. My only worry was for the slingshot, but then I figured a little washing would clean any pond scum off.

He stepped on the third log which wiggled and rolled two inches one way, then reversed and went the other way; it rolled again, two or three inches each way; then again, four or five inches in each direction.

"Oh, shit!" he screamed to my enormous delight.

Then that old log rolled seven or eight inches to the east, followed by a nine- or ten-inch roll to the west.

"Shiii … " hollered that no-good liar. His hands went straight up and the slingshot sailed into space, spinning round and round like a boomerang. He crouched and his hands came down in an effort to regain his balance. Then he leapt up and backward, like an uncoiled spring, his hands waving on the sides, something like a priest at high Mass. Then he went into some crazy back dive, perhaps five feet in the air, a bird with no wings, horizontal as a telephone wire!

He kicked and flapped and waved his hands, but it didn't help. He splashed down in that same position, kicking and flapping, then disappeared while bubbles rose up to mark the spot. My grin was so large I feared my face might split.

He stood up in the muck, soggy and dripping as a washed sock. I tried to wipe my grin off but it wasn't possible. He spouted numerous unpleasant statements about the swamp and the kids who brought the logs there and I think about me—though I couldn't tell for sure because by then I was rolling in the weeds and laughing so hard.

Finally I collected my wits and listened politely to Freeman's ideas, which were negative and hostile and directed, for the most part, at me. He slogged to the other shore where he said a few final words, shaking his dripping slingshot in my direction. I resolved to do better, to show that boy what form and grace and a real athlete are all about.

He shut up after I got started, no doubt fascinated by my talent. I put all my attention on the fact that I had to do better, no matter what. I moved fast enough to keep my balance, but not so fast as to misplace a foot and ruin that image of grace and coordination. I nearly made it too. With only half a log to go a feeling of superiority had already grown over me. I looked up to smile and give a friendly little wave from the middle of that last log which is when I hit a patch that was wet from all his splashing around. My feet slipped off before I could blink an eye; I was still smiling and waving, when I went off backward, at about forty-five degrees. I imagined I had more style and grace than soggy boy, but the result was identical when I slipped in the ooze and disappeared. I pulled myself up, another dripping sock, disgusted with myself.

Freeman was rolling on the ground like a sick hyena with gas pains. I was tempted to zonk him in the head with my slingshot to relieve him of whatever he was suffering from. But I controlled myself seeing as I still needed a friend, even a rotten, miserable one like him.

Freeman proclaimed himself the winner, having made the best entry; I gave him that point, though I got one for almost getting across, and another point when he found a fat black leech sticking to my neck. I yanked it off and tossed it at him. We brushed the dirt and sticks and particles of gunk off, what we could anyway, and commenced to squishing along.

We climbed the hill and made a general survey of the West-woods, though it hardly seemed worth the effort, given what little we could see. Freeman went to light two smokes, but the cigarettes were soggy and wasted, not to mention that his lighter stopped working.

"I guess this wasn't the best day for relaxing," I observed as he tossed the soggy pack into the weeds.

"Yea, but I know exactly how we're gonna get good and rested tomorrow," he replied. "I been thinkin' about it for a while now, and it's gonna make you one surprised and happy little boy. Plus it's somethin' I wanted to do for a long, long time!"

Thus it was with considerable concern that I followed him the next morning on my bike. We rode along Main Street, through town, and into the junkyard where we ditched the bikes; then we hiked through the fields around the west side of the Big Pond, not far from where we were the day before. We crossed the tracks and soon came to a stop beside a locked gate that led into the Goldberg Sump.

The Goldberg Sump was built three years ago, around the same time the Goldberg Electronics Factory appeared. A tall cyclone fence with rows of barbed wire glistening on top enclosed the place. A metal sign on the fence bore large white letters, on a red background: "No Trespassing! Violators will be prosecuted to the maximum extent of the law."

Past the fence lay the yawning cavity, something of an inverted pyramid, filled most of the way with glassy calm water. It was emerald green on top and darker as it went down, till it darkened and turned pitch-black in the depths. With effort, you could throw a stone maybe three fourths of the way across. On one side was a depth marker, which showed about seven feet sticking up.

A hefty lock and chain secured the gate, and thus the road, which looked to be for heavy equipment to move in and out. The road turned into a ramp that extended into the water. To the right of the ramp was a mud flat, the size of a living room floor, slightly above the present water level.

Freeman heaved a fist-sized rock into the muck of the flat. It created a big brown splash and a sucking sound, then vanished into the mud. He tossed another into the water, where a white splash rose up as the rock sank into the dark green depths.

"So whad'ya think?" he asked as the ripples flattened out.

"About what?"

"About our new swimming place! Our private, deluxe swimming pool!"

"You can't swim here. What do you think that sign says?"

"Aw jeez, Joey! Ain't nobody gonna come to this hillbilly hole! We can skinny-dip for a hundred years and never be seen by no one."

The only way in was to climb the hinges along the gate, then leap down. Which meant that if someone came by who frowned on kids being there, such as a Goldberg worker or a cop, there wouldn't be much chance to get away. Except maybe scramble up the other side and hope for the best on the barbed wire. And we'd need to get our clothes on first, which would not be pleasant with someone watching, particularly someone with an interest in capturing us. I explained this to Freeman.

"And what if JC came along with his goons," I added, "while we're floating out there like turds in a punch bowl? With our thingies hanging out, just begging to be lopped off? I don't think we should."

"Don't get weird now, Joey. Besides, I'm startin' to think JC is a bag of hot air anyway—all he ever does is send them damn notes and flip us off and try to scare us."

"So why do you think they put this sign up?" I rapped the metal with my knuckles.

"Oh hell, Joey! Every place puts them things up. It don't mean nothin'."

"It means: 'No Trespassing! Violators will be prosecuted to the maximum extent of the law!'" I tapped the metal again.

"Well, I'm dyin' for a dip, that's all I know. And on top of that, I want ya to teach me how to dog paddle, here in a nice calm place without no sharks sneakin' around."

I thought of being chased through the neighborhood by a cop such a short while ago, and I pictured a similar scene there in the sump.

"I can't do it!"

He shook his head like this was the saddest situation on the planet. "I've been wantin' to learn to swim on top ever since they put this place in. All I can do now is swim underwater. But I never went 'cause there was no one to do it with. And now you're gonna let me down!"

"I'm a coward."

He looked me up and down. "You only think you're a coward, Joey! You just need to get over that fence and you'll see. You got balls! And nerves of steel! More than anyone I know!"

"Really?"

"I can see it in your eyes sometimes."

"You're not pulling my leg?"

"I hear it in your voice sometimes too."

"What if someone comes by?"

"We ignore 'em and keep splashin' around. But I don't think that'll happen in a million years."

He had a point—what could anyone do if we were in there? Not a thing unless they wanted to come in and get wet.

"Suppose it's the guy with the key and he comes in and waits for us?"

"We pop out and run around him, one on each side to confuse him."

"Bare-ass naked?"

"That'll really confuse him. See what I'm sayin'?" He beamed and glowed like he'd just discovered nuclear power.

"You go first then."

He scrambled up the hinges, slid through the barbed wire and dropped in. I followed, casting common sense to the wind.

"You strip first," I said as we stood by the water's edge.

"Together!"

"No! It's your idea!"

He hemmed and hawed like a mule but finally took his clothes off, set them in the weeds, and waded to his thighs. He stood on the ramp, waiting.

"Hurry up now, before I turn into an ice statue!"

I packed my clothes in a tight bundle, one pant leg sticking out for a handle, just in case. We stood there in thigh deep water, debating who'd get wet first, my flesh turning to goose bumps, my pecker shriveling like a prune. I cast a glance at his and it wasn't much better, though I figured all that hair must have helped insulate it a little.

"If I'm giving the swimming lessons then you ought to go first. Besides, I need to see what you can do if you want me to help."

Right then a train whistle made us jump half a foot. We'd been so worried about someone catching us and who'd go first, we forgot all about the train tracks. And the fact that everyone on the train could see us standing there in our birthday suits!

Just as that idea was sinking in, one rickety smokestack engine rumbled into view, not more than a basketball court away, creeping along about twenty miles per hour. And may an atom bomb land on my surprised little forehead if that fossil from hell wasn't slowing to a stop, along with all the passenger cars it was towing, right there beside us!

I'd heard they were phasing these engines out, but there were still a few left. And I knew how they worked—they'd run out of coal and have to load the furnace to get moving again. It's a five- or ten-minute operation, then smoke bellows out like a blast of dynamite, black and thick as pea soup.

We looked at each other's horrified faces, wondering what to do. There we stood, naked as the day we were born, with five or six passenger cars stopping right beside us! A dozen or more eyeballs looking out the window of each car settled the issue—we dove under and swam like fish toward a stringy patch of weeds that grew along the edge of the bank to the north. We tried to hide under them but it was like trying to hide behind a flagpole.

It appeared every passenger had his or her nose to the window as we bobbed like apples before them! I made up my mind to hold my breath and find a large rock to cling to underwater; I hollered to Freeman to do likewise, then swam back to the ramp.

I stood up and hunted for a rock with my toes, exposed as a roll of film from the thighs up. Freeman's white rear end flashed at the passengers, then at me, then back at them, as he walked round and round looking for a rock to anchor himself to. My right foot tapped a boulder just as the train gave that last squeal of the brakes and stopped completely. There sat no less than fifty passengers, smack in front of us, gaping out the windows. I took air and went under, then clung to that rock like it was my old teddy bear. My feet floated up, but I didn't care about that end. The longest I ever held my breath was one hundred and eighteen seconds, in history class, but I believed now I would set a new record—I was not going to come up till that train left, even if my lungs burst and I died in the meantime.

But the next thing I knew, Freeman's huge hands gripped my sides and the big oaf rolled me over like a turtle then held me up in the air from below, my shriveled pecker protruding like a tiny periscope. And there was that train full of curious faces at the windows, each with free admission.

His hands clamped me like a vise while I kicked and squirmed and tried to roll around; I beat down on his arms, but to no avail. I saw people smiling and laughing and several of them pointing; one woman whisked away her little girl; in another window were two kids about Timmy's age, guffawing like this was the best show they ever saw. And the more I kicked and struggled, the more attention I attracted. I wanted nothing but to drown, then and there.

Freeman let go and I splashed to my backside. I sucked a lungful of air and swam like an escaped turtle. I paddled toward the bank directly beneath the train, praying to Jesus that the steep angle would put me out of sight of all those perverts.

My lungs caught fire and felt ready to explode but I paddled on, bound and determined to reach that bank. I thought I would die, but it didn't matter—I wanted to die if I couldn't make it to the bank. Faster, harder, faster; I spoke harshly to myself, ignoring all the signs a sane person would have to go up for air.

But I was rewarded at last as my hand hit the mud of the bank. I shot up and broke the surface like a dying man, wolfing air into my scorched lungs. I slithered onto the mud slope beneath the train. Slowly I raised my head to see if the train was visible. And there was the proof God still loved me; the train was out of my line of sight!

I looked back to see what happened to Freeman, not that I particularly cared. The flat green surface of the sump was the only thing visible with a few ripples moving across it.

What the hell? I wondered if maybe he'd drowned, and half hoped he did. I wouldn't have to worry about those dog paddle lessons now, would I?

But his head soon broke water beside me, laughing and shaking like he hadn't ever seen anything so funny in his life. He pounded his fists on the muddy bank then he grabbed his belly and shook like a wet dog, his shaggy private parts jiggling in the air.

He carried on for the longest time, till the train whistle blew and the engine belched dark smoke and made a loud chugging noise. The wheels rattled and creaked and started to roll, and soon enough the train and its demented passengers were gone. Freeman was still in hysterics, encased in mud that reached into his ear, though he didn't seem to care. Finally he settled down and appeared able to listen to what I had to say, which wasn't much.

"You jackass! You full-blown absolute jackass!"

That set him off again and he pounded some more on the bank, splashing mud and water all over; he rolled and shook his frontal region at the sky once more, and I hoped he might die laughing.

I swam to the middle and dove under to cool off, then sidestroked back and treaded water about twenty feet out, where I shouted, "You're the meanest, ugliest bastard I ever met!"

"Oh, that was hilarious!" he flopped about in the ooze of the bank.

"Things like that make JC seem like a good friend!! A smart one too!"

"Ya got no sense of humor, Joey! Anyways, none of them people could even recognize ya!"

I swam back to the deep water to stew in my own juices, and only after ten minutes or so did I crawl out on the opposite shore where I laid in the mud and wished I was dead. Freeman came by, crawling along the shoreline.

"Enjoying your rest and relaxation, sally mander?"

"You horse's butt."

"You gotta learn to take a little joke better. There wasn't no harm done, was there?"

"Oh no! I'd like to do that every day."

"You're still gonna teach me how to doggie paddle, huh?"

It was like nothing ever happened, and I still had an obligation to teach him how to swim! I wanted to kill him, yet how can you hate a guy like that?

"It's easy, Freddie. Just jump off the bank and land out as far as you can. If it's over your head, you'll soon be paddling like a dog."

"Aw, c'mon! S'pose I start to drown?"

"You don't think I'd let that happen, do you?"

"Stop messin' with me, Joey."

"What's in it for me?"

"I'm your best friend! And if you teach me, I'll never, ever do that again. Promise! And I'll even say I'm sorry."

The big oaf was too much. I held out for a while, but eventually I broke down and showed him the basics, how a little air in the lungs can hold you up, how to push diagonally outward, how to take little strokes with your feet and keep your nose up. "And stay calm no matter what; that's half the battle."

He caught on quickly and paddled back and forth, then around and around like a frog till finally he got cold and we laid out in the sun and the mud to warm up. It had been another long day. I was anxious to jump into bed and sleep like a rock, even knowing I'd probably have nightmares about the perverts in the train. But one more surprise awaited me; it was another letter on my pillow, this time with a canceled stamp, addressed to Joseph Simpson, 15 Maple Tree Lane, Sunnyville, NY.

"Looks like she mailed it this time, huh Joey?" said my brother from his bed.

"Go to sleep, Timmy."

I ripped it open, even knowing I probably wouldn't want to read it.

hi joey! i saw you walking down the street, and my heart skipped a beat. you look so divine, i wish you were mine. so talk to me, can't you see? i'd do anything in the world, if you'd ask me to be your girl. love, me!

Aw Jesus! I thought. What next? Why couldn't Maggie write such notes? And why did Annabelle have to get stuck on me? It seemed so unbelievable.

At least Freeman would be pleased, I thought. And I was glad I didn't stay up half the night thinking about it, the way I did last time. On top of which I had no nightmares, which was a great relief.

8

Freeman was putzing about his kitchen, where he'd told me to meet him. The radio on the refrigerator blasted out and Freeman sounded like a dying cow as he sang along, "Fever in the morning, and fever all through the night … " He swayed to the music and shook his hips to the beat.

Four bowls of Corn Flakes were parked in a neat line on the counter, covered with bananas. Freeman was in the process of burying them all in sugar, using a wooden spoon that he dipped into a large canister.

"Could I have some Corn Flakes with my sugar?" I razzed him when the song ended.

"And do I really have to eat four bowls?"

"You need the energy, son. But you only need to eat two bowls. The other two are Freeman's."

"But why do I need all that energy?" I played along.

"Because you are about to have another exciting day, filled with adventure! And you want to grow up big and strong. Like that Freeman kid."

"You mean big and ugly?" I took one heaping bowl from the counter and sat at the table. "Could I have a spoon, mom?"

"If you promise to behave and not give your mother a hard time today."

"I won't."

He gave me a spoon.

"But I might give that Freeman kid a hard time!" I stuffed my mouth with a large spoonful.

"Kids are such ungrateful little creeps these days!" He shook his head like an exasperated mother.

I laughed hard and banana mush shot up my nose while unchewed Corn Flakes went down my throat. I put my head between my knees and tried desperately to relieve the choking.

"I got another great idea," Freeman continued, oblivious to my condition. "We'll haul all the lumber we can with Matt's contraption in one night, stash it in the woods, then pick it up a few days later when the coast is clear."

I was doubled over on the floor, gasping for air, sugary mush stuffed in my nose, Corn Flakes rasping my throat. Freeman rambled on and monkeyed with the sugar.

"We'll do the final trips across Cranberry Boulevard as we need the lumber. It'll break things up and we can probably get done with Stoneridge in one night."

I gagged and choked and tried desperately to breathe; I felt certain I would die beneath the table, and he wouldn't even know it!

"Of course if we get enough energy from good meals like this, we might even do the entire operation in one night."

With an urgent push, I shot the banana ooze out my nostrils, enabling myself to breathe again. Freeman looked over at the strange noise and saw me laying on the floor.

Yellow mush flowed from my nostrils against the background of my red face.

"That's not a nice way to eat the breakfast I slaved over, son!" He acted like I was laughing, then went on as if nothing happened, except that I was greatly enjoying his jokes.

"Of course if you have a better idea on the lumber, I'd like to hear it."

I staggered to the sink and coughed furiously, spraying Corn Flakes and gobs of who knows what all over the place. I grabbed a glass of water and washed down the remains. It was like someone sandpapered the insides of my throat and nose. Freeman blabbered on, oblivious to my plight.

"Well, seeing as you have no better idea, I guess that's what we'll do. Now get yourself over here and eat your second bowl of cereal!"

"Christ, Freddie! I almost died! From a banana in my nose!"

"Well, that would have put a dent in things, wouldn't it?"

"Didn't you see me dying?"

"I thought ya was laughin'."

"It started out that way. Till the banana came out my nose."

"Ya okay now?"

"I hope so."

"Good! Then finish your breakfast, son!"

"For cryin' out loud, I am done! I don't want another bite for three days. Besides which, I got another letter for you."

He read it slowly, put it back in the envelope and kissed it three times. "Oh, I love this girl!" he said with a wide grin.

"I wish she'd address them to you, then. All they do is give me a headache. As you know, I'm madly in love with someone else."

"Don't be so limited, Joey. Why, if ya lived out west, in Utah for example, you'd have a couple of hundred girlfriends. Wifes, too!"

The calendar in Freeman's kitchen indicated it would be a near moonless night that Thursday. I had surprisingly little difficulty getting permission to sleep out since my dad had seized on the fact that I was better off around Freeman than the clowns who still played baseball. I imagined that my mom saw anything that kept me away from JC as a reasonable alternative—his reputation had gotten that bad in the past few years.

"Remember Jesus loves you!" she had begun saying in closing the brief conversations we had. As if by remembering that everything else would be just fine. Of course I was pleased to know someone loved me, though I would have been a lot more pleased if she said the same thing about Maggie. I mean, what can you do about the fact that Jesus loves you? Whereas if Maggie loved me I could think of lots of things to do, even if they were embarrassing at first.

Thursday rolled around and Matt came through with the board lifters, which he delivered to us in the front yard where we were playing fetch with James and Doc. They were made of garden hose, foam rubber and manila rope, all wound up in electrical tape.

The garden hose and the foamy part went around the neck, while five loops hung down on each side for boards—it was so obvious I couldn't believe I didn't invent the thing myself.

"I think you can carry ten two-by-eights. But you'll probably want to start with something less on the first run, until you get the hang of it."

"The hang of it?" joked Freeman, hanging one around his neck.

"Another neat thing is you can wear them on your waist when you're not carrying boards."

He put the other one on James's waist, and James beamed during the demonstration. Again it was so obvious, I couldn't see why I didn't think of it, unless it was because I wasn't an inventor. "And use them as whips if someone like JC comes along."

I smiled at the idea of whipping JC and his goons, and wondered why I didn't think of that too. While I was smiling and having that happy thought, Freeman piped up, "I think these'll work okay, Matt. Me and Joey here really appreciate it."

"No problem. I like seeing my inventions going to use."

"Speaking of that," I reminded him, "do you think we could see that underwater gizmo of yours now?"

"I can show you one of the early versions, but the latest one is still top secret."

"That's fine."

"Then step right this way, boys and girls!" He turned excitedly and motioned with his hand, then walked around the house and down the stairwell into the Freeman's basement, which I was not surprised to see was filled with junk of every kind—wooden and cardboard boxes, dusty boards, old carpets and clothes, metal scraps from who knows what, a bike with no wheels, barrels filled with parts from a thousand machines, and many other things that I can't remember. Matt marched us to a small table piled with yet more junk in a dark corner. Then he took what appeared to be a modified toilet seat off it—it was a ring of flat wood with a large hole in the center, the outside of the ring being about a half a foot across. The edges of the ring were different thicknesses, inside and out. I couldn't help thinking that it was a bit like a Hula Hoop, inasmuch as it was round with a hole in the center.

Matt held it in his hands in such a way that it framed his face, which had a wide grin on it. "So? What do you think?"

"What do I think?" asked Freeman. "I think it looks like a big asshole sittin' on a toilet seat, only the toilet seat's turned sideways instead of flat."

Matt kept grinning as if he had expected such a comment from his brother. "How 'bout you, Joey?"

"Well." I racked my brain for a kinder answer, but it wasn't easy. "It does look a bit like a toilet seat, but I'm wondering if you can show us how it works."

"I can't really show you, but I can tell you." He took the seat from his face and handed it to me in a horizontal position. "Put this dealie-bop flat underwater and what do you think happens?"

"I know!" shouted James.

"You be quiet now," Matt told him in a calming voice.

"It floats up. Anybody knows that." I moved the seat upward to demonstrate how I thought it would move.

"Exactly. But this puppy is different! It comes up sideways and keeps on going in one direction!"

Freeman and I stood there trying to picture what Matt was talking about, while our blank looks gave us away.

"Look, it's like this." Matt took the toilet seat back, held it in two hands, then moved it sideways and up at a slight angle, along the path that a sword might take if you swung it in front of yourself. "If I put this thing underwater and let it go, it's so thin and flat that it tries to shoot to the side rather than come directly up. It's like a knife when you cut through hot butter—you can push the knife forward, but not sideways."

"What makes it keep going one way?" asked Freeman.

"Look." Matt held the toilet seat sideways so we could see the edge. "One side is a little fatter than the other side. So the fat side rises a little higher, and up and away she goes, in that direction!"

His enthusiasm was contagious, but I had trouble seeing what he was talking about. Freeman stood there as dumbly as I did.

"It has to rise, right? But it can't come straight up, so it has to go sideways. It's like a sail—it can't go flat into the wind, but if the mast goes first it can cut into the wind quite nicely."

"So it floats sideways?" I said. "Like those swim boards that shoot out sideways at you?"

"You got it, Joey! But it just goes in one direction because of how it floats underwater."

"Smart little Joey." Freeman rubbed the top of my head, like a good dog. Then to Matt, "So why do you think anyone's gonna want an underwater toilet seat?"

Matt shook his head, like he had a moron for a brother.

"How can you be sure that's what'll happen?" I asked, trying to keep the edge off things.

"Because I've tested a zillion of 'em in the bathtub. And then when I get a shape that does what I'm saying, I take it to Herman's and use his little brother's pool. So it has a longer distance to travel and I can see how it really does."

"Herman knows about these things?"

"He's the only one, besides you guys. The latest models are at his house now. But the first ones are over there," he pointed to a huge pile of sanded wood pieces under the table that I hadn't seen. All manner of shapes were piled beneath the table, rectangular, triangular, square, a few circular, and several of them crosses between all the different shapes.

"You mean to say these pieces of wood glide underwater, like a bird in the air?" Freeman asked.

"Don't you get it? They glide up! What I'm working on now is to figure out what's the farthest I can make them glide."

"But what the hell good is it?" Freeman persisted.

"If these things were submarines they could move forward by gliding silently underwater. Then if you could make them heavier than water, say by venting a batch of air, they'd start gliding back down!" Matt was getting worked up as he talked, obviously in love with his own invention.

"I think we'll stick with the board lifters," Freeman announced bluntly. "Besides they already have submarines."

Matt shook his head, as if any further explanation would be useless.

"Well … " Freeman scratched the back of his neck in silence for a few moments. "Maybe somebody will want one when you get it all figured out. But I think we'll be happy with these board lifters. Huh, Joey?"

"This is pretty cool, Matt. I think I could have invented the Hula Hoop, maybe even the board lifters, if I ever thought about it, but I don't know about this one. It sounds mighty…unusual. But I'm still not sure I fully get it."

"Thanks, Joey. You'll get it when I show you the final version."

Matt set the toilet seat down and started away with James, then turned toward us and shook a finger in the air. "One more thing I almost forgot to mention. Herman told me this and said be sure to tell you!"

We pricked up our ears while he paused to get his thoughts together.

"So?" Freeman asked after some time went by and it appeared Matt forgot he was talking to us and had started thinking about something else.

"So," Matt came back to earth, still pointing at the ceiling. "All you need to do is drop a ping pong ball in JC's gas tank. The ball gets soggy when the gas leaks in, then it sinks and gets sucked into the gas line. Until it stops the car and she floats back up. Talk about changing density! Then it happens all over again and no one knows what's wrong! And the only way to fix it, if anyone figures it out, is change the gas tank. It's just a barrel of fun."

Freeman and I cracked up as we digested the idea of doing this to JC's car, then those two joined in and we laughed till we could scarcely breathe anymore. Putting a ping-pong ball in JC's gas tank was a welcome relief to the plan he'd been proposing for us.

Matt and James took off, and we sauntered toward Freeman's bedroom. Freeman claimed it was "time to do some more mathematics on our own little invention, even though you can't really trust the numbers like you can common sense." He also informed me that "Matt's still a dingbat, and if that little demonstration don't prove it, nothin' will."

"It sounded interesting to me," I responded on the way up the stairs.

"Whoever heard of a underwater flyin' toilet seat? That's the damnedest thing he ever came up with."

"I'd like to see it working. What gets me is how much time he's spent on that thing. Seems like he ought to be doing something else with his life." Then it occurred to me that I had no idea what else he could do with his life, so I let the subject die.

Freeman was soon scratching away on an envelope with his pencil, muttering to himself, shaking his head, crossing things off and writing new figures. I read a *Dagwood*, and it was probably fifteen minutes before Freeman lifted his head up from his calculations.

"Looks like six trips, Joey. Ten boards each, times two of us, times six runs, equals a hundred twenty boards. Times five square feet per board gives six hundred."

"You sure you did that right?"

"Does a bear crap in the woods?"

"Yea, but does a bear know his times tables?"

"Stop worryin'," will ya?" He swatted my ear several times with the envelope.

"This'll be enough for a real humdinger! And the girls are gonna love it! I get all warm and fuzzy just thinkin' about it. Not to mention swelled up pretty good," he grinned.

"So I see," I razzed him, nodding toward his fly.

That night we took off before Freeman's dad went to work. We figured we'd need the extra time to complete six trips with the board lifters. We planned to haul the lumber from Stoneridge to a storage location, about half a mile down the tracks, near Cranberry Boulevard and across from the fort site.

"We'll hide the goods somewhere around that neck of the woods," Freeman explained as we walked through the shadows along the streets. "At least 'til the emotional dust settles down and all them workers get over it."

"And hide the boards a lot better than last time." I winced as I thought of the train we nearly derailed, and of what Mario had said about cops looking for the culprits, not to mention what the workers must have thought when they found the lumber last time.

"Ya got that right, Shylock."

We arrived at the outer edge of Stoneridge and saw no sign of life. Still, we held back in a stand of bushes for a while to be sure no one was around. Freeman peeked through the branches and gave a report.

"Ain't a soul in sight, Joey. Looks like a graveyard, I'd say."

"Let's wait five more to be sure that cop isn't roaming around somewhere."

"Don't be such a confounded worrywart! There's no one but us here and some vacant houses out there. Besides, if that guy comes along he ain't even gonna see us in the dark."

"I say wait."

"And I say see ya later, alligator."

He started off and left me crouching in the bushes. I imagined I was a fool to follow but I figured I might as well get caught with him, since if he got caught by himself I'd be all alone and right back where I started, and that fate seemed even worse.

"You are the world's biggest ass!" I said when I caught up to him.

"Stop callin' me names," he laughed, "and start lookin' for boards, will ya, pokey wokey?"

We had a good idea where to look as a result of our recent nail run, and we soon came upon a huge stack of boards covered with a tarp along the side of a house. The aroma of fresh wood mixed with that of the warm canvas filled the night air. The silence and stillness was broken only by the sound of crickets, which seemed all around.

It pleased me that I had no paralyzing fears and no headaches or gas pains. Still, I was alert and ready to take off like a bullet, always aware of where Freeman was so if someone did come I'd be on the far side of him in an instant. It wasn't nice, but I reminded myself this whole adventure was his idea in the first place. And if one of us had to get caught, his parents would cut more slack than mine. So it made no sense for me to get caught, I firmly concluded.

"Look at this here pile!" Freeman exclaimed when his eyes lit on the canvas. "Why they must of been thinkin' of us when they stacked it up so neatly! I only wish they would of put it closer to the tracks!"

"I still say go for scraps. There's zillions of them all around here." I pointed to two piles of cut pieces of two-by-fours and -sixes, some quite long, that lay jumbled like pick-up sticks as examples. "Hoisting boards from a new stack will only attract attention."

"Which is why we gotta take the whole damn pile, Joey! That way they'll wonder if they even had a pile here in the first place. Not to mention that the new stuff will fit much better in the board lifters."

"I thought you said six runs was all we needed!"

"I did. But now that I see what's here, I say we take the whole pile."

"You're out of your mind, Freddie! They'd be after us in two seconds if we took the whole pile! On top of which that's criminal behavior!"

There was little doubt in my mind that the pile was worth $500 or more, though I really didn't know how much. I thought of what that visiting priest had said and I knew full well the hellish, eternal consequences this would have for my soul.

"That's what makes it excitin' and worthwhile—all that riskiness involved! Plus we gotta have it if we're gonna build a decent place."

"Hell, Freddie! I thought you were talking about something like a tenth this size."

"Don't be ridiculous! I told ya we'd need a real nice place, if we're ever gonna score with the girls!"

"You mean Annabelle?"

"Whoever."

"Well, I know her, and I don't think she'll even care if we have a fort, assuming she's going to come with us in the first place." I had absolutely no desire to get caught taking a stack of lumber that size, but at the same time I saw my error as the words left my mouth.

"Wait a dang minute! You mean all this work and we don't even need a fort?"

"Well, no … I mean, of course she'll care. And of course we'll need a fort! But we don't need some mansion, like that thing Matt was talking about."

"Look!" He raised his hands in exasperation. "We can stand here yakkin' all night, or we can start haulin'. I say let's start haulin'—it's what we came for!"

He untied his board lifter and hung it on his neck. "You gonna stand there like a two-by-ten yourself, or ya gonna help me out?"

I immediately had gas pains, a headache, and a guilty conscience, not to mention visions of hell and fears of dying along the tracks. What if the train came from behind and we didn't hear it, or what if I got my foot stuck in the tracks? I thought again of the stories my mom had told me about that. But there was no time to worry, at least not in the manner I was used to doing.

"So let's go!" Freeman implored. He slid the canvas off the boards revealing the neat white pile, about four feet high by five feet wide, of what appeared to be ten footers.

I put my board lifter around my neck and told myself that if things went right I'd have a clean soul in a day and a half, since it was close to midnight already. I would have walked away if I could have, but what choice was there? I had to have a place to take Maggie and this was the only way I knew to accomplish that.

Loading the lifters was much harder than we anticipated. If you put one board in, the lifter thing slid off to that side. We soon realized we had to put one on each side, with the neck loops on the ground, then lift the gizmo up with the loops on our necks. But even this was tricky, since you had to coordinate with the guy at the other end.

"Damn!" said Freeman after several failures. "That wing-ding brother of mine couldn't make a fly swatter that works!"

"It's not all his fault. We should have tested these things out, like he said."

"Let's try this." Freeman laid his contraption in a straight line on the ground and made me do the same, parallel to his, about six feet away.

"Now put all them suckers in the loops first, then we'll slip our necks under and rise up together."

I wondered if Freeman didn't have some streak of inventor in him too, and I kicked myself for not seeing that procedure first. This arrangement worked, though it was terribly rough on the neck, and I didn't see how we'd go half a mile that way.

"Let's take the last board out and see how that is," I suggested.

It made a big difference in neck pressure, and we didn't have that low board banging against our ankles.

"One last thing." Freeman set his load down again and tied off the slack in the end of the rope, motioning for me to do the same. "This way we won't have no confounded rope flappin' around our feet."

I convinced him to help me restack the extra boards and put the tarp back on the pile, so as not to create unwanted attention in case someone checked up on things.

"Good idea," he said. "Though you are a pain in the ass sometimes." He climbed back in his rigging. "Now let's get movin'!"

I glanced about to be sure no one was observing us. I had an eerie feeling once again that someone might be, though I saw no sign of it. The development sprawled in all directions, still, dark, lonely, barren, a bulldozed wasteland. I recalled how it used to be, with spruces and hemlocks, white and red pines, locusts, maples and other trees I learned the year I was in Boy Scouts growing amidst meadows and marshlands. It struck me then that the whole of Long Island must once have been a beautiful area, way back when the Indians lived there.

"You gonna stand there dreamin' about Maggie, or are we gonna go?"

We moved toward the tracks, four boards dangling on each side like barricades, in a way that would flag down anyone who glanced our way, no matter how dark it was. This was something Matt apparently hadn't considered, but it was too late now.

So I was glad when we picked up our pace along the base of the tracks since we were better hidden from view. I assumed we would continue there, given the visibility factor and what happened last time. But I should have known better.

"We gotta get up on the ties like we did before, Joey. To avoid all the weeds and rocks and crap down here."

"But I can't walk good on the ties. They mix my mind up something terrible. Especially when it's dark like this. Plus it might attract attention."

"It can't be no worse than walkin' through this junk."

"What if a train comes? Like last time?" Those dreaded butterflies lifted off in my belly, big time.

"Then we come back down. And we'll both be listenin', so we'll be sure to hear it."

"I don't want to. I'd rather take my chances in the weeds and stuff."

"I say try it. If the top ain't better, we can always come down."

I didn't want to spend all night arguing, and what more could I say? So we climbed up and got on the ties. It wasn't as bad as I thought, because I could watch Freeman's feet and see where to step. But I insisted we go up and down several times, to be certain we could do it quickly, in case a train did come.

"Look here!" cried Freeman, the fourth time we went up. "We gotta go up and stay up, or go down and stay down! I don't care which no more. But this is worse than mountain climbin', for Christmas sake!"

So we stayed up, since it's where we were and it really was easier. We listened for trains and remained alert for any signs of movement. I tried to keep my mind on the ties and the rhythm of the steps. Still, I couldn't help thinking about how much the lumber cost. Eight boards at five dollars apiece would be forty dollars; one half of that would be just twenty dollars, so most likely I wasn't stealing yet, but we had several trips to go. But then I had no idea how much the boards really cost, so who was I kidding?

Then, too, even at five dollars apiece, my part in the heist would not be one hundred dollars till the fifth trip—so maybe I wouldn't be stealing until the sixth trip, when the amount was actually over a hundred dollars. Then I wondered if you needed to include tax, and I resolved to ask that in confession. And what if the boards were cheaper at another store? And suppose they were on sale one week and not the next?

Good hell, I thought, there's also the possibility I could shift the weight to Freeman's end and cut my portion of the theft down! That sounded wonderful under any circumstance, and I made up my mind to slip more weight to his side at the next stop.

We soon broke for smokes and rested in the weeds, and even Freeman seemed to remember we ought not park on the tracks. He went off to water the bushes, which gave me a chance to slide my

174

lifters back about eight inches, so he had more weight and a larger portion of the goods.

"Ya know, Joey," he remarked when he returned. "I gotta say it: You're the best friend I ever had! And I mean it."

"Really?"

"You're the only friend, actually."

Of course I was flattered, and then I felt badly; he was the only friend I ever had too, besides JC, back in the olden days.

We grunted, got the lifters on, and headed off again. After a short time, Freeman spoke, "It's almost like these bastards are gettin' heavier. Don't ya think?"

"Oh, maybe a little. But I imagine you're just getting tired."

"I may be more tired than I thought."

"Actually, I'm kinda getting used to it. I almost feel like I could go all the way without a break. Provided you don't wimp out." It was an exaggeration, but I liked the sound of it and I did notice the boards were a good bit lighter on my end.

"Dang, Joey! You got some real endurance for a little runt like yourself." I liked that even more, no matter what the reason. To ease my guilt, I reminded myself that he was bigger and, of course, had gotten me into this in the first place; on top of which he was helping protect my soul from damnation. It's good to have friends like that, I thought.

By and by we came to a spot that Freeman said would be good for the storage area.

"It's almost right across from the fort site, and it ain't likely anyone's gonna find it. It's just like what I had in mind," he stated happily, veering off the tracks into the weeds. We soon found a tangle of shrubs of some sort, and slid the boards underneath them. We covered the goods with leaves and twigs and whatever else we pulled up in the dark, taking care to do a good job, then sat on top of the tracks for a breather.

"This could almost do for the framework," I noted. "And I still say we don't need more of the good stuff. In fact, scraps of plywood would probably be best for laying over the frame."

"Now listen up, will ya? I got it all figured out! We need the rest of that pile, and that may still be cuttin' things close."

"What do you mean cutting things close?"

"Well." He put a hand on his chin, looked down and shook his head. "First off, we haven't even made six trips. Right?"

I nodded.

"Plus we screwed up."

"What do you mean?"

"I was figurin' ten boards each, times two per trip. Right?"

"That sounds about right."

"So don't ya see? We're only takin' eight boards each trip. Not twenty like I figured."

Tired as I was, it took a moment for that to click. "You're saying we need fifteen trips instead of six?"

"Maybe more even."

I took a deep breath and sat in silence, wondering what on earth I'd gotten myself into.

"But she'll be one big sturdy mama when we're done, Joey! And that's what we gotta have if we're gonna get babes to visit."

"You sound like Matt, now. We're not building the Alamo, you know. And Annabelle's just not that fussy."

"But it's only gonna be half what I thought!"

"Well then … " I tried to picture a fort half the size of what I'd been thinking, and of Freeman and me and two girls inside.

"Well what?" he demanded.

"Well, I guess the girls will have to be real friendly."

"Have it your way, then," he replied, though I could see he was only saying it to shut me up. "Let's just get what we can tonight, then sleep on it real good."

We were halfway to storage on the fourth run, resting in the weeds, when I decided I'd had enough. Not only were we increasing the chances of getting caught, but also I was ready to drop, in spite of the weight shift trick. Sweat soaked my body, the lifter dug into my neck, and my jeans stuck to my legs. The only consolation was that I was too beat to think real hard about the consequences if we did get caught, not to mention if we got mangled by a train.

And a freight train did go by after a time, while we sat in the weeds and watched. The ground vibrated and sparks flew around the wheels. I pictured myself underneath them, realizing such a fate would sentence my soul to a good many years in purgatory; I wondered who I'd meet down there. The train squeaked and groaned, and open doors on the boxcars caused me to picture Freeman and me hopping into one, going who knows where, to have who knows what kind of adventure.

"How 'bout one last trip after this?" Freeman asked when the train had passed.

"No!" I responded instantly. "I can't do it! I don't want to do it! And I won't do it, either!"

"I've been recalculatin' again, Joey. Two more trips, and we might be done for good. Except for scraps to fill things in, like you said. Besides, we gotta finish what we started." He paused for a few seconds, letting that sink in. "Didn't the nuns ever teach you that?"

"The nuns can take a flying leap! I'm beat to hell and I'm not doing another trip!"

"Don't get so all-fired emotional. It was only a suggestion. A good one too."

"Baloney, Freddie! We got enough wood to make our own little Stoneridge. And Coney Island too!"

I was punchy and I knew it, but I didn't care. I had no intention of going back that evening.

"I'm worried you're losin' your mind now. We got thirty-two boards and that's all. We can finish the roof, maybe, or the frame and a side or two. But we'll still need more, that's all there is to it."

Part of me knew he was right, but I dreaded going back again. The thought of another load was too much. I had to hold my ground, no matter what. "No!" I said like a little kid.

He laid on a board for a few minutes, looking at the starry night sky. "All right then," he sat back up, "I won't push for no more boards tonight. But we gotta make one more trip for that roll of tar paper I saw on the flatbed. I'll carry it and you can just come along. You can't argue with that, can you?"

"It's three o'clock! It'll be light soon! I say go home and hit the sack."

"But we can sleep all day. We gotta take advantage of the night. Just one roll of tar paper. That's all I'm askin'. I'll even carry it, so all you gotta do is tag along for company."

"Tomorrow."

"Do it now and we can avoid the joint tomorrow. Then we can let things settle down for a few days."

"I need to settle down now! In my sleeping bag! On top of which we need to stop pushing our luck."

"But we need that tar paper bad—we can't have no leaky roof if we're gonna have girls come by." Then he put his hands on my shoulders, almost lovingly, looked in my eyes, and said in the kindest, sweetest way I ever heard him talk, "You'd make me ever so happy. On top of that, you're the most fun kid I ever knew!"

So it was that we dumped the last load of boards with the others, along with the lifters, and dragged ourselves back to Stoneridge for one lousy roll of tar paper.

I was thinking of my sleeping bag when Freeman pulled the heavy black roll off the flatbed and placed it on his shoulder.

"Blast! She's heavier than I thought!"

"And I suppose you want me to help you with it?"

"Naw. There's no place for you to … wait. By jove, you're right!"

He set the tar paper down and hunted up a piece of two-by-four, about four feet long, which he stuck through the center of the roll so the ends protruded like handles.

"Grab ahold." He pointed to the long end. "I'll take most of the weight, but you gotta tote that side so I don't kill myself."

"I thought you said I could watch!"

"That was before I knew better. Now grab that end and let's be off!"

We walked away from the flatbed, which, with its large round fenders and a split windshield, looked like it might be Henry Ford's first truck. But we hadn't gotten more than a hundred feet when Freeman turned around with a finger to his lips. "Shhhhhhhhhh!"

"What the hell?" I whispered.

"Maybe nothin'," he whispered back. "I'm not sure. But I thought I saw a light in the window, two houses over."

He motioned to the house we'd found the lumber next to.

"What kind of light?"

"Like a flashlight. But it's out now."

"You sure?"

"Shhhhhhhh! Hang on a minute." He wagged his hand to shut me up. "I ain't sure of nothin' yet."

The house was dark and quiet, the window openings black as coal. I couldn't see a thing. Chills went through me like hot needles through butter. Our feet and eyeballs were glued in place, and the rest of us as good as paralyzed. After half a minute I couldn't take it anymore.

"Let's go," I tried to say.

But no words came out, even on the second try. I tried sending mind waves to him but that didn't work either; I suspected because of his thick skull. I reached and tugged his T-shirt, nodding with my head to the railroad tracks.

He shook his head, "Yes."

We started moving out, and took about three steps each.

"Hey, you!" A voice boomed from the window as a bright flashlight washed over us.

"Aw, shit," said Freeman as we stood squinting in the light.

"Should we run?" I whispered.

"I don't think it's a cop. It sounds like a couple of kids."

"Yea, that's him all right!" Again a loud voice came from the window.

"You sure, JC?"

"I said 'That's him!' didn't I?"

We froze like rabbits in a headlight when we realized who it was.

"So it's gotta be him, don't it? Tony wasn't spyin' over here for nothin'!"

There was a shuffling of feet and a ruckus, then a third voice filled the air, "Well, let the party begin!"

I didn't recognize the voice, though it sounded vaguely familiar. More rustling and footsteps echoed from the empty house. The light went out and I could hardly see a thing, like I'd just entered a movie theater.

"Let's split!" I hissed.

"No, wait! I think there's only three of 'em. We can stand up to three punks, Joey! We gotta do it or we'll be on the run forever." We dropped the tar paper with a thud. "Get yourself a board!" he added.

I looked all around but didn't see any; it was so dark and my eyes were blinded from the flashlight. Then I remembered the board stuck through the tar paper. I slipped it out and held it like a bat.

"Get rocks!" I said to Freeman, though he was already doing just that.

We stood up, primitive weapons in hand, and turned to face JC and his goons. I could make out five figures walking toward us, one of whom had to be JC, and another one no doubt Tony. My legs felt like rubber bands; I wanted to collapse and die and end my misery before they did it for me.

"I should have listened to ya, Joey," Freeman exclaimed, though I was too petrified to appreciate his reassessment.

"So!" JC's voice filled the air. "It's Screamin' Freeman and his sawed-off little friend!"

"Stealin' things too! Tch, tch, tch!" mocked another voice that I was sure was Tony's.

"Look JC, a two-by-four! Ohhhhhh! I'm a scared!" It was a nasal voice that I recognized as Sandy Arnold's. Arnold was a classmate of JC's from St. Frances, who seemed to get in trouble as much as JC; though not for getting in fights so much as pulling pranks. He had once caused an uproar when he blew up a toilet bowl with a cherry bomb, and another time when he tossed a smoke bomb in the girls' room. And last spring he turned out to be the culprit who had slipped a jockstrap on the statue of the Blessed Mother the night before the May coronation. Even I appreciated that one, though it did rile up the nuns for a few days.

"So you had some fun knocking JC's teeth out, you retarded billiard ball?" I recognized Hank Powers from the ball games. He went to public school and was a year ahead of Freeman; his father was in the Air Force, and he had moved from somewhere in the last two years or so. I'd seen him around a few times—another leather jacket case with doodads dangling and jingling, like you might expect from a kinder-garten kid. I could see all that garbage glittering dimly in the moon-light, and when Powers moved, his chains rattled too.

"Let's use the two-by-four on their teeth, JC," suggested Tony cheerfully. "See if they like it as much as you did!"

"Don't worry, I can't hardly wait for that part. But first I think we should slice the peanuts off Dumbo here and see how he feels about that."

There was a click and the dull glint of a long blade, similar to the shine from objects on the leather jackets; it was in the hand of the fifth kid, who I was sure was Billy Ferguson.

All five thugs began surrounding us, not more than a few feet away. I felt certain we were about to die, bleeding to death with our family jewels lying beside us. But no sooner did I think that then I real-ized I wasn't so worried about dying as I was about thinking of a way to get out of there, and calculating what to do next.

"I didn't hit you with the bat, JC. You know that." Freeman spoke as if these guys were anxious to hear his explanation, or accept some apology and walk away.

"Say that again and maybe I'll cut your pecker off too, you fuzz-domed dweeb. I think it's time for you to just shut up."

"Herman did it!" I blurted out.

"Well, well, well." JC turned to me. "If it isn't Mr. Goody Two-shoes. Do you still play with your little toy trains, Saint Joseph?"

He moved in front of me and waved the blade of his knife back and forth before my face, as if he was going to cut my nose off, for practice.

"If you're trying to show me you've got balls, Joey, I know exactly what to do with them. Can you guess what I mean?"

He said the last part like a grownup talking to a little kid, while he continued flashing the blade in front of my face.

But he called me Joey, which was something. And I still wasn't sure just how prepared he was to use the knife on me. Was he bluffing or did he mean it? I was fairly certain he was ready to operate on Free-man, and that was scary enough. There I stood with the two-by-four cocked on my shoulder, a knife blade glistening before my eyes, three big shitheads and two little ones crowded around us. Freeman had two large rocks in his hands, and was on my left.

"Whatsa matter Joey the Simpleton? Got nothin' to say anymore?"

JC reached out with his knife and flipped my baseball hat off. The other buttheads laughed like this was the grandest of jokes.

"You still using that gooey green shit on your hair?" JC asked, messing my hair with his hand. I thought back to the time he criticized me for using my mom's hair-setting goo instead of Brylcreem, like he used.

"Leave him alone!" Freeman said, reminding me of how he spoke to JC at the baseball game, and again at Callaghan's.

JC turned to Freeman.

"I thought I told you to shut up! Or don't you hear too good?"

"I'll shut up when you make me, JC."

"Tony, put the light on this guy."

"You got it!" Tony beamed the bright light into Freeman's face. It was one of those rectangular battery jobs, with a red flasher that stuck out on top. Freeman looked white as a ghost, with his eyelids squished down and squinty.

"Get the freakin' light off me!"

"Why?" asked JC. "You're the star of the show now."

"Yea, big boy, what's wrong?" chimed in Sandy. "You don't like all the attention now?"

"Let's cut 'em off and make him eat them, JC!" laughed Billy, his chains jingling.

"Hey, let's make Joey eat one too!" added Tony, like it was the best idea he'd ever had.

"He could use some balls!"

They all laughed, but Tony was the loudest, carrying on like a hyena.

I was looking frantically for a way out but not coming up with any. Fears of dying flooded over me again. Billy held up his knife, which had a thin pointy blade, similar to a meat knife. He stood with

JC in front of Freeman, holding the blade alongside Freeman's face, twisting it back and forth like he couldn't wait to use it.

"Take your pants off, Dumbo! Let's see if there's anything worth operatin' on down there!" commanded JC.

"Up yours," said Freeman courageously and foolishly, I thought.

"He's afraid to show us, JC!"

"Maybe he's got nothin' there. That's what I've been thinkin' all along!"

"Eat shit."

"No, no, no," clarified Billy. "You got that wrong. You're the one who's gonna eat shit, Freddie Freeman! Now get your goddamn pants off!"

"Kiss my ass."

There was a moment of silence while JC and Billy looked at each other. I wondered if I could die simply by trying hard enough. They looked back to Freeman and inched even closer. Billy's knife was now by Freeman's neck and JC's by his stomach. It looked like JC was putting pressure on the blade since Freeman's stomach was pushed in perhaps half an inch.

"How would you like another asshole, asshole?"

"Fuck you."

"I don't think this boy is very smart," said Billy. I confess I was ready to agree, though I had no idea what else he could have done. Tony, Hank, and Sandy were standing quietly, smiling like it was a high form of entertainment.

"Maybe we could start with his earlobe," Billy said, tugging on Freeman's ear. I wondered if Freeman was going to use the rocks in his hand. It was becoming clear that my choice was to stand there and watch Freeman have his balls cut off, maybe even eat one myself, or else put up a fight like I'd never done before.

I'd been in two fights in my life, one with Henry Hodges and the other with Jessie Williams, both in fourth grade and both within two days of each other. Hodges beat me up because some older kid dared him to; Williams did it because Hodges told him how easy it was. That sank my spirits more than I care to think about, and it still does; and it's why I knew I wasn't much of a fighter.

But I was not about to let JC or anyone else cut Freeman's balls off, not without my doing something. I pictured the arc of my two-by-four crashing into JC's head, and I tightened my grip around it. My idea was to smash the side of his skull as hard as I could, just above his ear, then start swinging wildly at the other jerks, and hope to God that Freeman would behave in a similar fashion with the rocks, maybe nailing Billy in the head so we wouldn't have the two knives to contend with.

I was terrified, but also angry as I'd ever been. I tightened my grip and readjusted my body ever so slightly to get ready to bash in JC's skull. I would wait until someone moved to harm Freeman.

"Hang on a sec, JC." The voice was Sandy's. "I think there's some damn car comin' down the road!"

Everyone turned and looked where he pointed. I expected to see headlights, but there were none.

"There's no damn car!" replied Tony.

"Yea, there is. There definitely is. But it ain't got no lights on. Look close." I saw it, a dark form in the street between the houses, barely visible. The tires made a low crunchy sound on the gravel as the vehicle crept along. It disappeared behind a house, then reappeared; it did the same on another house, as we all stood in place straining our eyes.

"It's a freakin' cop!" said JC.

"No it ain't," replied Billy. "I can't see no light on top!"

"You got good eyes—what is it Sandy?" demanded JC.

"I'm lookin'. I think it does have a light on top … shit, yes! It is a cop!"

"Let's split!" someone exclaimed.

My heart let go with a holler of joy. I dropped the two-by-four like a bad guy in the movies who drops the gun when he's caught. No sooner did the board hit the ground than a colossal floodlight lit us all up, so blinding and bright that it made Tony's flashlight seem like a birthday candle.

Tony, Billy, Hank, and Sandy whooshed off like turds being flushed. The searchlight followed them as they dodged past a dump truck and a backhoe and continued on their merry way.

"Don't feel bad! You will see us again!" JC admonished sarcastically, then took off after them.

Freeman flew to the ground almost in the same instant. "Get down, Joey!" He didn't have to say it twice. In half a second I was stuck to the ground like a postage stamp. We laid there head to head in the rocks and gravel, quiet as corpses. The light swung by above us, then went back and focused on the fleeing parties, as they moved farther and farther away.

"I think we're safe," Freeman whispered after the car's headlights came on and began traveling after the fugitives.

"Hot damn!" I started laughing. "Hot damn, hot damn, hot damn!"

Freeman began laughing too; it was such an incredible relief. We laid there laughing and rolling in the dirt, unable to stop. My sides were splitting but there wasn't a thing I could do about it. In the distance we heard the siren of another cop car.

Freeman grabbed my arm and said, "I think the first cop got 'em!"

This sent me into hysterics. "We have to get out of here!" I gasped between laughs. "It's going to be light soon and those cops may be looking around." My cheeks were wet with tears.

Freeman whistled and sang while we walked down the tracks— "Whistle while you work"—over and over, while the roll of tar paper bobbed between us on the two-by-four. I broke into laughter every now and then, causing the tar paper to shake like a washing machine.

We slipped the roll in with the boards at the storage site then laid back and looked at the stars, speculating about JC and the fort and Annabelle, and wouldn't it be wonderful if JC and his friends got locked up for stealing boards? But light colors formed in the eastern sky and we soon headed for home and the cheerful welcome of two cozy sleeping bags, where I dozed off for a few hours.

"Joseph Simpson! Get up and get down here! I need to talk to you!"

I had pulled myself from the sleeping bag and tent some time before, arrived home around nine a.m., then slipped into my own bed for maybe an hour. But it appeared that luxury was over—you don't go slowly when my mom beckons like that.

I threw on clean pants, a fresh T-shirt, socks, and undies. I dashed to the bathroom, chewed a wad of toothpaste and splashed water over my face and hair. A few strokes of the brush and I walked downstairs, normal as I could, prepared to face the music, as they say.

"JC's mother just called and said JC was picked up by the police this morning! At Stoneridge."

"Really?" She had my interest all right.

"Do you have any idea what she's talking about?"

"How would I know, Mom?"

I squinted and shook my head, while my stomach bunched into a knot.

"She said JC told her you were there too!"

"What?!"

I looked at her with as much disbelief as I could muster up, though it didn't seem sufficient.

"JC said you and Freddie Freeman were there with him."

"Doing what?" I shook my head some more, and tried to act like I thought she was going crazy. I prayed to God that she wouldn't start asking about lumber or a roll of tar paper—I was reasonably certain it would cause me to break down completely.

"JC claims you were threatening him and his friends with switchblades, Joseph." Her eyes narrowed and zoomed in like gun barrels, in a way that normally would have caused me severe heart palpitations. But a flash of anger came over me then, along with a powerful urge to strangle JC. My mouth dropped open and my voice raised in indignation, "What? That's insane, Mom!"

"You honestly have no idea what he's ... " she started to ask, but I interrupted her.

"I don't even have a butter knife, let alone a switchblade!" I proclaimed.

She took a moment, evidently considering my reaction, along with the absurdity of the accusation.

"Well, I guess that is rather an odd thing for him to say."

"Why in the world would he say something like that?" I pondered aloud, silently thanking him for his lie, which worked so nicely against him. I even smiled a little to myself at the thought.

"So you and Freddie weren't even at Stoneridge last night?"

My inner smile disappeared and I coughed a bit, then started to take a breath with no idea what was going to pop out next. But at that very moment, bless his wormy soul, Timmy walked in the other door to the kitchen.

"Mom, are we going to the beach today?"

She turned his way. My mind was banging on all four cylinders to come up with an answer to that one, that wouldn't be an outright lie.

"Timmy, you talk to me in a minute! I'm having a discussion with Joseph right now."

"Oh."

The gun barrels turned back to me.

"Well?"

"I'm sorry Mom. What was that question before Timmy rudely interrupted us?"

"I said where were you last night?" Her voice was raised again, but not so severe.

"Oh … yea. Well, I slept out with Freddie, in Matt's old army tent … you knew that. And we took a walk around the neighborhood since we couldn't get to sleep. Then this morning I came home and read some comics in my room."

She was on hold, trying to X-ray my mind, when Timmy interrupted again, this time in a whisper. "Mom, I got Ryan on the phone and I need to let him know!"

Maybe I did love my brother, somewhere deep inside.

"Tell him 'Yes' Timmy, and start getting your things ready."

She kept her eyes on me, though I guessed she'd bought my answers, because her tone changed again. "You may go with us too, Joseph. If you want. I believe I'll tell Helen she needs to sit down and have a long talk with JC. I'm sorry if it seemed like I was accusing you unjustly."

"It's okay, Mom; you wouldn't be a good mother if you didn't look into things like that."

"You just remember, Joseph: Jesus loves you!"

Well, you can't beat that, I thought, as I slipped out the kitchen door into the fresh air and sunshine.

We learned through Matt, who learned through Herman, who had sources of his own, most likely one of his older sisters, that the cops suspected JC and his friends of stealing lumber and attempting to derail a train, despite their protests. Getting caught with switchblades late at night, in the middle of Stoneridge, was not a good thing no matter how you looked at it. On top of that, the cops found a key in JC's pocket that by chance fit a bulldozer. A small pang of remorse went through me, but it was overshadowed and diminished by my pleasure.

"That two-bit chickenshit!" Freeman slapped his bed as we discussed all this. "I doubt those jerks even got their stories straight."

The downside was that JC and the others were surely more ready than ever to do us serious damage, in retaliation. And thus we needed to be even more alert than before, ever ready to move fast in the opposite direction.

I had overheard my mom on the phone that morning and pieced together that JC's parents were at their wits' end, and considering sending JC to reform school.

"It would break my heart and make me cry," said Freeman when I relayed that bit of news.

Not long afterward, we went to the beach with my mom and the kids, though it was not nearly as interesting as the first time. I did some body surfing with Timmy, mainly to shut him up, while Freeman got another bucket of crabs for James and took a walk with Mary for shells, all of which greatly pleased my mom. And we saw JC's car in the parking lot by the concessionary.

"Someday we have got to play that ping-pong ball trick," I noted. "Let him give us grief just one more time … I almost can't wait."

"I'd do it right now," declared Freeman, "if only I had me one!"

9

Freeman and I sat in the front seat of the Mercury on the way home from the beach that day, which meant we both got to see, at approximately the same instant, the cop car that was parked in front of my house. It felt like my heart dropped about six inches. Hell's bells! I thought. Our little behinds will be soon hanging from the nearest flagpole! The cop was on the brick porch, pounding at the front door as my mom pulled in the driveway.

"Look, Mommy! There's a policeman at the door!" shouted Mary from the backseat.

"It's a real one too!" sang out Patrick, waking up from a nap.

"Good luck, you guys!" Timmy said under his breath, beaming happily.

My mom looked at Freeman and me as though we might be able to give her a quick explanation. We shook our heads negative, as if to say, "We know nothing!"

"You kids stay here," my mom commanded the passengers in back. "And you keep the windows rolled up!"

She turned icily back to Freeman and me. "Get out."

We walked together toward the cop, who met us at the base of the porch.

"You Mrs. Simpson?"

"I am."

"I'm Officer Maloney. I'd like to have a little chat with you." He eyeballed Freeman and me, as if we were surely the ones he'd come to see. "These your boys?"

"Joseph is." She put her hand on my head. "And Freddie Freeman lives next door." She nodded toward Freeman and pointed a finger in the direction of his house.

"We had a situation the other night," explained Officer Maloney. "And these boys' names were given to us by the parties involved."

My mom motioned for him to go on. I shot a glance at Freeman, who was staring stone-faced at the cop's belt. I tried to calm myself and do likewise.

"A couple of boys about this age were picked up at a new housing development the other night. They had switchblades, and we have reason to believe they were stealing things."

Maloney turned toward us, watching for a reaction. We stared blankly, though my knees felt weak and rubbery and my head was suddenly very light.

"I've talked to Joseph about this very situation," my mom replied. "I happen to know one of the boys involved, and his mother is a friend of mine."

Maloney now waited for her to continue.

"I have reason to believe that Joseph was not involved in this terrible situation, after speaking at length with both him and Mrs. Clancy."

"Do you mind if I ask the boys a few questions?"

"By all means. Please do officer." Both adults turned to us.

"So you know what I'm talking about?" asked the cop, as he eyeballed me.

"I heard somethin' about that," volunteered Freeman. "After Joey told me, after his mom told him. But we had nothing to do with it."

The cop now looked him up and down, as if in serious doubt, then turned back to me.

"Is that your version too?"

"Yes," I blurted out. "We never even saw those kids there!"

All eyes were now on me, and I could sense that Freeman was as unhappy as I was that I'd said anything, let alone that.

"I thought you said you weren't even there." My mom raised her voice in an accusing tone.

"Well, n … not the other n … night."

"So when were you at Stoneridge?" Officer Maloney sounded terribly curious. "We went there a couple weeks ago to get some used nails," Freeman spoke up again, before I had time to open my mouth.

"What does that have to do with the incident we're talking about?" the cop asked.

"Nothing," I sang out, trying to redeem myself. "I only m ... meant we never saw those kids there at all. And we certainly never saw them the other n ... night."

"So you were there on the night Officer Maloney is referring to?" My mom promptly sniffed the weak spot, undoubtedly aided by my stuttering.

"No!" jumped in Freeman. "That night we slept out, all we did was walk around the neighborhood, since we couldn't get to sleep right away." I breathed an inner sigh of relief. This was consistent with my earlier story, confusing though it may have been to Maloney.

"But you do know where Stoneridge is and you have been there?" asked the cop.

"Oh, I know where it is. I've been there three or four times," offered Freeman, sounding like innocence come to life. "I used to go there a lot, before them houses started going up. And I told Joey we ought to get nails there, so they don't go to waste." He looked to me. "Isn't that right, Joey?"

I shook my head yes.

"So if we weren't s'posed to be there," Freeman went on, in a respectful way, "then I'm really, really sorry. But there was no signs up or nothin'."

The cop and my mom looked at each other, almost like they had some kind of secret understanding, though it may have been my imagination.

"Joseph Simpson," my mom sounded like a nun, "let it be known from this minute on, that your going to Stoneridge is absolutely, positively forbidden! And I will talk to Freddie's mom about this matter in the near future. Is that perfectly understood?"

I shook my head and saw Freeman doing the same from the corner of my eye.

"Thank you very much, ma'am," said the cop. "I only wish there were more parents like yourself these days." He turned back to us. "You boys need to keep a clean record, and Mrs. Simpson here is telling you this for your own good. I'd strongly advise you to listen to what she has to say. Every word of it!"

"I appreciate that," responded Freeman without hesitation. "I wouldn't go back there for a million dollars!" My mom, Maloney, and I all looked at him.

"Well, maybe for a million. But you know what I mean."

My mom pointed us into the house, and as we walked into the front hall I heard Maloney say, "I have no reason to doubt them, ma'am. These other punks have been in too much trouble before. Though I admit your son does seem like the jumpy type. I appreciate your co-operation."

It was a close call, one I had no desire to repeat. When she got in the house and had shut the door, my mom exploded, "I don't ever, ever want to hear of you boys being around Stoneridge again! And you stay away from JC too!"

"Mrs. Simpson," rejoined Freeman, in a voice so sincere I practically believed him, "Don't you worry! I'll look after Joey here like he was my own little brother!" He put his arm around my shoulder and squeezed tight.

My mom rolled her eyes and I thought she even smiled a little, before sending us to fetch the kids and unload the car.

Our real problem, of course, remained. JC was still on the loose and a continued threat to us. We mulled things over and considered our options, but they always boiled down to the same simple plan: Lay low and keep working on the fort till it was suitable for the female visitors we had in mind.

We let several days go by, "for all that emotional dust to settle down a wee bit," as Freeman again advised me, and in the meantime we read comics, played rummy, watched Matt tinker with his various junk, and played catch with James and Doc.

"I sure am glad you guys found Doc and brought him home," Matt informed me one evening as we sat in the corner of his front lawn while Freeman chased James and Doc around, making strange loud noises and pretending to be a monster. "It gives James someone to hang out with and frees me up a lot."

Then Matt abruptly stood up, motioning me with his hand as he did so. "C'mon inside for a minute while those guys are running around, Joey. I need to show you what I've been working on."

I followed him down to the basement, and he walked me to the table where we had seen the underwater toilet seat. In the dim light he lifted up another odd wooden object. "This is the best design I've come up with, much better than that old toilet seat."

He held the object out for me to hold. It looked like a large guitar pick, about a foot across and two inches thick in the center, tapered around the edges, with what looked like long flat wings sticking out from the sides. I held the item in a way I imagined to be vertical.

"Looks like a Viking head with horns coming out of the helmet."

"I know. It also looks like fish fins and a flat fish body, huh? But you should see this thing scream through the water, Joey! It goes faster than you can swim."

I turned it over a few times, noting that the contraption did have a very fish-like shape. "It's mighty interesting," I lied, "but I admit I still don't quite see what good it will do."

"Like I said, it's a design for a submarine, but it'll go much faster than regular submarines. Plus it'd be super quiet and be able to stay under a lot longer. Still, I need to put a few more years into developing it."

"A few more years?!" I echoed in disbelief.

"That's no big deal. Look how far I got in the last six months. Give me another two or three years and I'll have it all figured out!"

"You'll be done with high school by then," I reminded him.

"But that's not the half of it, Joey," he went on cheerfully, as if he hadn't heard me. "This thing could glide like a bird in the air, only better!" He was talking fast and excitedly, waving his hands about like he had just made a fantastic discovery that would shake the world.

"You're saying this will fly?" I too was beginning to wonder about Matt's sanity, in addition to how I was going to get away from him.

"No, not this thing, Joey! But something like it, only bigger. Filled with helium so it's lighter than air! Imagine that! This very shape like you have in your hands, about the size of a school bus, but lighter than air so it glides up! Carrying passengers! Anywhere they want to go! Anywhere! Cargo too! It will change the world, Joey!"

I looked at the object I was holding and didn't quite know what to do with it.

"That's pretty neat. If you ever get this all figured out, I'm sure I'd go for a ride." I hoped that would shut him up since by now I was fairly certain that Matt had lost his marbles, and I couldn't figure how to break away, given his level of his excitement.

"Plus you can take off and land wherever you want, so you don't need an airport!"

I dumbly shook my head and rubbed my chin, pretending to be interested.

"Now if I can just figure out how to use pulleys and ropes to compress this thing, you could make it so you could fly by human power. Think of it! A human-powered airship! Why you might even be the first human to fly around the word by human power, Joey!"

"Me?!" I asked in amazement and alarm.

"Yes, you! I've been thinking a about it—you'd be the perfect pilot! You're not too heavy and you're in pretty good shape and you're a pretty smart guy. Even if you do hang out with Freddie."

"Well, thanks." I was at a loss for words, and though I appreciated the compliment, I was now convinced that Matt needed to see somebody, like a doctor, to get help in the mental department. As soon as possible.

He began buzzing my head with the stupid thing, explaining that it would make no noise whatsoever because there was no motor. Fortunately, Freeman's voice came down the stairs just about then. "Hey, are you guys down there?"

"So there you have it," Matt concluded. "You're the only one besides Herman I've told, and I don't want Freeman to know about it yet. Promise you won't tell him?"

"Okay." I would have promised anything to get out of there and change the topic.

We left the basement and Matt's Great Invention, and all four of us raided the kitchen, making hot dogs and peanut butter and jelly sandwiches, with Doc being the happy recipient of what we didn't finish.

It was about twenty minutes later, after Matt and James went off to tinker with something or other in the garage, that Freeman and I were cleaning up the kitchen. Freeman swept the floor while I wiped crumbs off the counter.

"So what were you guys doing in the basement? Or is that the kind of thing you don't want to tell me about?"

"Actually it is a secret," I replied as I went to clean off the table.

"Yea, I can imagine," he taunted me. "That sounds like the kind of secret I wouldn't want to talk about either." He put the broom in the closet and smirked at me.

"You moron. It's nothing like that. It's about Matt's invention."

"What? He showed you how to sit on a toilet seat?"

"You'd have to promise not to tell anyone."

"Don't worry 'bout that. I think I know how to keep a secret."

"You swear on a stack of Bibles?" It occurred to me that I sounded like JC did many years ago when he showed me that girlie picture.

"I swear on a stack of Bibles." He raised his right hand.

"Okay, then." I sat down in a chair and leaned back. "The secret is that your brother really is a fruitcake."

"That's it? I coulda told you that years ago. In fact, I think I did tell you not too long ago."

"Well, that's just the first part. The second part is that Matt thinks that water thingie of his can fly in the air."

"I told ya, Joey—he's dumber than he looks! His brain's got too many gears, or else not enough. I can't tell which anymore."

"Plus he wants me to fly the thing ... " Just the thought of that caused me to shake my head.

"Jeez!" Freeman pulled up a chair and sat down.

" ... around the world!"

"It's hard to believe the guy's my own brother."

"And he wants me to fly it without a motor, too!"

"He's off his rocker, Joey. If he weren't so helpful every once in a while, I swear I'd stop talking to him." He leaned back and stood his chair on two legs. "How the hell can anything fly without a motor?"

"He keeps saying something about it changing density, so it glides up, then down."

"His fat head is the only thing changing density around here. And right now I think it must be small as a pin."

I was going to tell him some more, but the door suddenly swung open, and in marched James, Doc, and Matt. We sat in silence and didn't know what to say. Both of us stared at Matt, like he'd just arrived from another planet.

"So you guys look like a bundle of joy," he exclaimed. "What's going on?"

"Nuthin'," replied Freeman. "We just finished cleaning up the kitchen."

"Mom will be happy. You should do that more often." Matt winked at me, and I felt guilty as all get out. I thought my face turned red but I tried my best to ignore it and act cool. I was glad that only the small light by the sink was on and the room was dim. James got a glass of water at the sink while Doc came to me for a pet, which I was happy to give him. Matt looked from one of us to the other, while I did my best to ignore him. "So you're talking about girls, huh? Don't let me stop you. I got more important things to think about."

He went to the sink and grabbed a glass of water for himself.

"Water's good for the brain, you know? You ought to have some, Freddie." He guzzled it down and put his glass by the sink, then came over and patted me on the shoulder like a long-lost friend before starting out of the room. "Drink a few million gallons of it and you might become smart as Joey."

"Yea, Freddie! Water's good for you," laughed James as he followed after Matt.

"All of which proves what I was sayin', Joey," Freeman said when they were out of earshot. I chuckled and acted like it was funny, but inside I felt lowdown and snake-like for having revealed Matt's secret so easily. What if he really was a great inventor? I wondered.

By and by the time arrived for action, though it was not so much the result of ambition as from the boredom of sitting around and reading too many comics. It was hard to say where our original ambition went, but it seems like summertime has a way of making desire and motivation get in the backseat, if not disappear entirely.

But boredom or ambition, it didn't matter—our immediate problem was to get the boards from storage to the fort site, then build what we could with what we had.

"It's just a tiny hop across Cranberry Boulevard," Freeman tried to encourage me, when I complained about all the work involved. "Gettin' the boards from storage should be a piece of cake."

"But there's traffic there now, and we'll be out in the open. We'll be sitting ducks if a cop comes by and catches us with all those boards!"

"I got a plan for that too," he calmly informed me.

"What? Use invisible paint?"

"We take only two boards at a time, see? And if a cop comes by, or anyone else, we say we found them two in the woods and was just makin' a small tree house. A lookout platform, actually, so as to make it more believable." He smiled proudly.

It wasn't bad, I had to admit. But I also knew we needed to have all the details worked out if we did get caught; and Freeman would have to do all the talking, that's all there was to it.

We disagreed as to the time for moving the boards. Freeman said go early, around six a.m., while people were still in bed. But I held out for late morning, since any kids actually building a tree house would more likely go then. Freeman finally came around to his senses and my way of thinking, so it was near ten when we dragged the first two boards from storage. We commenced to lugging them across the fresh pavement of Cranberry Boulevard, Freeman in front, me in back, "wiping up the rear," as he proclaimed.

We had both developed a great appreciation for the board lifters, since they spared much work and strain. But we didn't dare use them as they'd raise too many questions if we ever did get caught. The whole idea was to have to explain no more than two boards at any point in time, which was all we could carry without the lifters.

"It's a great way to get longer arms, ain't it?" joked Freeman as we marched across the smooth pavement, our arms straining with the two-by-eights.

"Maybe next time you should tie them to your ding-a-ling."

"Maybe next time I'm gonna tie 'em to your big nose, Mr. Funny Face!"

One car went by shortly after we crossed, but the driver didn't even seem to notice us, let alone care. A feeling of satisfaction came over me when those first two boards hit the ground at the fort site, and for the first time I could actually see the fort being built. We plopped ourselves down beside the lumber in the weeds and grass.

"This is almost too easy, ain't it Joey?"

"If you like your arms stretched out a few inches. That was killing me near the end there."

"So next time let's use the board lifters. We could cut 'em short and just carry two at a time."

"We'd still have to explain what they are," I observed. "And how on earth would you do that?"

"Bah!" He waved his arm in the air as if we hadn't had a similar discussion just the day before. "You need to stop worryin' and leave things up to me. It's gonna be the end of ya if ya don't!"

"It'll be the end of me if I do. It nearly has been so far."

"Ah, Joey—that's why I like ya so much. Ya always exaggerate and make everything sound like a great big adventure."

But we stuck to no board lifters and two boards at a time nonetheless, mainly because the lifters were still in his garage and neither of us was willing to go get them.

By the fourth trip our arms were adjusting anyway, and we were pleased there were so few cars. I was developing a large sense of accomplishment, and by late afternoon nearly all the boards had been moved. We had four boards to go, two that we were carrying and two that were still in storage, and we knew we'd be done soon.

And we would have been done, but for one big blue car, with long tail fins and whitewall tires, which approached from the north as we made our second to last crossing of the pavement. We stood on the side of the road waiting for this vehicle to pass, when suddenly brakes screeched, tires squealed, and the car slowed rapidly, causing us considerable surprise.

We were even more surprised when the car wheeled sharply into our lane and smoked to a stop in front of us. The window rolled partway down and a voice that I recognized as Mario Giovanni's bellowed out: "What in hell do you little bastards think you're doin'?!"

There was a long pause before Freeman responded. "Just goin' to the woods." Like it was the most obvious thing in the whole wide world.

The car was a dirty, dented, mud-splattered affair, with the word "Plymouth" written in a silver strip on the side. It looked like Mario was wearing the same jeans and suspenders as he'd worn the first time we had seen him, still with no shirt. He wore sunglasses, which made it difficult to read his eyes. But it didn't matter, since he shook his head in disbelief.

"And I suppose those boards just happen to be goin' the same direction you are?" Freeman looked at the boards, on one side then the other, like he'd never seen them before. An outburst of butterflies filled my stomach.

"Well, yea, I guess they are." He nodded his head.

"But we have plans for them!" I spouted out, as if that would make our possession of them acceptable.

"I'm sure you do," said Mario, opening the door and standing before us, his hairy muscles rippling in the sunlight and dark nipples staring at me again. "Why don't we talk about those plans for a minute?"

He motioned us closer to the car and pointed to the boards. "Now put 'em down, right there nice and neat alongside the car."

Freeman and I exchanged glances, but seeing no options did as he said.

"Now hop in the backseat there because I want you kids to be nice and comfortable. Real nice and comfortable!"

He pointed to the back door, and I followed Freeman in. Stale cigarette smoke filled the air. Black rubber boots and a general heap of junk lay scattered on the floor. Freeman pushed a stack of manila folders across the seat, then sat on a clipboard with important looking papers attached to it. I felt like a little kid with his hand in the cookie jar, though I knew the consequences here might be more serious—far, far more serious. My butterflies fluttered madly as Mario slammed the door behind me.

"Don't say nothin'!" Freeman whispered to me before Mario opened his door. "Let me do the talkin'."

"Don't worry. I said too much already."

Mario climbed in the front and picked up what appeared to be a microphone for a shortwave radio from the dash, like he was going to speak into it, then changed his mind.

He turned to face us and I noticed he had a large bent nose, which seemed to go well with his Diesel Power hat.

"I really didn't think it was you two!"

"What do you mean, sir?" asked Freeman, respectful as any kid ever was.

"You know exactly what I mean! What's your name, anyway?" He held a pen, which he pointed to Freeman, then made like he was going to write his name on a clipboard.

"Matthew Daniels," Freeman replied, mixing his brother's name and the plural of my middle name. "And my friend here's name is Tony Angeli. Do you want our addresses and phone numbers, sir?"

My stomach tightened, my palms got slippery, and I let out a fart that I could no longer hold. Fortunately the seat muffled the noise.

"I'll get to that in a minute! First things first, all right?" he barked.

"Yes sir."

Mario began scribbling with his pen, as if writing the names Freeman had given him. Suddenly he cocked his head, stopped writing, and glanced at us in a most unpleasant and suspicious way. Then he turned abruptly and rolled his window all the way down. Freeman started to laugh but quickly covered his mouth and turned it into a cough. God, it was a foul one! I wanted to open my own window, but didn't dare.

Mario turned to me, squinting like the fart had gotten to him bad, though he wasn't about to mention it. "Is that your name, kid?" he asked in a disgusted tone.

I nodded my head but kept my mouth shut.

"Sir," said Freeman.

"What?"

"May I explain something?"

"That's a damn good idea, kid! You punks are in a world of trouble."

"That's what I need to explain, sir. I don't think we should be."

Mario set the clipboard down and looked at Freeman like this was going to one of the most interesting stories he ever heard and he couldn't wait to hear how it went. I had considerable interest myself.

"And why don't you think you should be in trouble, Daniels?"

"'Cause we didn't do nothin' wrong, sir."

"What the hell do you call it when you steal lumber and drive a bulldozer all over the place? Is that your idea of doin' things right?" The guy seemed mad enough to reach back and choke Freeman, and for a moment I thought he might.

"That's just it, sir. We didn't do that. Nor would we ever."

"Look kid! I just caught you and your friend—what's your name again?"

"Phony … I … I mean Tony," I said, shaking my head and hoping my ears were not half as red as they felt.

"I just caught you and Tony walkin' off with the lumber! Or do I maybe need new glasses?" He took his sunglasses off and looked through them, then breathed on the lenses.

"I don't mean disrespect, sir. But we found those two boards in the woods." Freeman waved in the general direction we had come from.

"In the woods, huh?" He clearly didn't believe it, and he seemed to grow angrier as he worked his glasses back onto his head. "And I suppose they were just layin' in a nice neat pile, waiting for you to walk off with them?"

"Actually, that's right, sir!" I burst out.

Mario and Freeman looked at me with great interest, and I was instantly sorry for thinking I actually had something to say.

"And just what were you planning to do with those boards, Tony?" Mario asked mockingly.

Freeman kicked my calf then spoke for me. I was shaking like a leaf inside, scared out of my mind and picturing myself in a striped gray suit, hammering rocks alongside Freeman.

"We only wanted to build a little lookout platform. In a tree, sir. Those two boards were just what we needed."

"A lookout platform, huh?"

"If you look out the window, sir, you can see the tree we were headed for, right over there."

Freeman pointed out the windshield, and I ducked my head and squinted to see where he meant. Of course there was a tall tree in the distance, towering above the oaks—the very same tree we'd climbed to locate the fort site. Mario strained to see through the dirty glass, then turned to me.

"Is that the truth, Tony?"

"Scout's honor, Your Honor." I raised my right hand.

"I ain't no damn judge, kid."

"I'm sorry, Your Honor."

He winced like I was an idiot, then turned to Freeman.

"You can take me to the place where you found the boards, huh?" I expected Freeman to squirm, like I would have, but he didn't flinch.

"Absolutely, sir!" he exclaimed.

"Really?" I piped up, the word slipping out before I could think. I covered my mouth and coughed, trying to pretend I hadn't said a thing. Mario eyeballed me up and down, like I was the dumbest ass he'd ever met in his life. I thought I might be too. I squinted my eyes at the banged-up thermos on the floor, which said "anley" on the label, while my ears flared like hot peppers.

"Let's get out!" Mario instructed us. "And let's have a look what the hell you're talkin' about!"

I slid out of that piss-can Plymouth with Freeman right behind. Freeman then took the lead, with Mario second, and I picked up the rear. We led Mario to the remaining two boards.

"That's exactly how we found them, sir! That's exactly how we found them!" He pointed and emphasized the word exactly. "We even looked for footprints, but we couldn't find a single one."

If I didn't know better, I might have thought Freeman was telling the whole truth and nothing but the truth; my regret was that I did know the truth. So I was feeling mighty hot and uncomfortable inside, with everything I had ever been taught about truth and honesty suddenly falling by the wayside. It was clear at that moment that the bigger the lie, the better off we'd most likely be.

Mario examined me again as if to see if I agreed with Freeman. For once I managed to keep my flapper shut. I held the most solemn face I could, stared at the two remaining boards, and shook my head "Yes," like Freeman's words were as good as those of Moses, or Jesus, or Ike Eisenhower.

"So why didn't you come and tell us about these boards, the way we talked about a couple of weeks ago?"

"Why, when we found them this morning, we didn't think about that, sir," Freeman carried on. "All we could think of was how we didn't want them to go to rot in the woods. So me and Joey figured we better do somethin' worthwhile, 'stead of lettin' them go to the worms."

"I thought you said your name was Tony?" Mario raised his voice and pointed an accusing finger at me.

"That's what I just said," Freeman replied, while I nodded my head dumbly in agreement.

Mario looked suspicious as Dick Tracy but didn't say any more about it—I imagined because "Joey" sounds something like "Tony" and the whole situation was getting too confusing for him. Plus I was beginning to think he wanted to believe us, difficult as it might have been.

A long pause ensued before he said, "You kids ever hear of a punk named Justin Clancy?"

"No," said Freeman, at the same time I said, "Yes."

Again Mario's eyes darted from Freeman to me, then back to Freeman.

"Well, Tony here might know him," Freeman said, his twisted little brain working overtime. "He goes to a different school than I do."

Back to me again. I shook my head affirmatively.

"What school do you go to, Tony?"

"I … I go to … I go … " I had a brain fart and forgot what school I go to. "Tony here goes to St. Frances, sir."

"Is that so?" Mario was still staring at me like I had to be the sneakiest weasel he ever laid eyes on.

I raised my right hand, as in the Boy Scout's honor, shaking my head solemnly, like I finally got it straight who I was and where I went to school.

"You don't talk much, do you kid?" Mario said sarcastically.

I shook my head in the opposite direction.

"He's got speech difficulties, sir," Freeman informed him, and I wished to hell he would stop lying about me. Then again, I thought, it seemed I did have a speech difficulty, namely that I didn't want to say one more word to this baboon.

"Is that a fact?" Mario said slowly, as if trying to calculate Freeman's truthfulness.

"Plus he's in one of them special classes, if you know what I mean, sir."

"You mean he's re … " Mario started to ask, before catching himself and proceeding to look me over with a new point of view.

Damn you to hell, Freeman! I was embarrassed as all get out, because I knew I really must have appeared retarded.

Mr. Muscles took a breath, leaned on a tree, lit up a smoke. "All right," he said, as if some small amount of pity had crept into his heart. "I think you kids have got some problems, but I guess you're on the level. But I'm tellin' you, you better be glad I don't call the cops! They're mad as hell. Worse than my old lady gets," he paused as if to let that sink in. "And that's mighty damn mad! Now, they think they know who's behind this crap. But they're not gonna wanna hear about any more bullshit, from you or anybody else."

He glanced from one of us to the other several times, looking for a reaction. I shook my head No, like a retarded person, while Freeman shook his head Yes, like a retarded person. Mario ended up shaking his own head No, and I thought I heard him laugh to himself, as if he had concluded we were beyond all hope.

"Look," Mario added, after a moment of silence, "I'm gonna pretend this never happened, that I never even seen you punks! But I don't want to see you around here again. Ever! Or I will call the cops, and your parents can pick you up at the station. You get my meaning?"

Freeman said, "Yes, sir!"

"Now get these boards the hell out of here. Do the ones out by the road first. I don't wanna have to explain them to no one!"

We nodded, then walked fast toward the road. Mario followed and watched closely as we picked up the boards and scurried across Cranberry Boulevard, just as we had been planning to do before he came along.

"Stay the hell out and don't come back!" he shouted, before jumping in his car and roaring off.

10

With the lumber stacked neatly at the fort site, it looked like the hard part was behind us. But a number of difficulties remained. For one thing, we needed hammers, and a saw, a level, a plane, a tape measure, and a pry bar. "And don't forget a square and the dang shovel and bow saw one more time," Freeman reminded me.

With Matt's help we got the tools together, and then retrieved the buckets of nails, which fortunately were still in the sticker bushes where we left them. Then one dark night soon after we again snuck the necessary goods across Cranberry Boulevard. For the next five days we did not do much thinking, unless it was to think like ants. There was work to be done and no time for play.

We soon discovered we needed to hack away more oak trees, widening the fort space to make room for construction. We neatly dug out the grass that had been growing under the trees and set it in the shade for use on the roof later on, to provide coolness and camouflage. And we started digging the basement, though it wasn't long before we scaled that part of the project down quite a bit.

"This soil's way too rocky. It'll take us a century or two to dig a full basement, Joey."

We agreed that a small square pit in the center of the place, for dangling our feet, would work better than a basement anyway. So we spent several hours digging out old roots and rocks for that purpose. And it wasn't much longer before we determined to shave several feet from the overall dimensions of the fort, in order to stretch what lumber we had.

"It's JC's fault," Freeman maintained. "If that meathead hadn't screwed things up at Stoneridge we would've gone back another night, and we'd have twice as much wood as we have now."

I let him go on thinking that, and didn't mention the fact that I never wanted to go back anyway. "JC would screw up a wet dream," I said to keep him happy.

Most of the changes from the original plan made good sense and saved lots of work, especially for Freeman, who did the bulk of it. Plus they spared me from pretending to be busy, listening to him grunt and groan and invent new swear word combinations.

We brought in sleeping bags and a backpack filled with hot dogs, an almost empty mustard jar, four bread heels, the last of a box of Rice Krispies, half a quart of milk, and a chunk of Velveeta the size of a fist. I got permission to sleep out for several nights by acting like a saint and being extra kind to Timmy and the twins, which took some serious effort. But we had to go back home each day anyway, for tools, more food, and water, which we never seemed to have enough of.

At night we laid under the stars, on thick beds of grass that we'd tossed into frames fashioned from old locust logs, which we hauled in from the ponds area. The Milky Way blazed in the night sky and I saw more shooting stars than I had ever seen before. Freeman pointed to a moving white dot and told me it was a satellite, put up by the Communists.

"I wouldn't be surprised if they could hear our conversation this very minute," he said. "Which is just one more reason to cover the roof with earth."

"I don't give a hoot if they do hear us, so long as they don't discuss things with Mario, the cops, or my mom."

Gentle breezes blew through the oaks and crickets sang us to sleep.

The next morning Freeman began digging a number of good-sized holes for the support posts, so the place would be earthquake proof. While he did that, I heated a bucket of tar that we had salvaged from the junkyard over a roaring fire of oak branches; then I dipped the support pieces in so they wouldn't rot. The smell was horrendous, but the boards looked like something official by the time I got done.

"I'll bet they last five hundred years!" Freeman claimed. "That tar is the same stuff they found saber-toothed tigers and woolly mammoths in."

He packed earth around the posts with the butt of his shovel while I held them vertically. That was not hard, but trying to keep the whole arrangement square was another matter. We conceded eventually that squareness didn't matter that much because we could always cut the boards shorter if we needed to.

But it wasn't long before we saw the fly in that ointment. Namely, we couldn't stretch the lumber the extra foot or two where the posts were farther apart. We debated whether to put additional posts in or redo the originals. I felt we should redo the place and add more posts, since it was already scaled down something horrendous.

"It actually looks more like a shoebox than a mansion," I observed.

"I see that too. And I'm afraid if she gets any damn smaller, we're gonna need midgets for girlfriends."

"So why don't we redo the posts and add a bit more perimeter?"

"Yea? And who's gonna to redig all them holes through these miserable rocks? Not to mention dig a few new ones." Sweat shone on his body, and the thought of him digging more holes almost made me feel bad.

"I can see your point," I conceded.

"Ahh … let's just nail some pieces onto the eight footers to lengthen 'em and be done with it. I wish to hell Matt could invent us some board stretchers."

"But that will look like crap."

"So … we'll just bring the girls at night, and we'll only use one candle inside. That way nobody'll see how bad it is."

The final framework was a splendid example of a non-square. Thus we had to cut and bend the boards to make them fit around the support posts, or else bow them outward to reach the posts. And it took two full buckets of nails to fasten them to the frame.

"Maybe it's not too late to ask Matt for help," I suggested.

"Then we'd never get the thing done—he'd make us start over and turn it into a town or a dang city or somethin'." His hand swept in a huge semicircle, pointing to the surrounding acres of oak trees.

So we continued to sweat and toil like slaves in the heat, slamming hammers into nails and fingertips, grunting to bend boards into place, sawing like beavers and cursing when we cut them too short, which seemed like most of the time. But after a while we got a good part of the roof nailed down and the sides done and we sat back and examined the results.

"I knew we should have listened to Matt and drew up a plan." I couldn't believe now that we hadn't done what he said.

"Why? We couldn't follow it anyway."

"I still think we should have tried."

"It don't look that bad, Joey."

I sat on the kitchen table, which was lashed low between two oak trees, and tried to ignore the bows and wobbles in the walls, the unevenness in height from end to end, the cracks that seemed to be everywhere with light shining through, and the overall lopsided nature of the thing.

"Why, I believe you're right, Freddie. All I have to do is close my eyes and it doesn't look bad at all!"

"You really think we should start over, huh?" It sounded like he might be willing, and there could be no dispute that the thing looked like a pile of junk.

"It doesn't really matter what I think," I said with finality, wiping my forehead with the bottom of my T-shirt. "Because I'm done working for a while."

"Let's come back in a day or two, Joey. We need a little think time. Right now I feel like burnin' the son-of-a-bitch to the ground. All that work for a pile of crap!" He kicked the front of the place and the whole structure shook something terrible. "Anyways, it ain't gonna go nowhere, ya know?"

So we headed for the swimming hole, but only after Freeman promised to "never, never, ever, ever" hold me out of the water again.

"I'm gonna doggie paddle around for a while. You do whatever ya want," he said, before I even got my clothes off.

He spun around in his birthday suit and dove off the bank, hitting the water with a belly flop. Chilly drops shot back and landed on my neck and shoulders. Before long, his peach fuzz head came up by the depth marker.

"I'm so happy about learnin' to swim, Joey! I wanted to do it all my life! Why I'm so happy I could climb to the top of this here marker and do a dive off it!"

The marker stood seven feet out of the water that day, with the twenty-two foot mark on top. Small waves from Freeman's motions lapped at the fifteen-foot line.

"Do it, then."

"By damn, I will!" he shouted and slapped the water.

That oversized monkey began to shinny up, like an ape with no hair. He clung to the sides of the marker, straining and making funny noises, his big white rear end hanging out in space. His body arched like a bow, with that wooden marker for a string. Bit by bit he moved up, one hand and one foot at a time, his muscles tensed and rippling in the sunlight.

Fifteen foot, sixteen foot, like a native climbing for coconuts. Nineteen, twenty. He made it to the top, then wriggled and squiggled about on those last two feet, the marker wobbling and shaking beneath him like a willow branch. Then to my astonishment, he somehow stood and balanced like an acrobat on the very top of the thing, his bare feet perched on that skinny edge, toes curled like little fingers, his arms outstretched like Jesus. I thought he would dive off, with a spectacular arc from that height. And he might have, except at that moment the marker began leaning forward; slowly at first, but gaining speed as it went. If it was a dive he had in mind … well, he never got the chance. That wobbly, old marker kept on leaning, with Freeman on top. His arms were still outstretched like a savior, though of what I couldn't say, except it was not himself.

"Flap your buns!" I hollered, hoping that might help.

But he wasn't listening, and as the marker accelerated, he broke into a scream, "Arrrgggghhhh!"

It made my heart sing, and a big smile crossed my face. Then before I could blink, there was a loud *keeersplash*!"

Bubbly green-white spray went up on each side of the touch-down. The marker and Freeman sank out of sight, and only a few small bubbles floated where the marker had been. Freeman came up sputtering, one arm around the marker at the twelve-foot point. "I'd like to know who put that stinkin' marker in! I'd kick his ass in two seconds!"

"That was great, Freddie! You ought to try out for the Olympic diving team!"

"Maybe I'll try out for the Pissed-off Monkeys' Team!"

He calmed down after a while, and we laid on the shore in the mud flat by the ramp, basking in the sun. After some time, I noticed Freeman lifting oozy gobs of mud and dumping them on top of himself. His body was soon covered in a brown pile of slop, from his toes to his neck. I stared at this spectacle, trying to figure it out.

"What are you doing?" I was compelled to ask at last.

"Takin' a mud bath," he replied, white teeth shining through the mud on his face.

"Why?"

"It's what they call a beauty pack, see? My aunt said it's what they do in beauty parlors and people pay good money for it. It makes your skin soft and beautiful."

"What do you care if your skin's soft and beautiful? You're a guy."

"So? There ain't no law against a guy havin' nice soft skin. Is there?"

He threw several more handfuls on, and before long I had to try it myself, it looked so ridiculous. I covered myself with a thick frosting of that slimy muck, and it did feel good, though I couldn't imagine it would do much for my skin.

"Wow! Joey! I just got the meanest idea for the fort! Seein' you pile up that mud is what gave it to me! What we gotta do is bury the whole confounded thing like this—not just the roof, but the whole thing, sides and all!"

"What good will that do?"

"It'll improve the appearance of the place, for one thing, 'specially when we grow grass on it. And there ain't a soul around gonna find it when it looks like a measly little dirt hill. It'll keep the place cool in the summer and warm in the winter … like a blanket! And it'll be all quiet and peaceful what with the sound muffled by the dirt!"

It was brilliant. What else could we ask for, besides a larger structure? I could see Maggie's mouth dropping as she realized that this humble mound of dirt was our own private escape pad, our vacation home—hers and mine! Together! By George, I thought, maybe Freeman was as bright as Matt.

We sat on the swings in my backyard, in the cool of the evening, swaying slowly back and forth. The scent of fresh cut grass and honeysuckle filled the air, as did the gentle squeaking of the swings. We had been discussing the completion of the fort and, while we both liked Freeman's burial idea, there were still several complications before us.

"What about all the extra lumber? We'll need a ton of it to hold up all that earth and keep it from falling through the cracks."

"You're the one's been yakkin' about scraps since we started. Now's the time to figure how to get some, 'cause that's exactly what we need to finish the job."

"But everything's changed since JC got caught. You heard what Mario said. Not to mention my mom. I wouldn't go near Stoneridge again if you paid me! Not for scraps, not for nails, not even to look at the place."

"I knew ya was gonna say that. And that's exactly why I got plan B up my little sleeve." He tugged at the sleeve of his T-shirt, then pretended to give it a shake and catch something that fell out. He grinned. "Ya know that old house by the train station?"

"Hobo Haven?"

"Yea, that's the place, though I didn't know everyone called it that."

I thought everyone knew about Hobo Haven. That decrepit old house was three blocks from the train station, on a side street, though you could see it every time you went through town.

I'd been there twice with Timmy, a few years ago, but we were too scared to go in. Everyone said it was haunted. It was dark and spooky and home to bats, not to mention rats. Rumor had it there were countless rooms and closets and passageways, and that it was a hangout for hobos and drunks who wandered from the train station. All in all, it was enough to send shivers down your spine, and not a place I was keen on visiting.

"Well, we need thinner, flatter pieces to cover the sides and roof, right? And maybe a couple more support posts."

"I suppose."

"There's no supposin' about it. That's just what we need. And that old joint is bound to have it!"

I leaned back on the swing and looked at the sky. A half moon shone above the trees and a few of the brighter stars twinkled against the blue-black background.

"I'm still listening."

"So this old house has got the goods for us. We get most of it out of the walls, except for down in the basement where we get the beams for the roof. We use them big ol' four-by-fours that hold the place up. I reckon we could take a couple of 'em without causin' a problem."

I swung gently, mulling this over.

"But it would take forever to get that stuff out," I replied finally. "And how would we get it to the fort?"

"I think we could get it out in a day, first off. Second, it's only another half mile along the tracks, and it wouldn't take long with the board lifters. And thirdly, who's gonna stop us?"

I continued swinging, watching the moon as it appeared to move over the treetops.

"How do you get so many crazy ideas?" I asked.

"They just float into my head somehow. Kinda like soap bubbles in a breeze, I guess."

I laughed and dragged my feet to slow down. "You're busting my butt, Freddie."

"Maybe. But I just might help ya get to see Maggie's butt. That counts for somethin', don't it?"

I digested that idea for about half a second, then sat up straight.

"All right. So when do we check this place out, Mr. Bubble Brain?"

"Bright and early, Mr. Bubble Butt!"

We sat on his front steps the next morning, munching two sugary bowls of Corn Flakes, and I was very careful not to laugh while I was chewing. The topic of JC's court date came up. Freeman had learned from Matt, who had learned from Herman, who had learned from who knows where, that it would be in the middle of August.

"But it ain't like a jury trial to send him to the electric chair or nothin', which is a real shame," Freeman explained, crunching loudly as he spoke. "It's only so he can tell the judge he ain't guilty and cut some kind of a deal."

"What kind of a deal?"

"Go on prohibition or somethin' like that."

"What's that mean?"

"I can't remember exactly. I ain't a dang lawyer. But I hope they prohibit him from carryin' knives and drivin' a car; it'd save us a heap of grief."

"They ought to prohibit him from coming near us, too."

"I'd prohibit that clown from breathin', if I had my way."

Matt stepped out the door behind us then, shampoo in one hand and a brush in the other.

"You guys see Doc and James around?"

"Not lately," I replied over a mouthful of cornflakes, trying to swallow at the same time.

"Did Doc dig up the crabs again?" asked Freeman, eyeballing the shampoo.

"Not this time. He rolled in a dead cat and brought it home for breakfast. He stinks to high heaven."

We shared some chitchat about the fort, and Freeman informed him about our plans to bury the thing, carefully neglecting to reveal the main reason, which was how lousy it had turned out.

"Sounds like a good idea. I'm glad to see you two using your noodles a bit. It pays to have a good plan, huh?"

Freeman nodded, while I looked at the pattern of bricks in the porch steps.

"So you're going to get boards from Hobo Haven?"

"We don't think Stoneridge is such a hot idea anymore. Not after JC got caught," Freeman said.

"Maybe it's too hot," Matt laughed, shaking his head in agreement. I suddenly felt smarter and not so cowardly regarding my lack of interest in going back there. And I hoped Freeman felt dumber, given that it was his insistence that had taken us back to Stoneridge on 'the night of the switchblades,' as we had come to call it.

"You can use my dust masks and pry bars for those old boards, if you just tell me when," Matt offered generously. "You're going to need them."

"We're just scoutin' around today," Freeman replied, "but maybe tomorrow."

We followed Matt to the side of the house where we came upon James rolling in the grass with Doc. A foul stench filled the air, one of the worst I ever smelled.

"I told you not to play with him till we wash him off, didn't I? You're going to stink as bad as he does now!" Matt was clearly upset to find these two playing together.

"But ya get used to it!" cried James. "Then after a while ya kinda like it." Matt shook his head and turned to us. "I think you guys picked up the smelliest dog in the whole of New York!"

I thought of how I picked him up, or rather how he picked me up, and decided that might well be the truth.

"Have fun cleaning these guys," Freeman said to Matt, poking at me to get out of there. "We're off to check them boards at Hobo Haven."

We parked our bikes behind the dilapidated Hobo Haven, on the edge of a wooded lot that adjoined the overgrown backyard of the place. The old dwelling stood three stories high, with four brick chimneys rising above the roof, all with several bricks missing. Black holes took the place of shingles in odd places, while splintery shutters hung crookedly around boarded window openings. A few shutters had dropped off and vanished in the tangle of weeds below. It seemed an unlikely place to get boards from, but then again, I realized it might be the perfect place.

Freeman sat on the bumper of an old broken down car that had flat tires and must have been rotting for years in the weedy driveway.

He readjusted the slingshot in his belt, and it occurred to me that I never saw him without it anymore. I sat beside him as we looked the place over.

"Looks like no way in," I observed, given how boarded up it appeared. I thought of the time Timmy and I contemplated going in, then chickened out, blaming each other for being cowards.

"I know three ways." Freeman paused to light a Camel, then passed it to me. I raised my hand as if to say no, but then took a few puffs till it was short enough to snuff out. I had made up my mind I wasn't going to get hooked.

Freeman went on, "But I think we oughta go the basement way. It's least visible from the street."

We moved our bikes behind the old garage and laid them in the weeds. I followed him with what little enthusiasm I could muster up to a dilapidated concrete stairway that led to the basement.

"This used to be the servants' entrance," he announced, pushing back scraggly vines that grew around the area and into the entry.

Twisted brown vine roots clung to the concrete walls, and termity-looking boards lay scattered about. Spiderwebs hung everywhere, and numerous black and white bird squirts streaked the floor and walls. The cool damp air felt like it could easily support strange, undiscovered forms of life.

"Watch for rusty nails, or they'll poke right through your sneakers," Freeman warned. "Then you'll need a damn tetanus shot."

At the bottom of the stairs, Freeman squeaked open a wooden door that was hanging by a few loose screws and had a shiny white doorknob. The thought of long dead people once living there sent chills up my spine. We stopped to let our eyes adjust to the darkness and spookiness of the place.

"This stinks worse than a nun's crack," I said in a low voice, breathing through my mouth, so as not to get foul air molecules wedged in my nose.

"How would you know?"

"It's just a guess," I had to admit. "And a figure of speech, I suppose."

218

"Seems like every old house stinks the same way. It prob'ly comes from them witches people buried in the basement."

"What are you talking about?"

"A lot of old-timers buried witches in the basement. That's how they got rid of 'em back then, after it became illegal to burn 'em."

"Give me a break, Freddie."

"It's a fact. I saw it in a movie. This couple had a daughter who was a witch. You could tell from her bony face and her high voice, you know? Plus she could make things disappear and other strange things, like have a dog bark for no reason. I saw it with my own eyes; even ask my brothers. So they locked 'er in the basement where no one knew about her. For her own good, see? But they forgot to feed her for a time and she died of starvation. So they just buried her down there."

"That doesn't mean everyone did it. Besides, it was just a movie. Sounds like a stupid one, too."

"It makes sense, don't it? What else are ya gonna do with a witch if you're afraid for people to see her?" He looked at me to see if I believed him. "A neighbor got suspicious, and the cops found her in the end, though."

"That's nonsense. Ten to one we're smelling dead rats. Not that I like that idea any better." But even as I spoke, I glanced around to check for bones that might be poking through the dirt floor.

"There used to be thousands of witches. First they burned 'em at the stake, and thank goodness they got rid of 'em, too. We learned about it in history class."

"The only witches around these days are nuns. Who I get to see all year."

"You can think what you want, but that don't change the facts. Now get moving and stop being so disagreeable." He smacked my butt and pointed up the stairs.

Half the steps were missing, and the others looked like they might crash through if you stepped on them. So we put our feet on the sides, where the support was, and worked our way up the edges. I slipped once, but Freeman caught me and pushed me back upright.

"Stop thinkin' of Maggie and pay better attention, will ya?" he said.

The main floor was lighter, though still dark and eerie. But the air was better and I breathed through my nose again. Our footsteps echoed through the many empty rooms, and I wondered if I would dare go through this place by myself. It was hard to imagine.

"How do you expect us to get boards here?" I asked. "The walls are all plastered, and it'd take forever to get them out." I pointed downward. "Unless we rip up the floor, but even that looks like an ordeal and a-half."

"No one said it would be easy. Mainly what we need is to bring the right tools. Besides, some of the other walls may not be plastered. That's what we're here to find out."

"I don't like it. The whole place is creepy."

"Keep quiet till you see the kitchen," he said eagerly. "Up one more floor."

We climbed the next flight, and at least the stairs were safer. He led me down a long narrow hall into a good-sized room at the end, which was home to a long counter, a large wooden table, and an old cookstove with four burners and an oven.

"Someday we'll cook breakfast on this very stove, after we sleep out in the fort. And we'll have our honeys with us too, all lit up and glowing from a lovely night!"

"Why would they be lit up and glowing?"

"Well, mine will be anyway. Yours may be more like a sourpuss. Just keep an eye on me though, and you'll get an idea how these things are done."

He swept his hand over the stove and a puff of dust flew up, visible even in the dim light. Dirty pots and pans hung from hooks in the ceiling, and a smudged white washbasin sat on a small wooden table.

"This here's an old-fashioned sink. The kind they used before the days of plumbing. The girls can wash our dishes here." He patted the bottom of the basin.

But the room was stuffy and grungy, no place for a person in their right mind to prepare food, unless you wanted spiderwebs and mouse turds with dustballs mixed in.

Freeman rattled on like the place was fit for a king, and certainly the best kitchen he'd ever seen.

We stole up the last flight of stairs, our hopes of finding exposed, easy-to-get boards fading fast. Freeman marched me down a long bare hallway, where our footsteps echoed as if made by elephants. We paraded around the rooms, only to find plastered walls and not a single exposed board.

"It's not what I hoped for," Freeman admitted. "But there's one more thing I gotta show you, on the floor below."

He led me down a flight, back to a room we'd been in, then to a large closet that had no door. We stepped inside and he pointed to the wall.

"See that?"

I saw nothing in the faint light.

"Ya gotta look closer." He moved his finger in the shape of a large rectangle on the wall.

I leaned forward and looked again. A rectangle shape slowly came into focus, as if the wall itself had been cut with the piece put back in place. I could see two hinges and what appeared to be a ring handle on the opposite side.

"I didn't even know they had trap doors, till James and me found this thing last year."

"You brought James here?"

"Yea. He loves spooky things. At least when he's with me."

"So where's it go?"

"Who knows? That's what makes it so dang interesting. It's nailed shut from the back, I think."

I pulled on the round metal handle, but it didn't budge.

"You may be right. Though I can't imagine where the thing goes. We'd need Matt's pry bar."

"Maybe this is where they put them witches, Joey. I'll bet you anything that's it." I shook my head in disbelief.

"Before burying 'em in the basement, I mean. It'd be easy to throw food through a door like this, don't ya think?"

Before I could answer, a shuffling, scratching noise came from the other side of the door. There was brief silence, then we heard it again.

"What the hell?" I whispered.

"Maybe one of 'em survived somehow." Freeman spoke matter-of-factly, looking me in the eyes.

"That's insane, Freddie."

"Then maybe it's the ghost of one."

I shook my head and didn't know what to think, except it was clear we had heard something, and I didn't care to hang around much longer.

"Let's get out of this joint."

"Why? A ghost can't hurt us. They can't do nothin' but float around and scare people." Freeman appeared more curious than scared.

"Then how could it make that noise?" I pressed him.

"Well, they can make a little noise. But they can't stab you or strangle you or nothin' like that. The worst they could do is give you a heart attack. Which is why we gotta be calm and act like nothin's happenin'."

I couldn't believe he was so superstitious; all along I thought I was the one who might be superstitious. But my more immediate concern was the noise.

"Let's bolt … it's gotta be rats, and I hate rats!"

More scratching noises, louder. I had no doubt it was rats. I could picture the whole ugly family in there, clawing to get out, beady red eyes glowing in the dark, long wormy tails dragging while their fat bodies waddled about with tiny heads and glistening gray fur, sniffing for things to devour.

More scratching. We froze. It was distinct, definite; there was something back there.

"Let's get the hell out, Freddie!"

"No; it ain't gonna hurt us, and we gotta find out if it's a ghost."

I didn't care what it was, I wanted out. Something was trying to come through that wall!

"Now I smell it, too!" I had gotten a hint of some horrible odor, which at first I thought was my imagination; but then I inhaled through my nose and was certain. It was familiar, though I couldn't quite place it.

"Don't leave us here forever!" cried a voice from the other side. "Get us out now!" Freeman suddenly froze and we stared at each other in disbelief.

"Please help!" squeaked the voice, followed by vigorous scratching sounds, like nails raking across plaster.

I had no idea what it was, and no desire to find out. Nor did Freeman, who finally wheeled and took off like a rabbit, every bit as frightened as I was. We flew down the stairs, back through the kitchen and the hallway, and fairly tripped over each other to get down the basement stairs.

Freeman grabbed my arm, and we halted on the earthen floor of the basement. "Hold up here a minute and let's see what's goin' on!" He seemed to have gotten a grip on himself, though all I wanted was to get out of that musty, creepy place. But his grip wouldn't let me. My eyes darted frantically around, yet I could see almost nothing in that foul darkness.

A loud thud on the basement door made us jump into each other's arms, hugging like lovers do. Then the door swung open. In the light of the doorway stood a figure that looked to be the size of a giant. I was petrified and thought for sure our numbers were up.

Could it be JC, I wondered? Or a bloody ghost, like Freeman made me think?

"Hey, Freddie! You guys down here?" It was Matt's voice, and it immediately struck me that the voice upstairs was James. And the scratching was probably Doc's. Along with the smell! It suddenly all made sense. I quickly released my grip on Freeman, very glad it was too dark for Matt to see us holding each other like that.

"Yea, we're here," said Freeman, arms at his sides. "But what in hell are you doin' here?"

"I was washing Doc when I looked up and saw James take off. Chasing after you guys. Then Doc took off after him. I gave them a minute, thinking they'd be right back. But then I saw them racing like the wind and I didn't know where to—till I remembered you guys were coming to this place. Now I can't find a trace of either one! You seen them?"

"Not exactly."

Freeman explained the mysterious noises, and the fact they must both be upstairs that very minute still trying to escape from the back room.

Matt took charge and bossed us around, making us to look in this door and that, and I realized this must be the way the mind of an inventor works. It wasn't long before we found them both in a bedroom adjacent to the one we'd been in.

James had wet his pants and was bawling because we'd left him. Doc was still scratching at the trap door, which opened through a closet in that bedroom to the one we'd been in, and it was now clear where the odor had come from.

James calmed down, but only after Freeman gave him a big long hug and told him he'd never let that happen again. Then we explained how he'd scared us half to death, after which James laughed and said happily, "That's what ya get, guys!"

As we left the house, Doc abruptly took off into the adjacent wooded lot, bounding after something. We all called for him to come back, even though it was a relief to have him move away from us due to his incredible stink.

He disappeared in the underbrush and in moments the loud scream of a girl emerged from the direction he had headed. We all ran to see what was going on now. We found Doc licking the face of girl who lay on the ground, binoculars at her side.

"Annabelle!" I exclaimed.

"Doc!" shouted Freeman and Matt.

"Get off me, you big oaf!" shrieked Annabelle, struggling to get up. "Bad dog! Stinky dog! Get off me!" She pushed him away as she spoke.

Matt soon got Doc on the leash and pulled him aside, while Annabelle brushed leaves and twigs from her face and hair.

"What are you doing here, Annabelle?" I asked, not at all pleased about meeting her like this.

"Well, I was doing my observations of birds in these woods." She brushed her shorts as she spoke. "I do a half-hour observation every morning, and keep track of who appears and who doesn't. I was kneeling down when this fellow jumped me from behind. Boy, does he ever stink!" She was laughing now, like it was all quite funny.

"He just rolled in a dead cat. I was trying to wash him off when he decided to go for a hike." Matt pulled Doc in tighter on the leash.

"I know everyone here except you," she said. "I'm Annabelle."

"I'm Matt. Nice binoculars you have there." Matt pointed to the ground where they lay. "Those are some of the best." I looked down and saw the word Bushnell, which was written on the side.

"I don't know about that, but they work well for me."

She held her hand on Doc's head as he tried to lunge closer. "He is rather friendly, isn't he?"

"He's my best friend!" exclaimed James, flapping his hands in the air.

"I'll bet he follows you everywhere, huh? Unless he finds a dead cat." We all laughed at that. "So what are you boys doing here?"

"We were, uh, just explorin' the old house," Freeman said. "Lookin' for junk."

"Find anything interesting?"

"Not this time. The place has been gone over pretty good. But it's fun looking."

Annabelle suddenly noticed the slingshot sticking out of Freeman's belt. "I see you carry a weapon for protection."

I wasn't sure why she said this, but I did not get the impression she was happy to see it.

"Well, actually it's more for bir ... " Freeman began to say, then quickly corrected himself. "It's for barget practice."

Annabelle looked him over like she was not real pleased with him.

"What's barget practice, Freddie?" asked James, tugging at Freeman's sleeve.

"I'll tell you later," I said, trying to spare everyone embarrassment.

Annabelle mercifully turned toward Doc. "I've heard that tomato sauce works pretty good for cases like this. The acids are supposed to do something to the smell. Though I've never had to try it myself."

I was having trouble believing this was the same girl who wrote me the notes recently. How could someone as smart and pretty and grown up as this possibly be interested in me? Then again, there was her spiral notebook, the kind that opens on top, with the same light green paper as the notes, still lying on the ground.

I bent over and picked it up. A page flipped open as I did so and my eyes landed on a phrase: "You make me feel I'm soaring too, and fill my soul with dreams of … "

Good night! I thought. It's the next poem she's going to send me! I looked away from her face as I handed it back.

"Thanks, Joseph! It's nice to see you again. Though I really didn't think it would be so soon."

"What are you taking these notes for, anyway?" Matt knelt and petted Doc, apparently forgetting about Doc's stink, and evidently taken up with the sight of Annabelle.

"I read somewhere that if you were to watch in the same spot you'd see many of the same birds coming back every year. Though some of them stay year round, like woodpeckers. I was trying to verify if that's true, and see whether they come out at particular times of the day."

"So is it?" asked Matt.

"Well, I noticed that the woodpeckers do stay around. And a blue jay is sometimes here, but sometimes not. And swallows appeared in the spring, though it's hard to tell if they're the same ones as last year." She turned to look at her notebook and began flipping pages, as if looking for more information to give us about other birds.

"Well, this is all pretty interesting," I said. "But I think we need to get going. This guy needs a bath real bad."

"Nice to meet you, Annabelle," Matt said. "I'd like to see your notes sometime and hear what you find out."

"Me too!" added Freeman, who was standing a few feet back staring at Annabelle and grinning like a pervert. "I'd like to see it all!"

Everyone turned to look at him, as you might look at a dog wandering into a church during Mass. "Your notes, I mean. I'd like to see your notes." He pointed to the notebook in a sorry effort to redeem himself, and I couldn't help wondering if he wasn't becoming as big a dork as I was.

"I'll try to keep that in mind," replied Annabelle frowning, as she proceeded to dust the remaining pieces of leaf from her socks and legs with the notebook.

"You forgot these things!" James picked up her binoculars and handed them to her.

"Why thank you, James! That's nice of you!"

We took off and left Annabelle to her notes and the birds, Doc leading James, and James leading the rest of us. Freeman and I pushed our bikes and chatted with Matt, who asked me a few questions about the fort, and then several more about Annabelle.

"There's no way I'd want those boards even if we could strip them out. I'd be afraid of the smell and what might grow out of them, for one thing," I complained as we lay on beds in Freeman's room.

"That's two things, Joey."

"Right. And here's the third thing, you ninny. That place gives me the creeps!"

"Well, there may not be any boards in the walls anyway. Matt told me after dinner that back in those days they used chicken wire and lathe—that's them skinny little pieces that won't do us no good anyway."

"So there goes our future," I whined. "Like a fart in the wind." I thought to myself that I should have known everything sounded too good to be true, and our dreams were too far-fetched from the start. Maggie would never amount to anything more than a faded picture in my head.

"Don't be so eager to slit your wrists … frowny downy. Matt reminded me of one other place we might get them boards."

"The lumber yard?"

"Nope."

"Tear your house down?"

"Very funny."

"Well, don't keep me guessing."

"You ever been down to Cold Water Cove?"

Cold Water Cove is a wooded bay at the bottom of huge hill, the biggest in our neck of the woods. On a map it looks like a small balloon attached by the neck to the Long Island Sound. The beach there rarely gets used for swimming due to muddy water, a rocky bottom, large tidal changes, and a terrible stench when the tide is out.

But boaters frequent the cove since it has a large concrete ramp for boats; and by fishermen, at least at high tide, due to a massive, barnacled pier, that goes far out in the water.

"Everyone I know's been there, at one time or another."

"Okay then. North of the pier along the edge of the beach is an old wreck that has tons of lumber. All the boards we could ever want, I imagine."

"I have seen that. Timmy and I played on it once, years ago."

"So there's our answer. No one will give a holler if we take the whole thing."

I thought of the task of hauling lumber from there to the fort site. Running down the huge hill to the bay is a skinny, winding road with several S-curve turns, dangerous for bikes due to loose sand and gravel and poor visibility. I'd done it many times, and it was always necessary to ride the brakes and use great caution.

"I agree with the lumber part. Once again, that's good thinking by Matt. But how on earth does he think we can get boards from there to the fort site?"

"He said he could make two board haulers, one for each of us, that we can bolt to the axles on the bikes. All we have to do is get him a baby carriage with good wheels. Which shouldn't be no big deal. It'd be a pain goin' up, but we could walk the bikes on the steep part, then ride from there."

It sounded like work, but it also sounded far better than Stoneridge or the haunted house. I pictured the ship, laying on its side with weeds and even small trees growing from the various cracks. I had little doubt those boards would be easy to get and that they'd do the job well.

"Plus it'll be a nice relaxin' bike ride down there," Freeman said as an afterthought, "when we check it out tomorrow. And another day of relaxation is exactly what we need right now."

11

Freeman packed lunch and I broke the news to my mom, implying that we were merely going on a bike ride and neglecting to mention the real purpose of the trip.

"You be back by dinner, and you be careful on that road, Joseph! And remember … "

"I know, Mom! Jesus loves me. I love him too." I shook my finger teasingly at her. "And you be mindful around Freddie!" she shook a finger back at me. "He's an okay boy, but he is a bit different. And I still worry that he may not be the best influence on you."

"Of course I'm a good influence, Joey!" Freeman laughed as we rode along the flat part of Cold Water Road and I told him what my mom had said. "I'm gonna lead ya directly to hell, where all the fun and excitement is! Lots of crazy people, too!"

He howled like a lunatic, and I was glad my mom was not there to hear him. It was hard to believe that Jesus could love him as much as everyone else, given that he might well have passed for a twin brother of the prodigal son, if not a descendant of Lucifer.

We pedaled for several miles before we arrived at the top of Cold Water Hill, where we stopped for lunch: one peanut butter sandwich each, washed down with canteen water, followed by an apple, all from Freeman's backpack.

"Good lunch, honey bunch," I jibed him.

"Thanks. But I forgot the franks."

We laughed at the absurdity of our rhymes while Freeman put the canteen away. I noticed he was no longer wearing the slingshot, which I presumed was because of Annabelle frowning on it. But I didn't mention the matter since I imagined he'd already been embarrassed enough.

"I guess we should've adjusted our brakes a bit," Freeman re-marked, his mouth full of crunching apple. "This hill's gonna be some-thin' else."

"My brakes are good. It's these bald tires I need to worry about."

"I got them too." He kicked his front tire. "But what the hell? Ya only live once."

We started slowly, riding the brakes and keeping our speed to ten miles an hour or so. Freeman took the lead, his fuzzy head and protruding ears leaning first one way, then the other as he swung back and forth through the turns. His elbows stuck out like wings on a bird, his baggy T-shirt flapped in the wind, and his rear end hung off the seat, the way they do on bikes.

We gained more speed and Freeman skidded briefly on a patch of sand. He turned and grinned like it was a big joke. He skidded again on purpose. I relaxed my brakes to keep up with him, but I also kept an eye out to see what bush I could land in, in case things got out of hand.

One car flew past going down, forcing us to the side of the road. I felt a puff of air and road vibrations, and it occurred to me that death wasn't all that far away—all I would need was to slip in front of a car. But that thought soon passed as we coasted happily along enjoying the sunshine and fresh air, heeling on the turns, grinning now and then at each other. Freeman flirted with disaster by skidding several more times, on purpose.

We were sailing around a wide turn, about halfway down the hill, when a huge convertible roared up from behind, blasted the horn, then slowed down alongside us. It may as well have been a battle-ship on that skinny road; we were pinched onto the tiny dirt shoulder, where we bounced along, inches from the side of the car. The top was down and the radio was blasting, " … Charlie Brown, he's a clown. That Charlie Brown … ," so loud that the noise shook my body. The white interior of the car was packed with a wriggling throng of teenagers, most of them holding beer bottles.

"Git off the road, ya pissants!" one of them shouted as he threw an empty beer bottle in front of me where it smashed on a rock, brown glass flying everywhere.

"Ya damn road hogs!" hollered another.

As my eyes caught the dice dangling from the mirror, I realized the car was JC's, even though someone else was driving. The monstrous beast pulled slowly ahead of us, its occupants laughing and drinking and having a grand old time while a pizza box flew out and spun through the air, narrowly missing Freeman's head.

Freeman raised his left arm and flipped off the bunch of them as he bounced through the rocks and dirt, attempting to steer with one hand. I suspected immediately this was a mistake.

Sure enough! Brake lights flashed and tires screeched about half a block ahead of us. Long skid marks appeared on the pavement while blue tufts of tire smoke mixed with clouds of dust from the road. The car stopped, straddled across the double yellow lines. The driver turned to someone in the backseat and shouted over the blast of the radio.

"Ain't that the weenie who knocked your teeth in, JC?"

JC's wavy brown hair and air-filled head rose from the backseat. A blond-haired girl in a white sailor's hat and sunglasses wearing a tight red top, rolled off his lap. She was sucking on a beer bottle like a baby who couldn't let go.

JC spun around, then jumped on the seat. He pointed to Freeman with one hand and threw a bottle toward us with the other. "That's him all right! The one with him too!"

All four doors flew open and a body stepped or tumbled from each one while the others rumbled around inside, like they didn't know what to do. JC climbed over the trunk as if to make a beeline for us; but then he stumbled and rolled onto the road, hollering something about "these slippery damn socks!"

Neither Freeman nor I slowed down, partly because everything happened so fast, partly because we had no interest. Freeman swerved right, narrowly missing a door and the drunken body tumbling from it. I swerved hard to pass on the left, and there, not ten feet away, was another drunk teenager, flailing his arms as if in an effort to stop me.

Perhaps he saw the look in my eyes because he dove back in the car with a high-pitched yell while I sailed by not half a second later.

"Get in!" screamed JC to the others.

I glanced behind me and saw several drunken bodies scrambling about, doors slamming and dust shooting from the tires even before everyone was in.

Up ahead, Freeman pedaled furiously, accelerating down the hill. We still had another quarter mile to go, and it was the steepest part with two hairpin turns. My feet cranked like windmills. There was no choice save to go faster and hang on.

The next turn came quick, a dark curved tunnel beneath over-hanging trees. Freeman moved to the middle, where there was less sand on the road; I prayed to God there were no cars coming up. He stopped pedaling and heeled left. I followed as if on a towrope, petri-fied. He leaned harder and I realized that a few grains of sand, or one car coming the other way, and we wouldn't need to worry about JC anymore, or anything else for that matter—save what kind of ques-tions St. Peter had to ask.

The turn got tighter, Freeman leaned more. I wouldn't have thought it possible until I saw it. His left elbow was a foot from the pavement, and my own bike was heeled at the same death-defying angle. One teensy bit more and the tires would shoot out from under us! We'd be spinning on the road with that two-ton convertible tear-ing our flesh to shreds while its passengers laughed and howled and drank beer above us.

A loud squeal of tires came from behind as JC's car went into the turn. I hoped I'd hear a tremendous crash, that they'd fly off the road and slam into a nice fat oak tree there to meet their Maker, drunk as skunks and filled with evil intentions.

But no such luck. We pulled out of the curve and Freeman shot right like a speeding bullet, giving me a view straight ahead: a car popped into sight, headed right at me. It happened so fast I didn't even notice what color. I heeled right and the car flashed by with a deafening honk.

"Oh God!" I thought. "Could this really be the end for JC and his friends?"

Tires squealed, horns blared crazily. But still no crash. I glanced back and saw the convertible accelerating straight toward us. Some-how the cars had missed, to my profound disappointment.

Three teenagers now stood in front, waving and shaking fists over the windshield.

"Step on it, Freddie!" I shouted, pouring on steam myself.

My lungs were afire and my thighs burning. My eyes streamed from the wind and I could barely see. It wasn't possible to go much faster since my pedals were spinning without resistance. It looked like JC might have his way this time after all ...

I glanced back and the chrome grille gleamed in the sunlight, almost upon us, while the horn blared. The drunken occupants waved and shouted and one of them heaved another beer bottle toward us. It crashed to the pavement, the sudsy spray exploding amidst chunks of glass. I pedaled harder, frantically, though it didn't matter, as fast as I was coasting. Another yellow curve sign streaked by.

Freeman heeled right, and I could hear the radio blaring: "We're out to sink the Bismarck, the terror of the sea ... " A stream of sparks flew out as Freeman's pedal touched the pavement. I thought it was over.

But his bike came up, as mine leaned, and a blur of pavement flashed in the corner of my eye. I held my breath, prepared to crash and be mushed by the convertible. But up came my bike, like one of those punching bags you can't knock over. Then the turn straightened out.

Freeman's arm pointed right, as if to signal a turn. I had forgotten about the dirt path there which was a shortcut to the water, used by walkers who lived on the hill. It split off in a Y and shot across a small meadow before entering the parking lot of the boat ramp area. Freeman shot onto the path, bounced out in the meadow, then back to the footpath. I followed close, the convertible a stone's throw behind me, those drunken freaks screaming and honking and tossing empty beer bottles, hell-bent on catching us no matter what the cost.

As I bounced along the steep path there was a sound of metal on rocks, which was JC's car bumping and scraping in the meadow. I stood on my pedals to absorb the shocks, clenched my teeth, held my breath; my bike shook like a jackhammer, and it was all I could do to hang on.

Up ahead, exactly where our path entered the parking lot, sat a pickup truck with a dripping wet boat on a trailer behind it. To the sides of the path lay several large boulders, leaving no room for us to veer off.

We barreled toward the boat, on a collision course with death! It seemed a certainty that we would slam into that impassable wall and be killed in an instant, splattering like bugs on a windshield.

We braked hard, clouds of dust flying, the side of the boat seeming to expand into a field of white that I imagined would be the last thing I'd see on earth. Only at the very last second did the outfit lurch forward, as if the driver had seen us. The boat cleared away, its huge motor dripping water just inches to my left.

We blasted onto the parking lot. The convertible bounced and swerved and roared behind us. The drunken driver and brainless passengers showed no signs of fear, and no sign of slowing down, even when the car scraped a boulder on the right as it entered the parking lot.

But Freeman didn't slow down either. His feet pumped like pistons again and it was all I could do to keep up. The wind washed over my face and I realized my hat had blown off some time ago. Freeman zoomed across the parking lot, pulling a sharp right, then a left; he bounced over a curb, crossed a small patch of sand, headed onto the massive pier, and we drove straight down the center of it. So much for inspecting that old boat, I thought.

The pier shook as the convertible scraped over the curb and plunged after us. Freeman soared onward, pedaling madly, me right behind, even though I could now see it would do no good—there was nowhere else to go, and the end of the pier loomed before us!

But Freeman kept going like there was no tomorrow. I got set to hit the brakes, planning to swerve to the side so the convertible wouldn't run me down. I believed I might wheel around quickly and race back toward the parking lot and hope some fishermen or boater might be there to help, even though I'd seen no one except whoever owned the boat we almost hit. But there was Freeman, still headed full bore toward the small railing at the end of the pier.

It hit me then: Going off the pier was his plan! It was the only place where the lynch mob couldn't catch us. Who could have thought of it besides Freeman? But the tide was low, and the top of the pier was a good twenty feet above the water. It mattered not. He crashed through the waist high rail, and with splintered boards flying around him, launched into the air still pedaling crazily. I coasted behind, as if in a dream. And behind me was that infernal convertible.

I sailed off behind Freeman, realizing too late that I should have moved over so I wouldn't land on him and kill us both. The water looked a hundred miles away and everything suddenly seemed in slow motion. Freeman and his bike and scraps of railing drifted far, far below, like small toys, still in the air. I thought of the witch pedaling past Dorothy's window when her house was aloft in the cyclone.

My chest clenched, I couldn't breathe; my bike arched out and tilted downward. Flashing metal amidst white foam was all I saw as Freeman went under. I closed my eyes and expected to see my life go by, the way Sister Silvester said would happen. I wondered if I'd see Timmy when he was a little baby, or watch my mom changing my diapers.

But it was more like Superman punched me in the face and chest and kicked me in the stomach. Then came black, quiet, and stillness.

I opened my eyes but couldn't see a thing. I attempted to move my hands and realized I was mushed into the mud, twisted like a pretzel. I pushed and wiggled and worked myself free, like a cat escaping from a pillowcase.

I swam to the surface, which seemed four feet up, and gulped air. Pain was everywhere but my main concern was for Freeman, who was still underwater. Two empty bottles floated a few feet from my head, along with several broken boards, while obnoxious shouts came from the top of the pier.

"This one's for you!" hollered JC as a bottle came soaring down, landing so close that the splash hit my face.

It made me sick, but I was more concerned about Freeman—if he didn't show up in a very short while, JC would be the least of my worries. I feared he was stuck in the muck, unconscious and drowning that very minute. Another bottle whizzed down behind me.

The ugly, barnacled pillars of the pier rose toward the sky, where they supported JC and his numbskull friends and his two-bit car. I contemplated swimming underneath them to get away from the rain of beer bottles, but I realized I had no choice, save to dive under and grope about for Freeman.

I took several breaths and prepared to go down, but just as I gulped my last breath, Freeman popped up beneath the pier, beaming like a ray of sunshine. He said nothing, but his hands came up in a V as if to say, "No problem here, Joseph Simpson!"

I would have broken out laughing except another bottle splashed down by my shoulder, then bobbed up and floated near my ear.

"JC!" I shouted up.

"What, Simpleton?"

"I think Freeman's stuck in the muck and maybe drowned! Get down here and help me look for him!"

I dove under and swam around thinking it might give them food for thought. At least they might stop throwing the beer bottles. I found my bike stuck in the mud, and grabbed hold so I wouldn't float up. I stayed under as long as I could, then came up gasping.

"I think I found his bike," I shouted, "but I can't find his body! C'mon, help me!"

"Let's get the hell out of here, JC!" someone said.

"Yea, this is bullshit, JC!" a girl's voice squealed.

"C'mon! Help me, you guys!" I hollered.

The engine revved and someone barked, "We're leavin', JC! You comin'?"

"Yea, I'm comin'!" he replied loudly. But he leaned over the pier and called to me in a lower voice, "Ya need to find that ugly bastard! And fast!"

12

"So it wasn't the most relaxin' bike ride," admitted Freeman as we laid on the grass in his backyard, billowy white clouds floating in a pale yellow sky above us. "At least we found that rope to get the bikes out." He referred to an old ski tow rope with which we'd pulled the bikes onto the pier.

I had just finished complaining about the stress he was subjecting me to, and the fact that I might not live till twenty if I kept hanging out with him.

He sat up and grinned, a big weed wagging from his mouth, "Plus ya gotta admit, it was a mighty grand adventure!"

"If that's what you call it then I don't want another adventure till the day I die. I'd as soon be standing in left field with sweaty underwear up my crack. And I mean it! Hell, I'd rather sit through a history class than have another day like that."

He laid back down, deflated. "Jeez, Joey! I was just pullin' your leg. Don't be such a sourpuss all the time."

Maybe I was a sourpuss, but it seemed to me there was good reason for it. Still, I was glad he was only pulling my leg or it would have put a real strain on our friendship.

We stared at the clouds and said nothing for several minutes. It occurred to me to see how he'd like it if I pulled on his leg a bit.

"So, Mr. Happiness, how do you like all the kindness and affection JC has for you now?" I thought of JC's final words to me before leaving the pier, that I'd "better find that ugly bastard!"

"That SOB needs to be shot. And they can't do it soon enough!"

"Now who's the sourpuss?"

"That's a whole different matter, Joey. You're talkin' a serious thing here now."

"But he was interested in me saving your life. That's quite a switch, isn't it?"

"Very funny, Joey."

"I mean it. He surprised me too, that's for sure."

"What the hell are ya talkin' about? It's just more of the same old crap. JC has to rule the world and scare the hell out of everyone in it."

"But he said he wanted me to save you."

"Are ya losin' your marbles, Joey?"

Now I thought he was pulling my leg again. But he sounded serious. I wondered if perhaps he really hadn't heard JC before he went back to the car.

"Serious, Freddie. What did you think when he told me to save you?"

"He never told ya to save me."

"He sure as hell did! Right at the end there, when he leaned over the pier. He said, 'Ya need to find that ugly bastard! And fast!'"

"That ain't what he said!"

"What did you think he said?"

"I know exactly what he said. He said, 'Ya need to drown that ugly bastard! You ass!'"

"Jeez, Freddie. I was lookin' right at him."

"And I was right under him! I think I oughta know."

We argued the correctness of our positions and we each became more firmly convinced we were right. I knew what I heard, and it was consistent with our old friendship, no matter how big an ass JC was. But Freeman claimed to know what he heard, and I couldn't deny he was right there underneath JC when he said it. It seemed like a powerful big difference, but there was nothing we could do about it save wait and see how JC behaved in the future.

"Even if ya was right, Joey, which ya ain't, the only reason he would have said that is so he can cut 'em off later! Him and his wing-ding friends!"

I wanted to ask who sounded like a sourpuss now but I didn't think he'd appreciate it. So I let that go and contemplated how much the clouds had changed since I last paid attention, even though I was staring right at them all the while.

"Well, at least we got the air cleared up about Maggie, huh?" Freeman said after a time.

"And what's that supposed to mean?"

"I mean ya can't give me no more hogwash about her being in love with you."

"There is no hogwash. She is in love with me."

"Then tell me why in the world she's makin' it in the backseat with JC?"

I looked at him, shocked. "Are you trying to tell me that was her in the car?"

"I'm not tryin' to say it; I am sayin' it."

"That was not Maggie! I think I'd know Maggie Engles if I saw her!"

"I'm tellin' ya, that was Maggie Engles right there in the back-seat!"

"You are so full of horseshit! Why do you keep pullin' this stuff on me? Are you really jealous or something?"

"I ain't pullin' nothin', Joey! But I think you may be pullin' your own dang wool over your own dang eyes about this girl."

"You are one crazy mother, Freddie! Are you sure James didn't stick that bag over your head?"

I supposed that in the heat of the bike ride it was possible for Freeman to think he saw the Man in the Moon, but I knew what I saw and it wasn't Maggie.

"I can't believe you don't see it, Joey! It's like your brain steps out for a bite to eat every time it comes to Maggie Engles."

"I want to marry her, Freddie. Someday she'll have my kids." I pictured that, and it was very easy to do. It seemed like two or three kids would be just right. "And I might even name the first one Freddie, if you'll stop being such a dingbat."

He laid back down, as if that idea was too much to bear sitting up.

"What if it's a girl?"

"Why then … I'll call her … Frieda." I thought of the time he was going to name his kids after me, which brought a smile to my face, both the idea of it and the new turn of events.

"Aw, forget it, Joey. I gotta go home and go to bed."

We surveyed the fort one more time and checked over Freeman's calculations, which to my surprise appeared to be correct, in addition

240

to overwhelming. Even Freeman was surprised when we pictured how big a stack he was coming up with.

"It's almost like we gotta have our own lumberyard, ya know?"

"Maybe we should have Matt take another look," I observed once again. "Just to be sure we're doing this right. The idea of hauling all that lumber up Cold Water Hill just doesn't excite me. Especially if we figured something wrong."

"But there it is in black and white. I been over this three times now. Ya can't argue with these numbers, Joey."

"I'm not arguing with the numbers. I'm arguing with you. And all I'm saying is let's let Matt take a look and see if he's got some ideas before we go back to Cold Water Cove. Besides, we never really did check that ship out, you know."

"Don't worry, the wood's still there. I've seen it before and I don't really need to see that heap of boards again till we're ready to haul it."

"Plus we need to come up with a baby carriage. And unless Matt puts a big fat engine on these contraptions, that hill is going to kill us."

"I don't see what else he can possibly say that'll help us."

"I don't either. But that's all the more reason we ought to ask him. What's to lose, anyway?"

Thus I talked Freeman into enduring Matt's fantastic ideas one more time, and no doubt his criticism, on the chance he'd help us figure how to finish our own limited vision of an earth-covered fort. And so we brought him back to the fort site once again in a desperate attempt to milk his brain.

"First off, you need to tear this pile of crap down and dig a bigger baseme … "

"Wait a minute! Stop right there, Matt! We ain't gonna dig a bigger basement unless you bring us a bulldozer. And we're not tearin' nothin' down, and we're not makin' nothin' taller! That much is settled. So take a look at this thing, and tell us how to finish it up so we can bury the bastard."

"Help me get acorns, Joey!" James tugged my T-shirt, oblivious to the momentous powwow about to take place. I walked off a short ways, motioning him to be quiet so I could listen and watch, and we started gathering acorns.

Matt looked the structure over and shook his head while he did so, like it was considerably worse than the doghouse we'd built. He pushed on the frame and it wobbled back and forth; he stood on the roof and the beams sagged about six inches. I had actually convinced myself that our efforts were not a complete failure, but Matt's continued head shaking squashed my optimism.

"You really think that's going to hold a load of earth?"

James put acorns in my backpack, while I petted Doc for comfort.

"So what do we do now, Mr. Edison?" asked Freeman. "Joey and I think all we need is better supports and to cover it with boards so we can put dirt on top. But we don't have boards and can't think of anything else. And don't tell us to plant no forest and wait twenty years, 'cause we won't do it!"

Matt merely continued shaking his head, and I told myself I didn't have to feel bad just because he did that. But I couldn't help it.

"You've got some real problems," he declared finally as he finished the inspection, like we didn't know that and hadn't invited him for that reason in the first place. "Real serious problems."

"Yea, Freddie! Ya got real problems," echoed James solemnly. I motioned for him to be quiet.

"So are you gonna stand there takin' a dump on us, or are you gonna help us out?" pleaded Freeman.

"All you want is to bury the thing, huh?"

"How many times do we gotta say it?"

"No moat, no basement, no lookout tower?"

"Just bury the bastard!" wailed Freeman.

"Yea, just bury the bastard, Matt!" added James, who seemed almost as excited as Freeman.

"Well then, that's pretty simple. Why didn't you say so? Just use the old shingles behind our garage. They're not perfect, but they'd work for this job. I got them when they demolished that old house along Factory Alley."

He looked the fort over with what appeared to be a new outlook, put his foot on one corner like he owned it, and started talking like the boss of a construction crew. Doc went over and sat by his other foot, as if he wanted to take it all in too.

"You could stick four supports in the middle and shore up the sides with those scraps I have out back. Then tar paper the place and put shingles over the top, which you can do in no time, and she'd be ready for burying."

I couldn't believe it! Our construction problems had just been solved in the blink of an eye. Matt's most amazing eye, I thought.

Of course we took the offer, and that very night made four or five trips with James' little red wagon, toting Matt's donated shingles through the shadows and back streets, and grunting with them through fields and woods. It was monotonous and tiring, especially crossing the tracks, where we had to empty and reload, but by daybreak all the shingles were safe and sound at the fort site, more than enough to finish the operation.

Freeman said he'd never even thought of the shingles because they were hidden under a tarp and a pile of junk. Had I not been so happy, I might have said all manner of nasty things to him, but as it was, I bit my tongue and realized at the same time I probably never would have thought of the shingles either.

"Now we really gotta start humpin', Joey!" Freeman lit a butt for each of us as we sat on the kitchen table at the fort site in the early morning light.

"You better not start humping Joey, you damn horny toad! We got work to do," I replied.

And we did have work to do, though it wasn't till noon that we actually awoke in the hot sun to get started. We wolfed down cold black hot dogs on stale Tip Top Bread, followed by several mouthfuls of crusty marshmallows from the night before.

"De-licious!" exclaimed Freeman, washing it all down with stale canteen water. "I feel like Godzilla!"

"I thought I got a whiff of something funny around here."

"I'm not sure you really wanna discuss that one … stinky dinky." He swatted my head, grinning. "Though I s'pose we could get Doc to check things out."

"Forget it."

We chugged away like beavers, cutting, banging, cursing, yanking nails out nearly as often as we put them in, and bomping each another with boards on several occasions. We put up four more support posts, reinforced the roof and walls like Matt suggested, then laid tar paper over the entire structure. We sealed the seams with a rag on the end of a stick that I had dipped in hot tar.

The tar dried fast and made a sticky seal that Freeman said would surely work, especially since we had overlapped the tar paper so water would run over the cracks and not into them. I got tar on my shirt and my arms and nearly ruined my sneakers because the tar was impossible to get off.

"Use turpentine," Matt said when we made a trip for sandwiches. "I've got some in the garage." It saved my sneakers, but I had to trash the shirt and use one of Freeman's.

We nailed the shingles to the roof and tacked them on the sides, using small gray nails with big heads that Matt gave us for that purpose.

I never dreamed it was possible to make so many mistakes putting up a simple shelter, but we persevered and corrected most of them, and by and by the supports were up and the place was covered with tar paper and shingles and ready for the next step.

And that step was the hardest one, burying the whole affair. But we chipped away with shovels and buckets and several gallons of sweat, removing earth from a large hole a short distance away in the woods where we found reasonably sandy soil. It took three days to pile enough dirt over the thing to make a mound resembling a hill. And that was because we cheated by making dense brush piles with snaggly oak branches all around the sides and compacting and burying those.

After the burial, we dragged back as much topsoil and sod as we could and laid it on top of everything. It was brown and dead looking and, I strongly suspected, a waste of time.

"Don't worry. This stuff'll spring to life with the next good rain," Freeman said with an air of authority, and there wasn't much choice but to take his word for it.

After the sod was on, Freeman hung an old beach towel in the doorway. It dangled crookedly and let flies in, but also light, which we needed until we got candles. We soon tired of the towel, which was ugly, and the flies, which were everywhere, so we cut a piece of plywood very carefully, added hinges, and affixed a spring on top. It made a good door that opened inward and shut tight. It kept flies out, even though it walloped our behinds every time we went out; and it made the place quite dark, until Freeman swiped four candles from his mom's Christmas collection.

"We need beds inside too," he declared. "And before that, we need something to lay on the dirt, like newspapers."

I rounded up a bunch of *Wall Street Journals* while Freeman got gunnysacks from Matt. Then we harvested cotton from an old mattress in the dump, which we stuffed in the gunnysacks, and in short order we had two comfortable beds. We also found two floor mats at the junkyard, alongside a trashed car, and we used those to lay on the center of the dugout floor, like a carpet.

We stapled cardboard to the inside of the walls, and covered that with newspapers; we tacked up a second layer of cardboard and thus created a warm secure feeling on the inside. We made six shelves for the candles and other knickknacks, such as comic books, canteens, and food.

We finished the rock firepit, the outdoor table, and the latrine, which we moved to the woods after I convinced Freeman that no girls would use the thing where it was, and neither would we while they were there. We converted the large sandy excavation hole into a refrigerator, and made an insulating cover from crisscrossed branches and natural junk, such as leaves and grass, all bound together with twine. We built two benches for sitting on alongside the kitchen table.

"It ain't quite the palace I had in mind," Freeman admitted as we laid on the gunnysack beds, contemplating the fruits of our labors. "But it ain't too son-of-a-bitch'n bad, either."

"Amen to that." I stretched and yawned on the comfortable bed on my side of the fort, contemplating the many hours I would spend loafing about and reading comics, with no one to distract me or give me grief. No JC, no Timmy, no meddling mother poking her nose in my business. And, of course, no nuns. Just Freeman and me, at least for a while. It was a wonderful feeling and a tremendous sense of accomplishment, even though I never did get much time to think about it, let alone enjoy it.

"All we need now is—well, you know the next step, don'tchya lover boy?"

Freeman's plan was for me to have real film in the camera and take all the pictures, while he sat on a small canvas chair and smoked a cigar, if Matt could find one of each, while Annabelle practiced the skills necessary for her modeling career. Thus my immediate task, according to Freeman, was to convince Annabelle that he would make a good director.

"I really don't know if she'll go for it," I said, cringing to myself at the thought of even asking her.

"I'd pay her real money!" Freeman exclaimed, as excited as I'd ever seen him.

"But you don't have any money."

"I'll get some, Joey! Even if I have to mow lawns or clean toilet bowls somewhere!"

So much for my peace and relaxation. The dreaded time had arrived to approach Annabelle about launching the career we had mapped out for her, starting at our new resort in the great outdoors. I cowered and balked just thinking about it, and reckoned that I must have been temporarily insane to have agreed to it. I wanted desperately to avoid the encounter at all costs.

"Maybe we ought to forget it, Freddie. You could see for yourself that she has other interests now. You remember what I told you, don't you, that she's not the same person?"

"I remember exactly what you told me; you said you'd ask her and maybe she would!"

"But I didn't really think we'd get this far," I confessed, not caring if I ate crow if it would get me off the hook.

"Ya gotta do it, Joey! We didn't bust our hineys on this place for nothin'!"

"Maybe you should be the one to do it. You're the stud, remember? You could tell her I recommended you. I'd even write you a note."

"Ya gotta do it, Joey!"

"I don't think I can."

"Course ya can! Ya did it when ya was younger, for cryin' out loud."

"Now I'm older and smarter. And I've had time to think about it since we started building this thing."

"You're doin' it! That's all there is to it, and I don't wanna hear another word!"

I called her on the phone in Freeman's kitchen, around lunchtime, with him standing over me like a heartless slave driver. He pressed his ear to the phone with mine, while I informed Annabelle that I would like to talk with her.

"About what?" she asked, evidently adjusting to hearing my voice on the phone.

"Well … It's about, I, um … uh … "

"Tell her it's about a business deal," Freeman whispered.

"It's about a business deal."

"A business deal?" she asked, incredulously. "What kind of business deal?"

"Well, you know. The kind that makes lots of money."

"But I don't really need lots of money. I get an allowance, and I babysit if I need a little extra now and then."

There was a long pause while Freeman and I contemplated this announcement. A very, very long pause during which my armpits burst into a sweat.

"Well then, let's just talk," I blurted out.

"About what?"

Another long pause and my neck and face got hotter than they already were. Beads of sweat broke out on my forehead while my brain seized up completely.

"Tell her it's about a really neat house ya built!"

"It's about a really neat house I built."

"You built a house?"

"Well, kind of."

"And where is it?"

She did not sound like the sweet little Annabelle I used to know; nor did she sound like the one who had recently sent me two love notes. Oh God, I thought! I'm going crazy! Then again, I reasoned, it's probably because she's as embarrassed as I am, and she wasn't expecting my call. I was glad I at least had something to speak about besides the love notes.

"It's in the Westwoods." I tried with all my might to be causal.

"You built a house in the Westwoods?" She sounded yet more disbelieving.

"Well, not exactly. But it's something I want you to see. And I think we need to meet in person."

"Why me?"

Another long pause and my head felt ready to pop off my neck from all the pressure. I imagined she was waiting for me to tell her I loved her too, which I could never do.

"Tell her you like her."

"I like you."

"You do?"

Freeman was nodding his head frantically.

"Yes."

"You mean like as in 'like'?"

I wasn't sure what that meant, but it sounded okay under the circumstances. "Yes."

Another long pause. I could hear her breathing but I couldn't imagine what she was thinking.

"Okay. I guess. If you really think we need to. Where do you want to meet?" I looked to Freeman for an answer and tried to decipher his lip movements, which he repeated three times during another geologic pause.

"By the school. In back," I said.

"When?"

"Tonight at seven thirty," he whispered.

"Tonight at seven thirty."

"Okay. But don't get any crazy ideas, Joseph Simpson. It's not like the olden days anymore!"

"Don't worry," I said. "I know that."

I hung up the phone and shook my head. "Shit, Freddie! I can't do it! She's already suspicious!"

"They all say no at first. That's one of the main things ya gotta learn."

"But she meant it! I could hear it in her voice!" I was terrorized by the idea of asking her to take off her clothes in front of Freeman and the camera.

"It's too late, photo boy! You're on for seven thirty!" I felt sick and wanted to barf. I was faint and weak. I believed there was no conceivable way I could manage to do what I'd promised. I made Freeman help me to his bed, where I laid down to allow the blood to return to my head.

"Kill me, Freddie. It will be easier."

"I'll kill ya if ya mess up."

"There's nothing to mess up. It won't work."

"It has to! We already got the film!"

"I can't, Freddie, I can't!"

But my protests landed on deaf ears. A promise was a promise, said Freeman, about twenty or thirty times. I tried to read comics, but the best I could do was stare at the pages like a vegetable.

At seven o'clock we went to the back of the school, where Freeman climbed a sycamore tree and found a good branch to sit on, directly above the spot where I would meet my fate. I passed him Timmy's megaphone, which I'd had to finagle by letting Ryan borrow my slingshot.

"Now don't go wanderin' off once ya get talkin'," he admonished, "or I won't be able to hear ya. It's hard to move around and stay on the branch while I'm holdin' this confounded thing."

"I have no idea what I'm going to say!" I pleaded one last time, talking to the scaly tree trunk.

"Just open your mouth and see what comes out," he called down. "The main thing is her own dang notes. Remember them and you'll be okay. Ya still got 'em, don't ya?"

I felt the folded papers in my back pocket, where they'd been since I received them. "Yea."

"I think that's her now. Comin' around the other end of the building."

Sure enough, it was! I shut up and stared like a corpse as she walked toward me.

She was remarkably different from how I remembered her three years ago, and even though I'd seen her twice recently, it was a real shock under the circumstances, and the differences suddenly seemed enormous.

She was two or three inches taller than I remembered with bigger hips and what were clearly breasts, and her hair was fluffier and her eyes different. As she got closer, I thought her lips were redder, and I wondered if she had done something to her face too, though I couldn't say what. She seemed older and more like a woman, older even than just the other day. And I felt like I was still ten years old.

"You look like you've seen a ghost, Joseph. Are you okay?"

"I think so. I've had something like a cold today."

"Maybe it's hay fever or allergies." She sounded sympathetic, which made me feel even worse.

"Could be. My mom has hay fever, so maybe I caught it from her."

She smiled like I was joking, though I wasn't sure why.

"I was really surprised that you called. It appears you're having a very good summer."

"It's been interesting."

There was an uncomfortable pause, and I was about to thank her for the notes, when she said, "So you built some kind of a house in the Westwoods?"

"Well, it's not exactly a house."

There was another uncomfortable pause as I tried to figure out how to describe the place.

"So … you wanted to tell me about it?"

"It's more like a little fort, actually." It sounded ridiculous now that I said it, and I felt like a three-year-old kid talking to his mother. My face heated up and I tried to fight back the panic. Annabelle was looking at me for clarification, and I had to say something.

"It's a nice little place. In the middle of the woods."

"You built it by yourself?"

"Pretty much. Freddie Freeman helped a little."

"You two are hanging around a lot together these days, huh?"

"On occasion."

Another long, painful pause. I wondered what she thought of Freeman, but she wasn't about to say. I wondered what she thought of me.

"So … is that all you wanted to say?"

"Well, no. I, um … I wanted to thank you for the notes."

"What notes?"

"You know; the ones you put in my mailbox recently."

"I didn't put any notes in your mailbox, Joseph."

"What about these?" I said in alarm, pulling the notes from my pocket.

She read them carefully, shaking her head a few times as she did, then looked me in the eyes.

"I didn't write those notes. I think you can be a very nice person, but I don't love you."

"But you use the same paper! And I saw part of a poem when we were at Hobo Haven!"

"My notebook has paper like that. And I write poems about all kinds of things. Birds, for example."

"You didn't write these?" I asked in disbelief, waving the notes in the air.

"You thought it was me because of the same paper?" she asked in amazement. "Every store I know of carries notebooks like that. Is that what made you think I wrote them?"

"Plus you're the only one I could think of who … you know, after that time in the junkyard."

"I'm not sure why I did that, Joseph. But it was three years ago and I'd certainly rather forget it. In fact, I'm really not interested in talking about it. Ever again." It was the last thing I wanted to hear! Like a door slamming in my face before I got the question out. But at the same time I knew it was the best opening I was going to get. I was determined to say something, if for no other reason than to not have Freeman harass me later.

"Does that mean you don't want to do it ever again?" I forced myself to mumble.

"Excuse me?"

I couldn't believe she was making me repeat it. "Does that mean you aren't interested in doing it again?"

She looked at me as if I had slapped her in the face, as if I was the most brazen individual she had ever come across; she raised her voice, and it was like my mom scolding me.

"Is that what this is about? You built a little shack in the woods so you could take me to it and do a strip show for you?" She paused as if to visualize such a scene. "And maybe Freddie Freeman too?" she said even louder.

My head lit up like a torch atop my neck, and I was certain my eyes were bugging an inch out of their sockets. I felt like the lowliest insect ever to crawl across the face of the earth.

"Nnnn … nnnn … nnnnooo! That's not … not what I came here for," I lied.

"Well, then?"

"I … I … I … I just wanted to see you again. I thought you wrote the notes. And I … I … I figured you might want to see my fort," I stammered.

"That's all very nice. And I did think I might want to see you again. But now that I have, I think maybe you have some growing up to do."

It was like she read my mind. I was humiliated! Mortified! But I was also just a little bit mad; who was she to tell me I had some growing up to do?

I thought of Maggie and decided that if this was practice for the real thing, then I had better get with the program. I would need to do better. Much better. Starting immediately.

Besides, I asked myself, could things really get any worse?

"Actually, there was something else, but I don't know if I should even ask you now." I couldn't believe my own audacity, and I was amazed that the words were coming out of my own mouth.

"Oh really? Well, I suppose it never hurts to ask."

"I have a private swimming pool too, and I was going to see if you wanted to come to it."

She softened a bit here, breathing out and relaxing her body, I thought. I was pleased with my boldness. I hoped with all my heart that Freeman was taking this in, because if he missed it, I was sure I was going to have to kill him.

"Well," she spoke in a less irritated tone, "I guess you remember that I love to swim. But your own private pool?"

She raised her eyebrows, as if I might be a complete liar as well as a total pervert. I told her about the Goldberg Sump and how we swam there and were the only ones around. But in the middle of my revelation she started shaking her head, much like Matt had done when he saw our fort. I was unable to finish before she interrupted.

"That's a chemical dump, Joseph! It's filled with used solvents and solutions and toxic wastes! I'm surprised you're even here to tell me about it."

"It's not toxic! It's just green water!" I raised my voice, terribly upset by what she was saying.

"What do you think makes the water green, Joseph?"

I took a breath and held my chin up like I was going to give an intelligent answer.

"Besides," she continued, "my friend's father works there. I suppose he ought to know." She paused, and apparently had another mental picture, then looked at me like I was the equivalent of a worm. "And I suppose you wanted me to go skinny-dipping with you, and maybe Freddie Freeman too?"

My head might as well have been a huge pimple ready to burst what with all the blood pulsing in it. I would have felt bigger and had more self-respect if I were bacteria on a speck of fly dung.

And the conversation certainly appeared to be at a serious dead end. All I wanted was for her to go away, and for Freeman to come down, so I could beat the crap out of him. I breathed deep to steady myself, and maybe think of something decent to say. But before I could, Annabelle continued.

"You know, I really did like you, Joey. And I still think you're not a bad person. But I'm afraid you're becoming just like ninety-five percent of the other guys out there. There's more to life, you know."

"There is?"

"There are millions of good books to read. There's good music. There's bird watching and animal watching, which I've really been enjoying lately. And hiking. There's astronomy, which I happen to like. There are sports, like swimming and roller-skating, that I do regularly. Do you want me to go on?"

"No."

She shook her head and looked me in the eyes. It was a gentle, caring look, and at that moment I saw that she had turned into a very beautiful girl—as beautiful as Maggie, really, with the only difference being that I'd known her when she was younger. She was even wearing a nice perfume, which I suddenly became aware of. And I realized that I might really like her as a girlfriend. Except that now, of course, I'd blown the possibility of any kind of friendship.

"It's been good seeing you, Joseph." She smiled kindly. "I hope the rest of your summer goes well. Maybe someday I'll come see your new house, and tell you what kind of birds are around there."

She extended her hand and I shook it limply, feeling like it might take the remainder of my life to recover from this embarrassment.

Freeman leaped down after she left and whomped me several times on the head with the megaphone. He told me I should have pressed harder, that I screwed up bad, and that she was only playing hard to get.

"She's a fox too!" he added, like I hadn't figured that out. "Ya blew it, Joey, ya really blew it!"

"Kiss my ass, you big baboon!"

The next morning my mother came from behind and handed me a sealed envelope, which she said "a little birdie" had personally delivered. I was at the table eating Cheerios, with Timmy, Patrick, and Mary gathered around eating cereal too.

No sooner did my mom leave the room than Timmy chimed out with a huge grin, "I'll bet I know what that is!"

"Shut up, Timmy."

"Can I see?" begged Patrick.

"No."

"Is it from a girl, Joey?" Mary wanted to know.

"It's just an envelope!" I turned the envelope upside down on the table and continued eating like nothing had happened.

"I think it's from his girlfriend, Mary," Timmy announced in a teasing tone.

I shot him a glance that might have killed, if only he were smart enough to get it.

"Let's see, Joey!" Patrick reached excitedly for the envelope.

I swatted his hand. "No! It's to me and it's private. Now shut up, all of you!"

"You're a turd, Joey," Timmy mumbled into his bowl.

"Yea, I'm a turd with an envelope. That you don't have. Now leave me alone." I went back to stuffing my face with Cheerios, and pretended the kids weren't there.

"You used to be nice, Joey," Mary informed me.

This stung my feelings pretty good, but I could see her point.

"I still am, and tomorrow I'm going to do something with you and Patrick."

"Yeah!" exclaimed Patrick.

"Yeah!" echoed Mary.

"But not Timmy."

"I hope that letter has poop in it!" Timmy exclaimed, then stuffed his mouth with whatever cereal he was eating.

"I'd be jealous if I were you, too," I retorted.

I finished as quick as I could, then slipped into the backyard and sat under some bushes where I was hidden from view. The envelope had my first name on it, and inside was yet another note, which I read hastily.

Dear Joseph,

I'm sorry if I embarrassed you yesterday, but I do have other interests these days. I really do hope you stay out of that sump. It is a dangerous place! Also, I think the initials on your notes may stand for Maggie Engles. I can't think of any other girls around here with those initials, and from what my friends say, that would be like her.

I think you're okay and I hope we are still friends.

Annabelle

Eeaahooo! I was now certain of what I thought all along—Maggie really did love me! I was ecstatic. The notes were actually from her! Why didn't I see it before? "M.E." was Maggie Engles, not "me," like

I thought. How stupid could I be? So she wrote in lowercase— who cared? It was merely a poetic thing.

I looked carefully at the handwriting on the three notes. The first two were not at all like Annabelle's. In fact, Annabelle used cursive, not printing, the way the nuns insisted. I was beside myself with joy. I reread the two beautiful love notes two or three times every hour. Maggie Engles loves me! I sang to myself, over and over.

Later that day, Freeman sounded terribly depressed as he laid on a hammock in his garage. "Now I have nothin' to look forward to," he complained bitterly in reference to my colossal failure with Annabelle.

I could understand his problem, but, of course, I had little room for sympathy. I was overjoyed with my own situation.

As for the swimming hole, we both agreed that since nothing had happened to us yet, the place couldn't be as bleak as Annabelle had painted it. But we also determined not to put water from it into our canteens anymore.

"Just in case she has some idea what she's talkin' about," explained Freeman.

We stoked up a fire by the fort and laid on the cotton-filled gunnysacks, which we had dragged outside into the cooler air when the evening sky turned dark. I imagined we would discuss the recent turn of events, which I was more than happy to do. However, Freeman opened his backpack and withdrew a brown paper bag.

"It's what people do when things go wrong," he explained as he extracted a flat bottle with a yellow and red label from the paper sack. "I found two of 'em in my basement after New Year's. I always wondered if I'd ever use the stuff."

With that he twisted off the cap, gave me a salute with the bottle, and took a swig. Then he stuck out his tongue, grimaced horribly, and shook his head.

"Hot damn, Joey! This'll grow more hair around your jangler!"

He reached out to pass me the bottle.

"I never drank before," I told him, not reaching out.

"Me either. But I think it might do us some good right about now."

"I don't. Plus I've got all the hair I want. On top of that, Maggie loves me, remember?"

"Ya can't just sit there and watch me get drunk by myself, can ya? Besides, you've got reason to celebrate—the son-of-a-bitchin' fort is done, and ya got a beautiful girl who loves you—even if it does make me jealous as hell."

"You want me to get drunk with you?"

"What else are ya gonna do? It's time we learned about this kinda crap anyway."

I did not like the idea of drinking after all the things I'd heard about it. Such as that you could become addicted and spend all your money on it; it could ruin your liver, kill your brain cells, and shrivel up your brain; your life would be about ten years shorter; and you'd get hangovers and a big red nose, along with a bunch of other things I couldn't remember right off.

But at the same time I had to admit I was curious. And what the heck, I thought, maybe it was time to celebrate. Here we were at the fort we nearly killed ourselves to make so we could be free to do as we pleased; it was the middle of summer and my best friend was miserable. And Maggie loved me! If I was going to find out about drinking, it seemed as good a time as ever. Besides, I knew I wouldn't drink as much as Freeman, and after all it was just one night.

"Well … just a wee teeny bit," I said as I took the bottle, noting that the red and yellow label proclaimed it was Gordon's Distilled Gin, and that there was a little ugly boar head on it.

The clear liquid burned on the way down, my eyes lit up, and my sinuses cleared out promptly; it hit my stomach like a fireball, then flared out like something from the Fourth of July.

"Ho-ly shit! Someone actually paid for this stuff?" I sputtered.

"My dad did. But he forgot about it after he got soused last New Year's Eve. I remember he was howlin' like a wolf and actin' like a crazy person for an hour or two. Then he barfed and passed out in the living room and ticked my mother off something terrible. It was fun for us kids to watch, though."

"Does that mean you'll be barfing and acting like a crazy person tonight?" I thought to myself that it would be difficult to imagine Freeman being any crazier than he already was.

"I don't know. Ask me tomorrow," he replied, taking another swig. Back and forth went the bottle, the fiery substance dwindling by a slosh or two each time, me feeling more and more relaxed and happier and happier as the evening wore on, both of us babbling away about whatever came to mind, in spite of the miserable taste of the stuff.

"Now I see why Indians called this shit firewater!" I said loudly. "And why they liked it so much too!"

"It blows the cobwebs out of yer head, don't it? And here's what I decided, now that I'm thinkin' so clear: Annabelle can take a flyin' leap! Screw her, Joey. I never even knew 'er in the first place. So what in hell was I worried about, anyway? Besides, I need an older woman, one who knows what's what and what to do with it."

"Annabelle who?" I asked.

We fell on our backs laughing and I nearly spilled the bottle as I did so, though it wouldn't have mattered since it was almost empty anyway. Freeman finished the last of it and chucked the thing far into the woods.

"I ain't worried about JC no more, neither!"

"Why not?"

"'Cause if he cuts 'em off, I'll drink more of thish and grow some new ones!"

We rolled on our backs laughing again.

After we recovered, Freeman reached in his backpack and pulled out a second bottle, which he slid from the little brown bag and passed to me.

"Gowan, it's your turn for the honors, yer freakin' honor!" I opened the lid and took a swig, then looked closer at the label. The little boar's head looked terribly mean and nasty, even in the firelight. Its large fangs protruded menacingly at the end of a long twisted snout. Then it appeared that ugly little head was staring back. I soon became convinced it was looking at me in a very negative, evil way, like it was alive.

I roared out, "Ya lil pig, you're ugly as the devil!"

"What the hell are ya talkin' about? Are ya drunk already?"

"This lil pig's checking me out; I don't like it!"

"What little pig?"

"This pig-looking thing on the bottle!"

"Lemme see that thing again!"

I guzzled a gulp and passed it back. Freeman squinted and put his face an inch or two from the bottle. He stared and stared till I began to wonder if he'd fallen asleep.

"Ya may be right! The lil pissant 'pears to be alive! He's even winkin' at me, Joey!"

"Gimme me back the bazzard! I didn't see that part!" I put my arm out and Freeman attempted to pass the bottle, but it slipped from his hand and hit the ground.

"Grab the flicker before she spills all out, Zhoey!"

"Zhoey?" I said, looking around. "Who's Zhoey? I don't see no Zhoey!"

"Dalmatian! I can't even talk no more!" Freeman rolled toward the bottle like a worm, dirt and grass clinging to his clothes, then snatched it up and looked again at the boar's head, pensive as someone in his condition could be.

"He keeps winkin' at me!" he roared, obsessed with the label.

I burst out laughing and fell back again, heaving handfuls of dirt and grass in the air.

"Winkin,' blinkin,' Abraham Lincoln! G'im over one more time! And hang on to your baby bottle, will ya!"

I looked again and saw but one eye, which didn't appear to blink. "The piggy turned his head! There's only one eye now!"

That evil eye squinted and stared the way a nun does, like you're a worm on a hook and there's no way off. And it seemed to read my mind the same way the nuns do it. It gave me the creeps something terrible; I wondered if it wasn't the devil himself! I set the bottle against a rock, between Freeman and me.

"I don't want any more of that shit! I think it may be the devil on there, Freddie! Plus I think he's readin' my mind."

"Well … that wouldn't take too damn long, would it?" Freeman guffawed and slapped the ground repeatedly.

"I mean it! There's evil in his eye, and I think it's from Satan; we better get rid of it!"

"I intend to, Zhoey!" Freeman poured a huge swallow down his throat, while the liquid in the bottle sloshed in the yellow light of the fire. He looked at the moon and bellowed, "Ahhhhhhhhhhhhhhhhh-hhh!"

He put the bottle between his legs. "Satan's our friend, Zhoey."

"Really?"

"That's what that little pig is tryin' to tell us."

"He's not my friend! I hate him as much as I hate the nuns! But gimme another drink just the shame."

I gulped a mouthful, swallowed and belched. "It's unboarable going down, but it's boarable when it gets there!"

I laid back and laughed at my own words, thinking they were hilarious, while Freeman snatched the bottle from me.

"Don't board it to yourself, then!"

We laughed hysterically and spun in the dirt like damp firecrackers, holding our stomachs till we couldn't breathe anymore. Every time one of us came close to stopping, the other would start up again. This went on and on until I finally had to get up to take a leak. Which is when the world started spinning round and round, faster and faster, until it suddenly tilted off to the left causing me to take a flying leap into some oak trees so I wouldn't fall off.

At least I think that's what happened, though I can't say for sure. After that, I have some vague memory of sticking my head into a pile of leaves, which I intended to use for a pillow. And I think I remember Freeman laughing and carrying on a conversation with himself at the campfire, though I'm not sure of that either.

The sun was ablaze in a clear sky when I cracked my eyes and looked up from deep inside my head. It was not my room, there were leaves all around; and branches and trees. And flies! Thousands of flies! And the smell. What is that smell? I wondered, putting my hand on my chest. Is it beef stew? Oh, God! It's vomit! And the flies were going crazy now that they had been disturbed.

Deep breath; calm down. You can wash the shirt, I told myself. But my head! Oh, God! I closed my eyes, put my hands to my temples and had a vision of boar fangs coming out my mouth. Oh, God! I felt like I had a boar's head in place of my own. I sat up and stripped the T-shirt off, and felt like I might pass out. I flung the shirt aside and laid back down, away from the puke I had been lying in. My head seemed like it was stuck in a gigantic pair of vise grips, with someone squeezing and releasing them. Oh, God! Let me die. Please!

I sat up and the vise grips crimped down harder. Hell's Bells! I thought. I shook my head, but that made it worse. I laid back down, on my stomach, thinking maybe I could go back to sleep. But I was wide-awake, feeling like a zombie.

I reached up to see if my head was as furry as the one on the label, the way it felt. But I still had skin and my ears seemed normal; I checked my teeth and was pleased they had not turned into fangs.

Any quick movements, and the image of a boar's head with beady squinty eyes floated before me—maybe it was a picture of Satan, and perhaps they put it on the label because Satan was inside the bottle. Anything seemed possible at the moment.

I started crawling toward the fort to find Freeman, but it was too hard, so I dragged myself to my feet and commenced with baby steps, trying not to jar my brain any more than I had to. My head ached like never before. But there was no Freeman.

What now?

I pushed open the plywood door only to find an empty fort; I retreated dejectedly to the firepit, and saw what looked like burnt stew in the ashes, which I took to be Freeman's vomit. At least it smells better cooked, I thought. I listened for snoring noises, but heard none. Two birds flew by, one chasing the other, but there was no other movement. I dragged myself down the trail and didn't get far before nearly tripping on Freeman's head. He was decked out across the path, snoring like a grizzly bear, though most of his body disappeared into the scrub oak.

I made a shadow over his eyes with my foot, but he didn't stir. I picked up an acorn and dropped it on his head. Nothing. I dropped a second acorn from a greater height. His eyelid twinched, but he continued snoring. I knelt down and drew a weed across his face, like an insect crawling. Nothing.

I poked his ear with a twig; I picked up a pebble and set it in his ear. He kept on snoring. I put another pebble between his lips, and effected a change in the tone of his snoring. I gently inserted the fat end of a weed in each nostril, then sprinkled a handful of grass over his hair. He was a sight to behold, but still snoring like an old man.

I crawled to his feet and took some matches from my pocket. Ye olde hot foot, said a voice inside me that I was sure was Satan's. I stuck two matches into a hole in the sole of his sneaker, lit another match and touched the tips of the first two, then sat back smiling. The matches burned in the still morning air, and my smile grew as they got smaller. I smelled the rubber from his sneaker, then another smell that I took for a sock, or possibly his foot. The peaceful atmosphere exploded with a loud scream, "Ooooohhhhh, son-of-a-bitch!"

Freeman was soon dancing about, swatting his foot; he whipped his sneaker and sock off, and continued swatting as he hopped around. My headache grew worse from laughing, but I enjoyed myself more.

"What's goin' on? Where the hell am … " He got quiet, sat down and reached for his head with one hand, the other still holding his foot.

"Oh, Jesus H. on a firecracker!" he uttered, shaking his head as pieces of grass fell off, and the remaining weed dropped from his nostril. "I think I had too much to drink."

It was a slow process, but we gradually reentered the world of the living. Freeman tossed the second bottle as far as he could into the trees, swearing he'd never touch another drop, while I vowed I'd never even look at one. The bottle crashed on a rock, and I wondered what the little piggy on the label was doing then.

Freeman loaned me the extra T-shirt he had in his pack, and I crumpled mine into a ball and stuck it in one of the paper sacks.

We each had fifty cents in our watch pockets that we'd gotten from my mom for babysitting, and which we had been saving for emergencies. I reminded Freeman of that, and to which he replied, "Well, this sure as hell is one of 'em!"

He checked to make sure his own fifty cents was there, then added, "And some mighty strong coffee is what we need right now!"

We hobbled like old men with polio toward Jericho Turnpike, that was about a fourth of a mile to the south, along Cranberry Boulevard, then another eighth of a mile on it, to a small café, the Silver Bird Diner. The place, mostly visited by truck drivers along the turnpike, reminded me of a large aluminum airplane with no wings. We slid into the bathroom by the tiny, dirty sink, and washed up the best we could; then we pulled ourselves up to a table and ordered coffee. Freeman claimed dark coffee with extra sugar was the best cure for problems of this nature, according to his dad.

The friendly waitress appeared to be about seventeen or eighteen. She had long black hair, a body with many nice curves to it, a sweet, soft voice, and a nametag on her light blue uniform that said Vera. One button was undone on the button-down top of her uniform, revealing a pink bra underneath, which promptly caught my attention. As she leaned to set our cups down, the bra hung loose, causing my eyes to fix upon her beautiful breasts, where they remained until the cups were full. She set the coffeepot down, reached in her apron pocket and dropped four aspirin on the table.

"I happen to think you boys might need them," she said with a smile.

Freeman and I looked at each other, then at her.

"Refills are free," she added, before we could thank her. "And it appears you handsome devils are going to need a few!"

Then she bent closer and whispered in my ear, "Looks are free too, honey."

My face sizzled as if it had been dunked in hot oil! Freeman laughed so hard that some water and chips of ice sprayed from his mouth.

The pretty waitress, whose green eyes reminded me of Maggie's, only smiled more.

"If you boys want dessert, be sure to let me know. There are lots of things around here for boys like you … " she raised her eyebrows and added in a deep sexy voice, "to nibble on and enjoy."

She took the coffeepot and wiggled away while I melted into my seat.

"Jesus!" I uttered, pouring a mountain of sugar into my coffee with a hand that wobbled like a duck. "How red was I?"

Freeman pointed to a basket of bright red tomatoes on the cover of the menu.

"You think she likes me?"

"Sure. Who wouldn't? It's fun to be around people who turn that red."

We drank three refills each, and used up half the container of sugar. Freeman also made me drink three large glasses of water because he said we were dehydrated and water would help with that. I was working on the last one when Vera came back with two plates of toast, which she set before us.

"This will help soak up any nasty things that may have gotten in our little tummies. If you want more, just let me know." Her green eyes twinkled and produced in me a warm, familiar feeling; as I was noticing this, she gave me a wink and proceeded to another table.

"She does, Freddie! She likes me!"

"I think she likes me more. Check this out."

He pointed to the back of the bill upon which there was a little note: "Hey, big boy! What's your name? I'm usually on midnights."

I was disappointed, but on the other hand I could see she was too old for me, and besides, I had Maggie. And if dreaming of Vera could restore Freeman's spirit, what did I care?

The bill was forty cents, but Freeman insisted we leave a dollar seeing as she'd been so kind to us.

"But why should I spend a week's allowance just to be embarrassed?" I protested.

"Ya got a peek, didn't ya? Besides, maybe she's got a younger sister."

As we headed out the door, Vera brushed by us, but paused long enough to give a friendly smile. "You boys come again, you hear? And anytime you come, be sure to think of me!"

She winked and whirled away, her dark hair flowing over her shoulders and her white skirt clinging to her rear end and thighs.

"Freddie!" Freeman called after her as she slipped around the counter. She raised her right hand and waved to acknowledge she'd heard his name.

13

Freeman's intention solidified, we agreed to go back on the mid-night shift, as Vera's note suggested. Thus we turned in early that next night at the fort, on the cotton-filled gunnysacks, planning to sleep for four or five hours, then rise and return to the Silver Bird Diner, around the time she got to work.

But a large thunderstorm came up soon after we settled in, so we propped open the door to watch the lightning, which lit up the glistening wet oak trees in ghostly white flashes. It was pleasing to note that the fort did not leak despite the pelting rain outside. We felt warm and cozy and secure, in addition to convinced, finally, that we had done an okay job on our country home. I also realized that Freeman was right about the sounds being muffled—I could hear the thunder but it was greatly toned down and without the loud clap that makes you jump ten feet.

I watched the tree from which we had discovered the fort site blowing to and fro in the distance and thought that we really should build a small lookout there, like Freeman told Mario we were going to, and like Matt suggested.

After a while the rain subsided and we laid back down. Before long I lapsed into a dream, in which I was climbing that very tree while Freeman began hammering steps into the base of it.

Freeman's banging resulted in a violent shaking of the tree, back and forth like a whip, which made me lose my grip and shoot out as if from a catapult. I screamed as I plummeted toward the earth, but at the same time I spread my arms, like skinny little wings.

This caused me to continue horizontally through the air, gliding down at an angle like a seagull. I would have continued gliding except I began to flap my hands, the way James does when he gets excited. I thought of Matt's invention and it occurred to me that I too had invented a new way of flying. I was wishing he was there so I could show him.

Then I thought of James. "So! This is why that guy is so happy when he flaps his hands! That little rascal has sure kept a good secret! He's been flying even before Matt dreamed up his invention!"

I kept flapping and soon leveled out, then found if I flapped harder I could go back up. I flapped faster and faster, until I was rising vertically, then somehow I appeared in front of my own bedroom window, where I saw my mom and Timmy, who were having a talk.

"Hey!" I shouted. They turned to look, as I flapped madly in front of the window.

"Oh, wow!" said Timmy. "I never knew Joey could fly like that! I wanna fly too, Mom! Joey never does anything with me anymore." He looked longingly at me and for a moment I felt badly that I didn't do more things with him.

"This is unusual," my mother answered. "Not many children can fly anymore. The nuns stopped teaching it when I was in eighth grade—kids were having too much fun and they were afraid it would lead to sin. I'll bet that's another stunt your brother learned from Freddie Freeman!"

Then they turned to each other and continued talking, as if I had disappeared. I burped loudly at them, then flew higher till I was level with the roof of the house. I flew above the chimney and looked into the dark black hole at the top, which reminded me of hell and sent shivers down my spine. I circled a maple tree in front of the house, fluttering the leaves with one hand, listening to birds chirping.

I soared to Freeman's window and hovered outside; he was on his bed, talking to Maggie and Vera who were listening to him and smiling as if they were madly in love. All three were oblivious to me. I started to flip them off, then realized I needed both hands for flying, and that I shouldn't waste energy on such stupid things.

Up I went again, above the rooftops, then around the neighborhood. I flew over the sidewalks, as this was easier than flying elsewhere; I found I could travel over them without flapping. Since I was so high, no one saw me, except kids, who could read my mind. They looked up and waved quietly, like it was the most natural thing in the world for me to be flying by. I smiled and waved back.

I passed my house again and this time saw Timmy and Ryan in the backyard, Ryan playing with model cars and Timmy writing in a notepad. Ryan pointed and Timmy looked up. "I thought he was still up there!" said Timmy, shaking his head. "He never takes me anywhere anymore!"

Ryan winked, like it was okay, then went back to playing with his cars. Timmy went back to the note he was writing, which he seemed to be taking very seriously. I spiraled higher, then glided to JC's house where I saw Mrs. Clancy doing dishes through the kitchen window. She looked out but didn't see me. I flew closer, just yards in front of her. She didn't blink, evidently I was invisible to her. I hovered even closer, looking into her face from only a foot away. She squinted as if to look at something small in the distance. I realized that to her I was a little bird and it was as if she were looking at me through the wrong end of a telescope.

"Harold! Come quick!" she called. "There's a rare bird out here! I believe it's that species that never gets in any trouble. I do wish JC were home. It would be such a good example for him!"

Her husband came and squinted out the window.

"No it isn't, Helen! It's one of those blasted Joey birds! He must have escaped from his proper habitat somehow. Get the BB gun before he gets away!"

I banked left and flashed away like a swallow. I regained altitude and was soon high above the neighborhood, with houses sprawling in every direction. I knew as if by magic what people were doing in their houses; watching TV, doing dishes, sleeping; one couple was fighting, with the guy throwing dishes; an old man was reading a magazine and trying to have a bowel movement; one couple was having sex, and I hovered over that house longer than the others; two little girls were playing school and had made their little brother sit in the corner for being bad.

Suddenly a huge dark cloud blew in and swallowed me up, blocking out the sun. It became difficult to fly, and I had to flap my hands extremely fast to stay up at all. Lower and lower I sank, feeling cold and wet, until I could vaguely make out something underneath, in what was now a thick, damp, gray fog.

At first the form beneath me was merely a dark, solid shape, moving slowly along, but then I heard voices, indistinct at first, but rapidly growing louder and clearer. Soon I could make out JC and his friends, in JC's convertible, hollering and screaming because I was about to land in the backseat.

"Let him land! It's what we want!"

"No! Step on the gas! We're done with him! He's bad luck!" said JC.

The car was badly damaged, with a front fender hanging off, taillights broken, the windshield cracked in several places, no muffler, and the car itself caked with brown mud.

The first voice shouted, "Move over! Make room!"

"No! We can't let him in! Oh God! He landed!"

I was on the backseat then, dripping water all over it, but I had my eyes closed, or else the fog had thickened; I couldn't see who was shaking me back and forth, back and forth, like a doll. All I knew was that I wanted to go back to sleep.

"C'mon! Get up, ya lazy bum! You can't sleep here forever!"

I strained to open my eyes but it was still dark, which was good because I didn't want to see who was shaking me.

"C'mon, Joey! The night's still young, but it won't wait forever."

"Oh, man! You won't believe the dream I had, Freddie! It all started in that tree over there … " I pointed to the lookout tree, eager to tell him what happened.

"Save it, Joey. We ain't got time right now. We gotta go see if Vera's workin' tonight."

And thus it was that we headed for the Silver Bird Diner so Freeman could visit his newfound sweetheart and strike up a conversation, and presumably make something good of it.

As we strolled along Jericho Turnpike toward the diner, we passed a small dirt road, which led to a dumping pit that had been bulldozed into the south side of the Westwoods, and that I'd been to a couple of times with my dad. It was perhaps a quarter mile from our fort, as the crow flies, but it might as well have been a hundred miles due to the barricade of the scrub oak. Freeman pointed down the road as we shuffled past, claiming he'd heard from kids at school that there was often parking and necking going on down there, by those fortunate enough to have cars and girlfriends.

"Maybe we ought to take a quick look," he said as he gazed longingly down the road, like a moth fixed on a light. "Just to see what's goin' on tonight. If nothing else, we oughta hear some interestin' noises comin' from the woods."

"I thought you said you didn't have time to hear about my dream?"

"This is different though; we might learn somethin' educational."

I didn't really want to, but we took a detour down that dirt road in hopes of advancing our education. And sure enough, we came upon three cars lined up along the side, near the end of the road. But there was no one around, no sign of life, no noises whatsoever. What was of considerable interest, though, was the middle car—it was a fat red convertible with two large dice hanging from the mirror!

"Can't we ever get away from this jerk?" I wailed in despair, wondering how it was we kept bumping into JC. "It's like I have the same dream, over and over! A broken record, only a million times worse!"

"A hundred dollars says the whole flock of 'em is in the woods doin' it!" surmised Freeman, ignoring me completely and evidently dismayed that he wasn't there himself. "Though I gotta admit I got a mind to put a dog turd on the driver's seat."

"Too bad we don't have that ping pong ball with us now," I said, knocking the gas cap with my knuckles, thinking that I really ought to start carrying one.

"Ya think there's anything worthwhile in the glove box?" Freeman inquired, leaning over the passenger door to examine it. "Holy Mama, Joey!" he pointed. "Get a look! There's the keys just a janglin' from the ignition!"

"Don't even think about it! Don't EVEN think about it! We do not need one more problem now!"

"Problems?! This is a golden opportunity, Joey! We go for a little spin and have some fun while he's bangin' up ... ," he hesitated for a second, and I knew he was thinking 'Maggie,' but he continued, " ... some poor girl. He won't know the difference. Besides, don'tchya think he owes me one after pokin' me with a switchblade—not to mention chasin' us into the muck on our bikes and all the other stuff?"

Before I could say a word, Freeman was in the driver's seat, experimenting with the shifter. "It's a piece of cake, driver boy. Matt showed me how to work these babies in the junkyard two years ago."

"Don't be insane! If we got caught stealing a car we'd be in deep shit. Deep, deep shit!"

"No one's stealin' nothin'! We're just gonna borrow it for a bit. We'll bring 'er back good as new! He won't even know it's gone."

To my horror he turned the key and cranked the engine, which started smoothly and made a deep throaty sound that caused the back of my neck to tingle.

"Runs good, don't it? I gotta say that much for it." He threw his head back and laughed maniacally, as if he'd lost his mind.

"Turn it off, Freddie! Let's get out of here!"

"Get in and we will!" he laughed louder, bobbing his head like a deranged person and slapping the steering wheel several times.

Then he shifted into reverse, gassed the engine and slammed into the car behind; there was a crash and a shattering of glass, which I took to be taillights or headlights, or both, while the parked car jumped several inches.

"Damn! That's one touchy clutch pedal, Joey."

He shifted and popped the clutch again. The vehicle lurched diagonally into the road, scraping the passenger end of the car in front while a loud metal crunching noise filled the air.

"This boat's leavin' for deeper water! All aboard that's comin' aboard!" He laughed insanely.

"Damn you, Freddie! I can't believe we're doing this."

I climbed into the passenger seat and hated myself, realizing at the same time that if I didn't he'd most certainly leave me behind to face JC by myself.

Just as I settled in and slid down for safety there was a commotion in the woods, and as I turned to look, a figure was emerging from the trees, bellowing and screaming, "What are ya doin'? Get back here, you bastard! That's my car!"

It was JC in his underwear, enraged and chasing in our direction with a club-like stick in his hand.

The car leapt forward, the tires spun in the dirt, the rear end fishtailed back and forth. I was pressed against the seat and turned my head to see where we were going.

"Hold yer hat, racer man!"

We flew down the dirt road, bouncing in and out of mud puddles, scraping bottom, brushing against protruding branches, Freeman intent on acceleration, hands clasped to the wheel like those of a little old lady.

"Slow down!" I screamed as we neared the end of the road, which made a T into the busy Jericho Turnpike.

"Don't be a backseat driver now, will ya? How 'bout some tunes?"

He jammed on the brakes and slid to a stop about one foot before the pavement, reached over and turned on the radio full blast. On came the fast, cheerful beat of "Happy Organ," so loud it vibrated the dashboard.

I opened the door to jump out but Freeman stepped on the gas, and as the car leapt forward my door slammed shut.

"Don'tchya be a weenie now! We got places to go and things to do! Grab yer bloody hat again, will ya!"

With that we spun onto Jericho Turnpike, where fortunately there were no cars coming due to the time of night.

"Sit back and relax! Everything's under control!"

There wasn't much else I could do, though relaxing was not at all that easy. I wanted to kill Freeman, and I felt trapped like a prisoner in his insane world.

"Where do you think we're going?" I hollered above the blare of the radio and the whistling of the wind.

"You'll see! Just enjoy the scenery and leave the navigatin' to the captain!"

At least we seemed to be doing the speed limit, and not drag racing in a way that would attract attention. I noted that Freeman probably could pass for seventeen, though I thought it best if I sank down further into the seat, which I proceeded to do.

"Your captain is happy to have you aboard!" he yelled. "And we hope you will enjoy the ride—we've got lots of places to go!"

"Captain Cocksucker!" I screamed back, now realizing he had no intention of returning soon. "The quicker you get off the main road the happier I'll be!"

He laughed ecstatically and replied, "Ya read my admirable mind! Admiral Asshole!"

With that he cut a sharp left, pressing me hard against the door as JC's convertible roared onto Cranberry Boulevard, operated by that grinning nutcase who was supposed to be my best friend.

It was dark with no streetlights, there were no other cars, and the road was wide, so I reasoned we were safe at least for the moment. The radio was blasting, "Me and Sheila go for a ride … ," and the cool night air rushed over my face while the dark forms of trees flew by on both sides. Freeman beamed with pleasure in a way I'd never seen before, while his hands tapped on the steering wheel to the beat of the music. I had to admit to myself that it did feel exhilarating, and I suddenly wished all the nuns I ever had could see me now.

"Here's the result of all your beating on me for all those years," I would have yelled at them. "Cruising in a stolen car with Freeman! How do you like them apples, ya old windbags?"

And I wished Timmy could see me too. I felt so very alive, even though it was like a bad dream at the same time.

We passed the spot where Mario had stopped us and I wondered what Mario was doing that very moment. It crossed my mind to try to drive down the path to the fort, but I stopped thinking that immediately for fear Freeman might read my mind and actually try it.

"Hang on!" he howled as the car began swerving back and forth, the way I often do on my bike. "Let's see how good this baby handles!"

"Cut it out! You're going to tip us over!"

In response came a screeching of tires as I was pressed yet harder against the door, then flung the opposite way, which forced to me to grab the door so I didn't land in Freeman's lap. Then slam to the door, then back toward Freeman, who was laughing like a maniac. Back and forth I went, like an insect in the jar of a crazy kid, who would not stop till the insect was dead, or maybe paralyzed. I wanted to jump out but we were going way too fast.

"Stop, Freddie! I'm getting sick!"

Freeman lifted his head to the sky and laughed harder still, swerving more and not looking where he was going. I wanted to beat the hell out of him, even more than I would have liked to do to JC, but there was nothing I could do about it.

"Slow down! Please!" I screamed.

"Aw jeez, Joey! It's like a big bumper car! I never knew it was so easy to drive one of these things. Ya wanna give it a spin?" he replied as if he hadn't heard me.

"I want to go back! Now!"

"Just one more little test; we gotta see how she handles in the dirt!"

He turned out the lights and the car cut a sharp right off Cranberry Boulevard into a large dirt field, where workers had dragged bulldozed trees and debris from the road construction in preparation for burning. We bounced off the pavement traveling at what seemed like fifty miles an hour. Freeman pulled another sharp turn, making us spin in a circle in a huge patch of mud. We slid sideways through a gigantic puddle. Water splashed from the tires in a wall, then splattered over the car as we passed underneath, traveling backward and hardly slowing down.

"What are you doing?" I cried, filled with despair, fright, and anger.

"Takin' a little bath! Like mother always said!"

Nothing I could say would slow him down as we spun around and around in that muddy field, banging one way and the other, splatters of mud and sprays of water flying over us; it occurred to me that if there ever was a heaven, Freeman must have thought he was in it. Round and round the uprooted trees and rocks we went, moonlight glistening off the waves in the puddles and the slick mud and the sprays sent up by the tires, me growing sicker and sicker by the minute.

"Stop the car!" I shouted into the night, about half a second before I puked onto the seat between us.

Freeman nailed the brakes and my head banged the dash while the tail end of my barf splattered onto his hand and the gearshift.

"Jesus, Joey! Why didn't ya tell me to slow down?" I launched a second barf onto the dashboard as I turned and tried unsuccessfully to eject it over the side.

"Now JC's really gonna be pissed!" Freeman said, though I knew he didn't care, due to the evil smile on his big ugly face.

"Why can't you ever listen to me?" I moaned, one hand on my stomach and the other on my head where I had smashed the dash.

"All right, you win; let's go back!"

He gunned the engine and we shot into the road, but as we did we passed over a small tree stump. A dull thud came from beneath the car, near the center of it. As we moved onto the street, there was a scraping of metal, and the sound of the engine increased noticeably.

"What the ... " said Freeman above the ruckus and the infernal radio.

"Muffler!" I said, looking back and noting the long black item laying in the road.

"Well ... it sounds better without it, don'tchya think?"

"This is it, Freddie! Our asses are going to be hanging from a flagpole after this little joyride!"

"There ya go worryin' again! Most of it's nothin' a little soap and water can't fix. And the rest is just a muffler and a couple of dings here and there."

"I wish tonight had never happened!"

"Grab yer hat before it blows off yer little noodle!"

My head pressed against the seat and we accelerated down Cranberry Boulevard, still without lights. It's hard to say how fast we got going in the next minute or so because without the lights I couldn't see the instrument panel; but I believe the car had accelerated to the maximum speed before Freeman started braking, which he did only because Jericho Turnpike was coming up. When he turned the lights on the red needle was pointing to fifty and we had slowed down from what seemed like twice that speed.

"You're going to kill us if you don't cut it out!" I bellowed over the squeal of rubber on the pavement.

The smell of burnt tires filled the air as we slid up to the red light, but it was a welcome relief to that of my vomit.

"Grab that rag in the backseat, will ya, Joey? Then wipe up some of this puke. It's the least we can do for the guy."

I did as told, noting the rag was more like a dress of some sort. But it worked well enough and I wiped off the dash and the seat before chucking it into the back again. I was most eager to return the car, and I had visions of dropping it off at the turnpike end of Lover's Lane, then splitting. I believed there was a good chance that there'd be many people, even cops, at the scene of the original crime.

But Freeman surprised me once again as he swung sharply into the Silver Bird Diner parking lot where we lurched to a stop under the dark shadow of a large pine tree. He turned the key and killed the obnoxious thumping of the engine.

"What now?" I sighed in a state of hopelessness and resignation, noting that the right front fender was sticking out sideways, flapping about and hanging by a thin piece of metal, remarkably like in my dream.

"We go see my girlfriend! What else do ya think? I'll even buy ya ice cream this time!"

"Aw shit," I said, tagging behind like a puppy that had no choice in the matter. I wanted nothing but to jump into my bed and forget the night had ever occurred, then wake up in the morning and find it had all been a bad dream. I thought how much I had so desperately wanted a friend only a few weeks earlier; now I wondered about my sanity.

We sat by a window near the door and slurped our homemade sugar water, waiting for Vera to emerge from the back. I was glad the mud splatters on us weren't as bad as I had thought, and the wetness was rapidly drying. And I was glad there was hardly anyone in the diner to notice anyway, just an older couple in the corner who were making eyes at each other, and two old men at the far end of the counter who were talking over a meal.

A plump woman with a wrinkled face appeared seemingly out of nowhere to serve us, her gray hair pulled tight in a bun, with dark red lipstick and a name tag that said "Camille."

"You gentlemen are up rather late this evening." She beamed, putting a pen to her notepad. "Taking care of important business, I suppose," she added with a twinkle in her eye.

"Well, sort of," Freeman replied, obviously flustered at not seeing Vera.

"And just how might I help you now?" Camille had a most friendly smile, despite her wrinkles.

"Umm," said Freeman, apparently embarrassed yet determined to ask. He breathed deeply and continued. "You know that girl with the dark black hair that works here?"

"Vera?" Camille rolled her eyes and sighed.

"Yea, that's the one. I was hoping to talk to her."

"You mean along with every other guy in town?"

"Umm … I mean … well … is she working tonight?"

It did my heart good to see Freeman stumped like that.

"Oh, I'm not good enough for you, huh?" she teased. "Well, let me tell ya—anything she's got I've got a whole lot more of. And my line's a whole lot shorter than hers, honey." Camille laughed, her chunky arms and plump bosoms shaking as she did.

"Um … it's not that," stammered Freeman.

"Oh, wonderful!" she teased, putting her hand around Freeman's head and stroking his ear while he turned red as I imagined I had ever been.

Then she added as she continued stroking, "Well, honey, I have bad news for both of us. That girl was supposed to be here at midnight, but since she didn't show up this evening, I'm filling in for her. Though I do believe I'll kick her behind if she ever does show up. It's already almost one o'clock!"

"Oh." Freeman exhaled, clearly disappointed.

"So now … " Camille put her pen to her notepad. "Do you want something to eat, or would you like to sit here and cry about Vera?"

"Two ice cream cones, please."

"Vanilla, strawberry, or chocolate?"

"One vanilla," he replied.

"One strawberry," I added.

"Anything for two handsome young bucks." She smiled broadly at Freeman. "Christmas!" he said as she walked away. "She's not exactly what I had in mind."

"Well, don't look now, but I think there's something else you didn't have in mind, walking through the door behind you."

Freeman turned to see the new customer go straight to the counter, where he slammed his fist down several times causing the silverware and cups nearby to jump and rattle.

"Vera!" he bellowed loudly. "Vera! Get the hell out here!"

Vera didn't answer, nor did anyone else, but all the customers looked on in disbelief. After a moment, Camille appeared from the ice cream machine, vanilla cone in one hand and strawberry in the other.

"Mario! I told you yesterday she doesn't show up every night! Now you're going to have to leave before I call the cops again!"

"I'm not leavin'! She's my damn wife for Chrissake!"

"But she's not here tonight, Mario!"

"I know she's around here! And look at this, will ya?"

Mario held up a long wrinkled piece of clothing that looked a lot like the uniform Camille was wearing.

"It smells like puke for Chrissake!" he screamed, flinging it on the counter in disgust.

"And I got it right there in that freakin' car of that freak who's been screwin' her!"

"Well, I'm truly sorry for you Mario. But it ain't my fault, see? I just work here. Just like Vera's supposed to do every now and then."

Mario stumbled then regained his balance by grabbing the counter at the same time screaming, "She's hidin' in the back, ain't she?"

"You've been drinking again! What do you expect her to do if you're going to bury yourself in the bottle every night?"

"I only drink 'cause of her, ya old bag! Now get her out here before I have to beat the crap out of everyone in this place!"

"You moron! Sober yourself up and act like a normal human being! And don't ever call me an old bag!"

Camille reached from behind the counter and stuck my strawberry ice cream cone on Mario's nose, from where it protruded momentarily like a rhinoceros snout. Everyone in the place snickered and tried to hold back laughter, it looked so ridiculous. Mario grabbed the cone in a rage and threw it furiously at Camille, but she ducked and it spattered on the wall behind her.

"Now that does it! I'm callin' the police!" she screamed. "And the sooner you're out of here, the better off you'll be!"

She headed for the phone on the wall, and Mario suddenly turned around as if to see who was watching him. In another moment he saw us staring at him, and he stared back at us for what seemed like half a minute.

"Hey! Ain't you the retards who was stealin' the boards?" Freeman shook his head negatively, but it did no good. Mario stormed to our table and began pounding on it.

"What the hell are you doin' here? You're friends of that jackass, ain't yas?" We shook our heads.

"Mario, you leave them kids alone! They're innocent bystanders and you got no business talkin' to 'em!" Camille was dialing and trying to keep track of Mario at the same time.

"They're thieves!"

"You get out! Now!"

We said nothing, though I feared Mario would mush our skulls together. The veins of his forehead protruded and saliva sprayed over us as he spoke.

"Ya little bastards! I know yas had somethin' to do with this!"

We continued shaking our heads innocently.

"Now, Mario! Get out before the cops get here!"

Mario stomped back to the counter where he made a grand sweep with his arm, sliding cups, silverware, napkins, ketchup, and various containers off the edge. As they crashed to the floor, Camille was talking frantically on the phone.

"Ya ugly dog! You're all a bunch of dogs!" Mario roared to everyone in the restaurant as he kicked at the mess on the floor. Then he turned and stalked out of the place, stumbling against a chair and knocking it over on the way.

We looked through the glass and had to squint to see him due to the darkness and the reflections. He walked a wobbly line toward JC's car, nearly tripping over his own feet. He paused to consider the vehicle, like it might somehow be the source of all the problems in the world, then proceeded to kick the dangling fender.

The fender, hanging by that strip of metal, shot forward then snapped back and thwacked him in the shins. He shouted something, then jumped on top of it, as if doing so might kill it, but he slipped and fell backward, landing soundly on his rear end. The floppy fender swung forward, then flew back and whacked him in the chest.

He grabbed the metal angrily and commenced to wrestle with it, like he might be struggling with an alligator. He rolled over, twisting it, then shifted to his knees, prying at a different angle. With great effort, he stood up, still prying and bending, till he finally tore the piece off. There he stood, hugging that hunk of metal as though it might escape if he didn't.

I couldn't imagine what he was thinking, but next thing we knew he flung the fender violently at the side of the car where it clanged and bounced back to the pavement, then spun around two or three times and came to a stop.

He shouted at it for a few moments then came back to kneel under the window, nearly in front of us. He picked up a huge rock from the garden, carried it to the front of the car, raised it over his head and then brought that boulder down with a crash to the windshield.

We could hear it breaking, though it was hard to see clearly in the shadows. He was about to do it a second time when Camille burst out the restaurant door.

"They're on their way, Mario! If I was you, I'd get out! Now!"

The rock came down and smashed the windshield once again, and rolled to a stop on the hood. Mario turned and started toward Camille, who jumped back and dead bolted the door. She turned and said to us, as Mario pounded with two fists on the glass behind her, "Y'all are witnesses! You hear! This time he's done it! I want you to please remember what you just saw and be ready to tell the cops!"

Mario was still pounding and hollering obscenities when the flashing red lights shined through the restaurant windows. Three cops appeared in two cars. "You're hidin' her on me! I know ya are! She belongs to me, godblam ya! I'll beat the piss out of her!" I could hear his voice muffled by the glass.

I felt sorry for him but there was not much anyone could do. Meanwhile, the flashing lights helped focus Freeman's and my attention on the gravity of the situation. The shock of seeing Mario go insane wore off quickly.

"Say as little as you can," whispered Freeman. "Nothin' if possible! Ya gotta get this right or we're dead meat!"

The panic in my eyes must have told him he had my undivided attention. He leaned forward, speaking urgently. "Okay … we was sleepin' out at my place and couldn't sleep, so we took a walk. That's all ya gotta remember—nothin' else, 'cept what ya saw Mario do! Ya hear me?"

He grabbed my wrist and squeezed hard, like it was the most important thing I had to get straight in my life. Which seemed true enough at the moment.

"Got it."

I suspect it was the shock of all the events together that rattled my system enough for me to think clearly and talk like a normal person, and I imagined I did a pretty good job when the cop sat me down on his front seat, taking notes under a small yellow dash light.

"And you were here for how long before this guy came in?"

"Maybe ten minutes."

"And what were you here for?"

"Strawberry ice cream."

"Your friend's name again?"

"Freeman. I mean Freddie Freeman."

"And he lives next door to you?"

"Yes."

"And you don't know anyone who works at this place?"

I wasn't sure what the cop knew or what Mario had told him, but I was pretty certain he was trying to make a connection between Vera and us.

"Not really," I said, trying to stay calm.

"What do you mean, 'not really'?"

"Well, I've seen the name tags of the waitresses. And, of course, they're pretty friendly."

"Is that all?"

"Yes."

And so it went, with no real hard questions asked, like did you help steal JC's car, or how was it we found your puke on Vera's uniform? Or did it ever occur to you that it was Vera with JC in the sand dunes way back when? Or have you ever had the pleasure of meeting Mario before this evening?

It was a crazy night and there was no way we could go to sleep. We laid on the outdoor beds, but red lights still flashed in my brain, and a thousand thoughts raced through it.

"I thought something about her looked familiar. I just couldn't place her in that uniform," I observed as I tucked my hands under my head and gazed at the Milky Way, breathing the cool, fresh air.

"I was thinkin' the same thing. That long black hair and somethin' about her voice. And the way she moves! Damn, Joey! Now I've seen everything!"

"How do you think JC got to know her so well? That's what I can't figure out."

"He must have met her in the café and got her into his blasted car somehow. It's all I can think of. And it's why I need a car! But why on earth does she keep seein' a jerk like him? That's what's drivin' me nuts."

"And why is she married to Mario? She must have mental problems, though you'd never know it from looking at her." I swatted at a mosquito that had been buzzing around my ear. It felt like I got him.

"Poor old Mario. I could almost feel sorry for the guy, Joey. Except for his stealin' Vera from me. What a butthead!"

"How about JC and his new jalopy, if you want something to feel sorry about?"

"That SOB deserves it after what he done to us. Not to mention monkeyin' with Vera, while that schlump Mario's runnin' around like a wild fruitcake."

"But wouldn't you monkey with her yourself if you had half a chance?" Another mosquito or else the same one was buzzing around my ear, but he didn't show any interest in landing.

"That's a whole different story—I ain't no schmuck like JC."

"But she's gotta be eighteen or nineteen."

"I like that. She'll know how to treat me."

"But she's a married woman!" The mosquito landed and I brushed my hand hard over my ear. But just as quickly as I did, it was up and buzzing again.

"She can get a divorce. And she ought to! That drunken bum is no better than JC."

"How can you even want a woman who goes after clowns like them?"

"Why, that's easy! I'm the one she needs to straighten her out. Ain't that obvious?" I laughed for several seconds until it dawned on me he was serious. Then I rolled to my side and pretended to be coughing so as not to hurt his feelings.

"What do you think they'll do with Mario?" I managed to ask in between coughs.

"Prob'ly let him out tomorrow when he sobers up. Then some judge'll make him pay for fixin' the car."

A pang of guilt went through me as I thought about what we'd done to the car, or rather what Freeman had done to it. I wondered how Freeman could live with himself, but then I remembered he didn't have a conscience like I did. I was fairly certain he had none of those voices in his head forever telling him what's right and what's wrong. No little whispers saying "Do this," or "Don't do that," driving a guy crazy, the way they did to me. I was pleased the mosquito seemed to be buzzing around Freeman now.

"That ought to put a smile on Mario's face," I replied, for want of anything else to say.

"It'll make me happy! And it'll serve him right for callin' you a retard, Joey!"

He laughed and slapped his thigh a few times, and my pity for Mario vanished quickly. It occurred to me that any real sorrow I had ought to be for myself for acting like such a retard.

"So, Mr. Einstein," I said sarcastically, "what's your next step for winning Vera over?"

I heard a hard *thwack* and pictured Freeman's hand swatting the mosquito. "I gotta find out where she lives and pay a visit. Right now I'm wonderin' if Camille can get me her address."

"And risk getting caught by Mario?"

"I'll work somethin' out. You oughta know me that well by now."

It was true. I had no doubt he'd find a way to see her, given a little more time. I was amazed he still wanted to see Vera now that we knew she was Mario's wife, but at the same time I recalled someone on TV saying that love is blind, and this looked like a perfect example.

Then too, I had my own problems in the love department. I'd been putting off looking up Maggie, and I well knew why, though I hated to admit the possibility: What if she told me no? That the notes were not really hers? That she had only been flirting with me, like Freeman kept saying? That she didn't mean anything the way I was taking it?

Life would be hell! I'd never be the same again. I might even start looking forward to school, which would mean that life was worse than hell. In addition to which I was a coward and I knew it, and I was surely not worthy of someone as perfect as she was. Not to mention the horror of having nothing to say when I did see her. I had worked long and hard on my list of things to talk about, but it didn't amount to a hill of beans. I had five topics and they all sounded lame: the weather, Father Sedrick, how her eyes got so green, the fort, and what classes we'd be taking in September. I needed more, but for some reason my mind went on the fritz whenever I tried to add to the list.

So I had put off working on it, let alone looking Maggie up. And now I knew I'd hate myself all the more if Freeman actually made contact with Vera, as it appeared he would. A long silence passed and I nailed two more mosquitoes while Freeman swatted at a few more of his own. I was glad there were crickets galore that evening, producing all manner of comforting cricket noises.

"You know the difference between JC and us, Joey?"

"No. What?"

"We got no balls, and he's got 'em all."

It was a sorry, pitiful statement and a huge pill to swallow, but I knew there was much truth to it.

"What about a red convertible? You don't suppose that's got something to do with it?" I couldn't bear the thought of us taking all the blame for being losers.

"Yea, then why's he got one and we don't?"

"He's older and he's got a job?"

"If we had any real balls, we'd be buyin' a car for Matt and payin' him to drive us around."

"At least we have a nice place to go to," I reminded him.

"Yea, but who have we taken here so far?"

"Hell, we just barely finished the thing," I pointed out.

"We got no balls, Joey. That's all there is to it."

"Speak for yourself," I retorted.

But I knew it was so. At least partly so. I got butterflies just thinking about seeing Maggie; and I was flooded with fear at the thought of inviting her to the fort. Yet at the same time I knew I was miserable and that something had to be done soon. Real soon.

Eventually we drifted off and gave our troubled minds a much-needed rest.

It was late the next morning, as we munched stale Corn Flakes sloshed down with canteen water when Freeman brashly announced, "We gotta make it happen, Joey! We can't sit around and take this crap no more! Now here's what we're gonna do … "

Thus he laid out his plan for action, which he claimed was "guaranteed to kick us both in the pants," in a way we sorely needed. I was to figure out some way to see Maggie, he said, while he arranged to see Vera, some night very soon. We would report to each other thereafter to offer congratulations or condolences, depending on the outcome. At first this seemed like a splendid idea, but on second thought I saw a glaring hole in it.

"Suppose one of us gets lucky and the other guy gets shot down? It'll be all the worse for the loser!" Who I deeply feared would be me.

"That should encourage you to do a better job, Joey. Besides, what've ya got to lose?"

Of course he was right. Neither one of us could possibly be worse off than we already were. Or so it seemed to us both at the time.

We gave Matt ten comics to put in a phone call to Herman, since it was rumored that Herman could find out anything in the world through his various connections, and Matt knew him well enough to ask. It seemed like a good deal, especially since they were Freeman's comics.

Herman called back in less than an hour and informed us that Maggie lived in the trailer park to the west of the Silver Bird Diner. He also told Matt he'd help Freeman anytime, and be sure to tell Freeman thanks for what he did at the ball game. In addition, he gave Matt a phone number that was supposed to be Maggie's, which I promptly memorized.

At first I was sorry to learn that Maggie lived in a trailer park, since I'd always heard nasty things about people who live in such places. But on second thought I realized it was my dad who said those things, and they generally had to do with how much money people made—and I could not have cared less about that.

Matt appeared to be done talking by and by and went back to fidgeting with the gears of an old clock on the kitchen table. Freeman disappeared to use the bathroom but the second he was gone Matt turned to me.

"Herman said there are rumors going around about that girl, Joey. But I didn't want to say anything in front of Freddie."

"What kind of rumors?" I challenged him.

"He wasn't real clear, to be honest. But he said his sister said something about Maggie going out with older guys and … well, I don't need to tell you what older guys do."

"How would Herman's sister know anything?"

"You know how girls are. On the phone all the time yakking to all their girlfriends. It's like tom-toms in the jungle or Indian smoke signals or something."

"Well, I can't worry about rumors and what other people say. And I wouldn't even want to imagine what girls say about me." Of course I did worry about rumors, and I often tried to imagine what girls said about me. But I sure didn't want Matt to know that.

"Good point," he replied. "And you're probably right. Girls are jealous by nature and that makes them say all kinds of things. No point getting too worked up over it." He tinkered with the clock as he talked, evidently trying to unstick a few gears. "Still, I'd be a little careful if I were you."

"How do I 'be careful'?" I probed, trying not to sound offensive.

"You know. Just think with your big head and keep your pants zipped up, till you're good and sure about everything." He winked like that made some kind of sense. I was not happy, of course, to hear any of this. But at the same time I realized that behind any rumor about Maggie there had to be some other female jealous of her good looks. And while it was nice of Matt to avoid discussing this in front of Freeman, what did it really matter? Even if there was some kind of problem, I was obviously the person who could help Maggie overcome it.

"One more thing, Joey. What did you say that other girl's last name was?" I scratched my head. "What other girl?"

"You know. In the woods. By Hobo Haven."

"You mean Annabelle?"

"Yea, that's it. What's her last name anyway?"

"Flannigan. Annabelle Flannigan."

I picked up the back of the clock that Matt had removed and examined it.

"You know where she lives?" he asked.

"Harmony Court. In that big brick house at the end of the street."

"She goes to the academy, huh?" He reached for the back of the clock and I handed it to him.

"That's right. Why? You interested?" I asked.

"Naw. It's just that I got an old telescope I don't use, and she might want to have it."

True to his word, Freeman went back that very night to the Silver Bird Diner and schmoozed up to Camille. He soon found out what appeared to be a remarkable coincidence, which he revealed to me the next morning, on the swings in my backyard: Vera lived in the same trailer park that Maggie did! Neither one of us had an exact address, but it was not a big trailer park and Freeman was sure we'd find both places in a very short time. And he learned that Vera had called in to quit work that very morning, according to Camille.

"Which I don't mind one bit." He folded his arms, mimicking exactly what Camille had told him. "But that's because she's a jealous old bag, Joey," he added.

Camille also said she wasn't sure what the love of Freeman's life was up to now, and she didn't particularly care. She reminded Freeman that she was free herself and sure would appreciate a young buck like him—anytime!

"You really can't lose then, can you?"

"Aw Jeez, Joey! I'd rather be a monk!"

He assured me he was going to find Vera's trailer that very night and snoop around to learn what he could, even knock on the door if it looked like Mario was out.

"That's insane!" I balked, though at the same time I could offer no better plan if he was serious about Vera.

"Life is insane. But ya can't let some stupid little fact like that slow ya down," he replied.

My task was simpler, though no less nerve-wracking. Freeman correctly observed that I was already stalling.

"You could have taken step one yesterday," he pointed out mercilessly. "Besides which, what other choice do you have? Give up and forget about girls?"

It was the chilling truth and I knew it was so. The plan was for me to call Maggie and talk about things in general, relying on my list of topics, which was now up to seven and included where she'd moved from and what her astrological sign was. I would end the conversation by inviting her to visit the fort the next day. I imagined it would be easier for a cat to learn how to dance than for me to make the call, but, like Freeman, I could see no other option.

Freeman went off to help Matt dismantle a lawn mower engine, while I spent a good part of the day pacing around and around my room rehearsing what I'd say when I got on the phone with Maggie. After lunch I practiced in front of Freeman in his bedroom.

By late afternoon, I was worn out and ready to sleep for a couple of weeks, so stressful and overwhelming was the whole idea. I told Freeman I had to have a break and was going to check out new comics

in Callaghan's, to take my mind off The Most Important Phone Call of
My Entire Life.

"Go do it then. I need a good long nap after listenin' to ya anyway."

So I went downtown alone, my head so stuffed with words it was
like learning my catechism all over again. I was eager to bury my head
in a comic to relieve the tension. But a surprise was awaiting me, and it
blasted apart my well-laid plans like a cannonball. I was passing Rhinehart's Jewelry store, not twenty feet from the door to Callaghan's,
when some girl stepped out the door and into my path. I bumped into
her and nearly knocked her off her feet.

"Why don't you watch where you're … " the girl began to say,
before pausing. "Say, I've seen you before, haven't I?"

The girl was wearing dark sunglasses and a floppy straw hat so
it took a moment to realize this was none other than Maggie herself!
Blood rushed to my head and throbbed through my brain; everything
I had practiced was forgotten in an instant, elusive as answers to a ge-
ography test. My tongue moved of its own accord.

"And your name is … don't tell me! Maggie, isn't it?" I was pleased
I could sound so casual, when in fact I was boiling over with emotion.

"Yes. But I can't remember yours." She snapped her fingers as if
to help recollect. "Where have I seen you before?"

I imagined she was as flustered as I was and wanting to act as
cool as possible, so as not to embarrass either of us too much. On the
other hand, I thought, what if she really didn't know who I was? What if
I was just another guy she had bumped into and flirted with, like Freeman kept insisting? For an instant I was nearly consumed by doubt,
but then I remembered the love notes in my pocket and her warm
smile at church. Of course she knew! Damn you for making me crazy,
Freeman!

But then again, we both needed to play everything down to
avoid embarrassment. To acknowledge the powerful feelings we
shared would be far too humiliating. I was determined to do my part.

"Umm … I'm not real sure." I scratched my head a few times. "But
it had to be somewhere. Otherwise how would I remember you?"

"Lots of people know me. And you do look so familiar … Was it in school? No, I don't think … It seems like I saw you sitting somewhere … "

"Is it possible I was kneeling?"

"Oh yea! That's it!" She shook a finger in the air. "You're the guy I saw when we went to church that day!"

There! It was as I thought! There was a limit to how much she could pretend she didn't know me.

"That's right!" I raised both hands. "Joey with the notes!" I blurted out.

"Excuse me?"

"You know, Joey with the notes!" I winked and made up my mind to ignore my flushed face, along with the blank stare on her face.

"Oh." She looked down and acted like I had lost my mind. I assumed she was embarrassed, and to tell the truth, I didn't blame her.

"So … you're getting jewelry," I said, feeling like my brain was not connected to my tongue, or to any other part of me for that matter.

"A ring." She held out her hand and revealed a large silver ring with a turquoise stone, though I wasn't sure if it was that ring she was showing me or one of the smaller ones on three of her other fingers.

"It's pretty."

"Aren't you the guy who hangs out with Freddie Freeman?" she asked coyly, making me think of my conversation with Annabelle. Of course I assumed she knew the answer—after all, she knew where I lived, since she had delivered two love notes. But I played along anyway.

"Oh, yea. Once in a while."

I wasn't sure if it was a blessing or a curse in her eyes that I knew Freeman; so I assumed it was a curse and made up my mind to say as little as possible on the subject.

"Were you with him the other night?" she asked eagerly. "Everyone I know is talking about what happened!"

"What night do you mean?" I tugged at my ear, trying hard to be calm and casual. "Why, the night he stole JC's car!"

I imagined her friends were in the woods that night at the end of Lovers Lane, and I wondered how much anyone knew, and what kind of rumors must be flying around. Of course I knew the cops were involved after our escapade at the Silver Bird Diner, but I really didn't know who knew what.

"I umm … I did hear about that, come to think of it."

"I was so glad he did that! JC needed to learn a lesson!"

I wasn't quite sure what she meant, but it was my opinion JC needed a lot of lessons. And I supposed it didn't really matter: If she was glad about JC's car, why so was I! And she darn well ought to know I had a hand in it.

"Yea, I was with him, come to think of it." Her face beamed like this was truly wonderful, and my mouth moved in response without assistance. "If you want to know the truth, I was the one who put him up to it."

"Oh, I loved it! He had it coming to him!" She clasped her hands and seemed genuinely pleased.

"Well, he has given us a little grief in the past, you know?"

I realized she must be acting this way not so much because she cared about JC, but because she saw it as a way to talk to me while she avoided the issue of how madly in love she was. My chest puffed up and I think the redness of my face may have diminished, at least for a while.

"I am so glad someone finally gave him a dose of his own medicine!"

I shuffled my feet. "I can't even remember how I got the idea, but Freeman usually does what I tell him."

"Weren't you worried about the cops?" She acted as if I was her hero, and I felt ten feet tall.

"Naw." I put my hands in my pockets, shook my head like it was nothing. Like I stole cars every day, just for kicks! It did not occur to me to ask how she knew JC, or why she thought stealing his car was such a great idea, or even how she knew we did it. But she seemed happy, and that was all I needed to know.

"Next time, I think you ought to pop JC in the kisser a few times too!" She swung her fist in the air as if to show what she meant. Her turquoise ring gleamed in the sunlight, along with the little ones beside it.

I confess that seemed a bit nasty, coming from her. But at the same time I believed it was a superb idea, and certainly one that had occurred to me on a few occasions. And who in their right mind didn't want to punch JC's lights out? Besides, wasn't this girl merely trying to show that she liked me, and having trouble expressing herself?

"Well, then, next time I will!" I punched the air twice to show I meant it.

"I'd love to see that," she laughed. "Just you let me know when you're going to finish JC off, okay?"

So … she has a good sense of humor, I thought, convinced she was joking that I would finish JC off. I like that in a girl.

"Of course I'll let you know. Maybe we can do it tonight, huh?" I joked back. She laughed some more, then turned abruptly as if to walk away. "Well, it's been nice talking to you, but I really need to get going now."

This caught me by surprise, but at the same time I realized it was time to act or else blow my golden opportunity, which I would regret forevermore. My armpits were hot and wet and I was flustered and embarrassed, but nothing was going to stop me now! I was determined to take that first big step and break the icy wall of embarrassment that obviously stood between us.

"Why do you have to leave? I wanted to talk to you some more."

"I have to meet my sister. She's picking me up in a few … "

I was not about to let her get away like that! I cut her off, feeling bold and courageous as I did. "Well then … what time would you like to see me tomorrow?"

"What?" She looked at me like I'd lost my mind again, and I figured she must be one very good actress. Another plus for this girl! I noted. But in my frenzied condition, I didn't really care what she was thinking; I had but one goal before me.

"I'd like to show you the vacation house I built!"

Her eyebrows danced above her sunglasses, and I felt embarrassed for a moment.

"A vacation house?"

"It's way back in the woods. Where no one will ever see us!"

Her eyebrows went up higher and she said nothing. But after a moment she rubbed her chin. I recognized it as another sign that she was madly in love and too stunned to talk, not to mention ecstatic that I'd sprung the question.

"I can meet you here tomorrow at ten and we'll be there in twenty minutes!" I spouted out. Oh, I was delighted, and nearly beside myself with happiness!

"Are you out of your … " she started to say, then paused again. I was certain she was going to say, "Are you out of your mind with love, like I am?" but I imagined she was too embarrassed to say it. And I didn't blame her a bit!

There was a long silence and my heart melted as I looked at her. She took a breath and heaved her beautiful chest. "You do know quite a bit about JC, don't you?"

"Oh, a fair amount. I've known him since he was in third grade!"

"Really?"

"I used to be his best friend!"

She shook her head and relaxed, and the warm smile that I loved came to her face. It seemed like a strange interest, yet it furthered my belief that she must be so much like me—she just needed something to talk about, besides her true feelings for me.

"Okay, Joey. I'll meet you right here at ten o'clock tomorrow. I'd really like to learn a few more things from you."

With that, she turned and departed in the direction of the train station. Her blond curls bounced beneath her hat, the way they bounced that day in the grocery store; the tan, smooth skin on her shoulders shone in the sun, her hips moved so gracefully. Oh so very gracefully! And she wanted to see me the next morning and learn more about me! I was an expanding bubble of happiness, almost ready to burst. Just wait till Freeman got the news!

14

"Maybe you have been right all along," he conceded after I relayed the story as well as I could.

My heart did a handspring, or perhaps it was a cartwheel; Freeman's words were music to my ears. We were laying on the beds in his room and he raised up on an elbow to deliver his next thought.

"But somethin' still sounds a little fishy, Joey."

"The only thing fishy is you're jealous as hell. Not that I blame you one bit." I tossed the pillow from James's bed at him, but he ducked and it flew by.

"I ain't jealous. I'm in love with Vera. But she's married and I don't have a car. And I imagine JC is after my ass big time, and prob'ly Mario too. I don't have time to be jealous, Joey!" He flopped back and looked at the ceiling. "Besides, I'm glad for you and I hope it all works out. You need a girl as much as I do—maybe worse, the way you act sometimes."

I let that last remark go. "All right … what is it that sounds fishy then?"

"The fact that she doesn't 'fess up to the notes right off is one thing. Also that she seems so interested in JC."

"I told you, she's embarrassed about the notes. Who wouldn't be? And she likes to talk about JC for the same reason—she's too embarrassed to talk about us! She's madly in love, Freddie! That's how you are when you're in love! There's no other explanation!"

"Then I guess I'll keep my mouth shut, Joey. You got all the answers, so there's not much else I can do."

I imagined he was shutting up mainly so he could think about Vera, and, of course, he was right. My mind was made up, and even though I had a horrible case of the jitters, I was bound and determined to take Maggie to the fort and show her what I was made of. It was the chance of a lifetime and nothing anyone could say or do would slow me down! Maggie, oh Maggie! Maggie, oh Maggie! my mind kept singing over and over, like a broken record stuck inside me, or perhaps it was my heart.

Naturally I said yes when Freeman asked if I wanted to tag along with him to the trailer court that night. He claimed we'd find where both girls lived in short order, then snoop around Vera's trailer and learn whatever we could.

"But if I end up knockin' on the door, you gotta hang back in the shadows. Okay?"

"You don't have to say that twice! You think I'm going to stand there and risk having Mario open the door? Just because you're nuts doesn't mean I have to be."

Fortunately my mom had stopped giving me grief when I inquired about sleeping out, and simply said, "Okay." I don't think she ever ceased worrying about my soul, but she seemed to have resigned herself to the idea that I really did need a friend, even if it was a character like Freeman. I couldn't help but wonder whether my dad had greased the wheels, but then again I didn't waste much time worrying about it.

We left Freeman's around nine thirty, so it must have been close to ten that night when we got to the Trail's End Trailer Courts. The extreme darkness was the first thing that struck me about the place. Clouds blocked the moon and shadows from the trees covered the streets and small yards like a blanket. The two working streetlamps were dim and surrounded by leafy branches, so they did not provide much light.

"I guess we gotta go up close and look at each mailbox from an inch or two away," Freeman announced in a discouraged tone. "But there's only about ten streets in here, so I guess it can't be too bad."

Which would have been true, except that several places had slots in the doors instead of mailboxes on the street. And it seemed like every other place was home to a dog, and that all the dogs did nothing but bark for a living.

"Blast it! I didn't figure on this sort of crap." Freeman exclaimed halfway down the first block as we stood by a mailbox trying to read the name with his cigarette lighter. "If we get lucky their places will be ones with mailboxes. I think we should check all of the mailbox places first, then worry about the others only if we need to."

"You mean if these blasted dogs don't wake up the neighborhood first." We held to the shadows and slinked back and forth through the streets, creeping up to each mailbox like thieves in the night, in an effort to locate the women of our dreams. But by the end of the second to last street I was ready to quit, and I let that be known.

"No!" said Freeman. "Just one more street. They have to be in here somewhere."

"What if they don't have mailboxes? We'll never find them."

"Just one more street," he insisted. "Just check the mailboxes on one more street!" It was the urgency in his voice that drove me on. After all, where Maggie lived was not a major concern; she was going to meet me at ten o'clock in the morning, and we would fulfill our destiny elsewhere. But Freeman was getting desperate and I owed him the chance to make a fool or a corpse of himself, as the case might be.

It was the second to last mailbox on the last street, not far from where we started, in front of a long heavy equipment trailer, where I made out the name "Giovanni" in the feeble glow from Freeman's raspy lighter. "Here it is!" I shouted, causing a dog in a nearby trailer to bark several times.

Freeman, who had sat down on the equipment trailer for a smoke, came over and checked the name on the mailbox, then lifted me a foot off the ground with a bear hug. "Damn good work, admiral!" he exclaimed, before dropping me down.

"Now what?" I asked.

He pointed to a small, high window near the far end of the trailer, which emitted a dim yellow light.

"I'm gonna take a peek. You wait here." He passed me his half-used smoke. "Puff on a cancer stick while you're waitin'."

I leaned against what appeared to be an old dark Ford in the driveway, the kind that reminds me of a hot dog on wheels. I inhaled and blew smoke out my nose as Freeman moved across the grass toward the small, lit window. He walked up close to it, then came right back.

"Come with me! I gotta lift ya up so you can see. It's too high for me."

When we got to the window he knelt down and motioned for me to sit on his shoulders.

"Gimme the butt so no one sees it through the window."

I did what he said and was soon sitting piggyback atop his broad shoulders, a few yards in front of the little window.

"Get closer. All I see is a wall."

He moved in and my view expanded. It was the bedroom I was looking into, and there lay Vera on the bed, on her stomach, in nothing but pink panties and a bra that was open in back, her dark hair laying over her shoulders. On the nightstand beside her were three open beer bottles, along with an ashtray filled with cigarette butts. The yellow light came from a small lamp with a pale crooked shade, on the side of the bed. The softness of her body in the dim light filled me with longing.

"Whad'ya see?"

"Shhhhhh! It's nothing!" I swatted him lightly on the side of the head, and soaked up the scene as well as I could.

"Is she in there or what?" he whispered.

Her hips moved and one breast became partly exposed, like a small water balloon. I sat frozen on Freeman's shoulders. It was the first real live breast I ever saw close up like that. A hot flash swept over me and a throbbing developed down below.

"I'm gonna dump ya if you don't tell me what's goin' on!"

"Let me down then." I feared Freeman might feel the swelling in my pants anyway. I scrambled to the ground and sat cross-legged, motioning for him to do the same. But just as I was preparing to describe what I'd seen, headlights turned a corner and a car raced up the street wavering back and forth, as if a little kid was driving it. Back and forth went the lights till suddenly the vehicle shot onto the grass and skidded to a stop in the middle of the lawn, not thirty feet in front of us.

"It's Mario!" Freeman said as the driver's door flew open and a body stumbled out. "Drunk as a skunk!"

My instinct was to jump up and run but Freeman clamped his hand on my arm and signaled for me to follow. We scurried on all fours through a break in the skirting beneath the trailer, a short way from the front door, where we crouched like puppies in the shadows. We watched as Mario staggered to the door, which was in the middle of the trailer. He was oblivious to us hiding there, perhaps two car lengths away, when he turned the doorknob several times.

It didn't open, and he began banging.

"Vera! Open the damn door!"

The door remained shut, and Mario banged all the harder. "Open the door, Vera! Now!"

"You're drunk again!" came a muffled cry from inside.

"I ain't drunk! I just had a few drinks! Now lemme in!"

He pounded as he spoke but the door remained shut. Freeman shook my arm, as if to indicate this was going to be one exciting show.

"You parked on the lawn, you drunken moron!" came Vera's voice.

"It's my lawn, ain't it?"

Mario began kicking at the door, running back and kicking again, several times, before we heard Vera's voice again. "All right! Stop kicking and I'll let you in!"

The door swung open and Mario disappeared inside. Freeman grabbed my shirtsleeve and dragged me back out and closer to the door.

"We gotta hear this, Joey! Every word!"

The door remained ajar and we stopped a short distance from it. We could see into the living room but we only heard the voices of Mario and Vera.

"Every night you leave me in this two-bit shoebox while you're out drinking! We'll never get out of this hole with you drinking your paychecks away!"

"I started drinkin' when you started seein' that young punk!"

"I was trying to teach you a lesson!"

"Oh, great lesson! The cops come around asking how did this kid get a copy of the dozer key, so everyone can figure what kind of girl I married! Yea, that was a real great … " There came a loud crash, like a plate breaking.

"And why did I start seeing him? You got drunk and put your paws all over my sister first! How many times do we have to go through this?"

"You tell me, Vera! Who's the one who taught her how to flirt the way she does? And who taught her to smile at guys like that?"

"Every girl should know how to do that. It didn't mean you had to put your filthy hands on her!"

"Yea? And who bought her that low-cut blouse? Who's the one she tries to act like? What was I supposed to do when she started acting the way you showed her?"

"She's fifteen, for God's sake! What were you thinking?"

"That didn't stop you from teaching her to act like a whore!"

"You pig!" I feared Vera's raised voice might pierce my eardrums, and it sounded like another plate crashing. "I only wanted to teach her how to get a real man!"

"That's exactly what she was gettin'!"

"And here's what you get!"

"Aaaaaaahhhhhh!" screamed Mario as sounds of crashing and banging came through the living room door, as though someone were falling down." "My God, Vera! Don't kick me there!"

"Let's see if you try to touch my little sister again!"

More thrashing and banging filled the air. Freeman put his hands to his ears as if to block the sounds. I shook my head in disbelief. All I could imagine was chairs being thrown about, bookshelves falling, lamps crashing. Lights came on across the street. A couple in their pajamas came out next door, but the woman pushed the man back inside after a couple more crashes and shouts.

"I never should have married you, Mario! And I wish I never had your kid!"

"Don't say that!" screamed Mario. "Good God, how can you say that?"

"It's true, you piece of crap! You don't care if you wake him up with your drunkenness! You don't even know where he is right now! You're no kind of father!"

"I married you to raise my son! But you're a whore! I knew ya was a whore the first time we did it!"

"Why you … !"

Slapping and punching sounds came through the door, and I imagined it was Vera assaulting Mario like a tiger, but there was no way to tell who was after who, or even whether someone was being hit.

But it didn't really matter. Red lights were soon flashing at the end of the street, and we dashed back under the skirting.

By the time the third police car arrived, four cops had handcuffed Mario and bent him over the trunk of a car. One cop stayed with him, holding his face down. Ten or fifteen neighbors materialized, seemingly from nowhere, and were told repeatedly to stand back and go home, though no one seemed to be listening. We peered out from our hiding place, enjoying the show in spite of our cramped condition and the stench of cat turds.

"You sure you're all right, ma'am?" one officer was asking Vera, who stood on the front steps in a loose bathrobe that ended above her knees, as we could see from the shadows below.

"I'm fine. Just don't let me ever see that man again!"

"This is the third time in a week, ma'am; I don't guess the judge will let him out for a few days. You might want to think about getting some help in the meantime, ma'am."

"I'll be with my family in Hartford by the end of the week."

"I'd advise it, ma'am," said the officer.

"You whore! Go ahead and screw him, too!" shouted Mario from the street. "But you can't take my kid away from me!"

"Shut up!" said the cop standing over him as he banged Mario's head into the trunk. The officer near us stepped closer to Vera, shaking his head. "That poor schmuck will never learn. Some people never change."

"Oh, that's so true, officer." Vera touched the cop's elbow.

"Bastard!" hailed Mario from the street.

His head banged down again with a dull thunking sound. Freeman touched his own head, as if in sympathy. My face grimaced as I imagined how he must have felt, but at the same time I thought, "Who's the retard now, Mario?"

It was another ten minutes or so before all but one of the police cars had disappeared, and the crowd evidently went back wherever it came from. I was anxious to crawl out and stretch my limbs, not to mention get back to Matt's tent where our sleeping bags were and catch some sleep. I'd had enough for one day!

One cop sat in the car waiting for the last officer to break away, but he seemed unable to.

"You just don't know how much I appreciate your being here," Vera was saying. "I can't imagine what I'd do if you hadn't come by." She was standing inches from the cop and she stroked his arm as she spoke. Light from the living room illuminated the V in her bathrobe that went almost to her waist.

"It's a pleasure to come around. Any more troubles, you just call that number I gave you there … anytime!"

"You're sure you wouldn't like a cup of coffee?" She continued stroking his arm.

"Well, you know I would … but my buddy there needs to get going." The cop motioned to the car in the street.

"You sure he can't come back and get you in an hour or so?"

"Well, that wouldn't be … aw, hell. Lemme see."

The policeman walked to the car and bent over by the driver's window. Low voices could be heard for a minute or two, then the engine started and the car drove off. A moment later the cop was back.

"No problem. I can call him on the radio whenever I want."

"Oh, I like that idea, Officer! Won't you please come in and … um, give me a hand?"

The tone of her voice reminded me of the way she sounded the day we met her in the café. I thought of her lying on the bed in her panties, and I was filled with jealousy toward the cop, who silently followed her into the trailer.

The door shut, and although I couldn't see too well in the shadows, it looked like Freeman's face dropped several inches. He breathed out and I felt great sorrow for him. My best friend, stripped of his life's dream in less than thirty seconds!

At the same time, I realized how lucky I was to have a younger girl waiting for me the very next morning. I wished there was a way I could share my joy, but I could think of nothing to say that seemed appropriate. We walked to our summer home lost in our own thoughts, and all I remember saying as we crawled into our sleeping bags was, "Get some sleep, Freddie. I think that will help a bit."

"Yea, right," he mumbled, dejected as I'd ever heard him.

15

I sat in the warm sunshine on the sidewalk, my back to Rhinehart's Jewelry store, waiting, wondering, worrying; excited and at the same time filled with fear. Would the dream of my life stand me up on our first date? The very first date I ever had? My watch said 11:10 and I'd been there over an hour. Could she really have changed her mind? What was the first thing I'd say if she did show up?

"Hey, kid!" the clerk hollered from the door of Rhinehart's. "Why don't you go find somewhere else to sit?"

"I'm waiting for someone."

"Sit somewhere else, will ya? You're makin' a bad impression here."

"But I'm supposed to meet her here!"

He looked me over like I was one sorry case, while he contemplated what to say next. "I'll give you ten more minutes. Then I want you out of here!"

I looked frantically up and down Main Street for the Girl of My Dreams, but still no trace. Cars came and went with people traveling here, there, and everywhere, but no sign of Maggie. My heart was sinking fast and I could see my dreams vanishing, much like Freeman's had. Eleven thirty rolled around. The guy from Rhinehart's poked his head back out.

"Looks like you lose, kid. Time's up, huh?"

"Yea." I rose sadly and began trudging off. Just as I did an old brown Ford pulled to the curb. My heart stopped as the passenger door swung open, and out stepped the girl with blond hair and green eyes.

"You are here! I didn't know if you'd really show up."

As the car pulled away, I heard the woman driver shout, "He's a cute little boy, Maggie!"

She had on a pink skirt that barely went to her knees, and a tight white blouse that revealed breasts that were the perfect size for her body. A large brown purse hung by a strap around her neck. Sunglasses wrapped around her eyes, her blond curls bounced just like I remembered, and she wore the same straw hat she had the day before. She may as well have been an angel, descending to pay me a visit.

"So ... you're going to show me your vacation home?"

"I'm really glad you want to see it!"

"I'm not really certain that I do. But maybe some of the things you can tell me will make up for it."

I wasn't sure what she meant, but her words were music, and the sight of her a feast for my eyes. "It's about a fifteen- or twenty-minute walk. I guess I should have told you to wear jeans and sneakers."

Her flimsy sandals did not look comfortable, and jeans would have been much better for the woods.

"I guess this will have to work." She waved her hand vaguely over her outfit.

"Anyway, I'm not real keen on sneakers and jeans. They're so tomboyish, if you know what I mean."

I promptly forgot all that I had planned to talk about as I took in this remarkable sight. But it soon became evident that it didn't matter. When Maggie began talking, there was scarcely time for me to utter a sentence anyway.

"You know, my sister is such a pain! She made me babysit this morning just because she's too busy with her petty little problems to deal with her own kid."

I had started walking, and now she was walking beside me making me feel ten feet tall. The Woman of My Dreams walking beside me! Oh, but I was delighted.

"I swear she thinks I'm a slave!" Maggie went on. "And I had to watch my nephew the last few nights so she could 'work things out with her husband,' who's a complete creep!"

She spoke sarcastically and moved her hands rapidly as she did, making me think at first that gnats were bothering her. But I soon realized it was just the way she talked.

"I don't know why she even married him. Oh well, I do know. It's because she had to. Well, she didn't really have to, if you know what I mean."

"Umm-hmm," I said repeatedly, nodding my head to indicate I was listening.

On and on she talked, without ever keeping quiet long enough for me to recall the topics on my list. Then again, I thought, I no doubt would remember them if I weren't straining so hard to listen to what she was saying.

"Of course it's a crying shame that Sunnyville has so few guys to look at," she declared at one point.

"I'm glad there's a few!" I beamed, thinking of my own lucky self, proud to be at the top of her short list.

"Oh, there's a few, there's always a few. I could never stay otherwise. And then there's problems with the school, like how boring the classes are. Hang on a minute."

She stopped to take off a sandal and shake it out, grabbing my arm for support.

"Damn pebbles," she said, then continued her complaints about the school. "I can't even take dance or home ec, for Pete's sake! And the cliques around here … brother! They are something else … "

"Umm-hmm," I mumbled, "umm-hmm."

"You know, I was so very interested in the things you were talking about yesterday!" She paused as if to be sure I was listening properly. "I can't believe you've known JC since he was a little kid. Or that you were the one who wrecked his car!"

Again I wondered what kind of rumors must be going around. But only for a second, because Maggie suddenly stopped walking and looked at me like I was supposed to respond. My mouth opened seemingly without my assistance.

"Well, we used to be friends. Way back in third grade."

I didn't want to talk about JC, not in the least, but he seemed to be a major interest for her, and I couldn't figure how to change the subject.

"So … what happened?"

"About what?"

"About you know, that you're no longer friends."

I resumed walking, forcing her to tag along. "He turned into a know-it-all. Everything had to be his way. He was always right and everyone else was always wrong. Especially me."

"That's not so bad, is it?"

"It was to me."

"Plenty of people like things their way. It's a sign they know what they're doing."

We had come to the junkyard, and I debated whether to ask if she wanted a rest. But that might mean coming up with even more things to talk about, and I didn't want to press my luck. So I kept walking, following the zigzag trail that meandered through the junkyard. I was disappointed when I suddenly realized that Maggie was actually a bit taller than I was, which I hadn't noticed till then. I imagined she'd grown an inch from the time I'd seen her in the grocery store. But I wasn't going to let something silly as that slow me down.

She kept asking about JC, and I kept giving the shortest possible answers.

"So how long ago did he move to Sunnyville?"

"Probably five years ago."

"Has he gone to St. Frances all that time?"

"Yep."

Why couldn't she think of something else to talk about? Was she really that interested in JC? Well, I reckoned, at least I wouldn't need to use up my own topics till she got done. And I couldn't deny that JC was an odd enough character that anyone might find him an interesting topic of conversation, at least for a while.

"Why don't we sit down and rest for a minute?" I said at last, hoping that might put her mind in a different groove and get her mouth moving on another topic. I pointed to a log and we both sat down.

"He goes to church every week, does he?"

"As far as I know."

"Has he gone out with any other girls?"

I hesitated, not sure if she knew about Vera. "What do you mean 'other girls'?"

"You know. Has he gone out with a lot of girls?"

"Oh, a couple." I thought of rumors I'd heard about him and two girls from Freeman's school, in addition to what I knew about Vera and him, but decided not to bring those matters up. I couldn't tell if my answer satisfied her, or if she decided she didn't want to know any more.

She paused for a moment, as if contemplating my response, which gave me a chance to recall the topics on my list. I made up my mind to change the record. I would use my topics to get her mind off JC.

"Beautiful weather, isn't it?"

"Yea. I love sunshine."

I stretched my arms and tried to pretend I was feeling casual and relaxed, but nothing could have been further from the truth.

"So … have you ever been to confession with Father Sedrick?"

"No. But I'm ready to start walking again."

She got up and I did too, and we continued toward the fort.

"Well, don't. He asks way too many questions."

"Oh." She glanced at me quizzically as she adjusted the purse strap around her neck, while proceeding to walk with her head down. We continued a ways before I could remember my next question.

"How did your eyes get so green, anyway?"

"My mother has green eyes."

It seemed like several minutes before I was able to recall what else was on the list.

"Oh, yea! I can't wait to show you the fort!"

Maggie stopped in her tracks.

"I thought you were going to show me a vacation home?"

"Well, I am. But you can call it a fort if you want."

"I like 'vacation home' better."

"Yea, I can understand that."

Silence and a lengthy walk ensued, while I struggled to dredge up the next topic. Maggie did not seem overly enthused, but at least she was walking beside me.

"Now I remember! Have you figured out what classes you're taking next year?"

"No. I don't worry too hard about that sort of thing till school starts. Plus I know they don't have the classes I really want."

"Oh." My mind seemed to be racing as fast as my heart as I struggled to recall my last few topics.

"So … what's your astrological sign, anyway?"

"Cancer. But I don't believe in that sort of stuff."

Another flat tire! I vowed next time I would have a much longer list, and I would think of follow-up questions. I had one subject left, and I knew I had better develop it.

"So … where did you move from?"

"Connecticut."

"Oh. That's a nice place, huh?"

"It's okay."

That shut me up like a sealed envelope, and I could see that I needed to learn how to expand on different subjects better. Conversation with girls was definitely not my strong suit. Right then I didn't know what was my strong suit, or even if I had a suit. A painful silence followed until Maggie asked, "So, how long before we get to this place?"

"Oh, not much farther."

I was glad one of us still had a brain that worked. We were almost at the trail to the fort but as we approached the scrub oak Maggie froze in her tracks.

"Whoa! Hang on a second here! You expect me to go in that place?" She pointed in the direction of the woods.

"Don't worry. There's a real nice trail."

"I hate the woods! They give me the creeps. Who knows what's going to jump out at you?"

"Nothing's going to jump out! I've been coming here all summer."

"It looks like a jungle!"

"But the trail makes it … you know, makes it okay." I didn't know what else to tell her.

"What about snakes? I hate snakes!"

"I never even saw one in here."

"That doesn't mean there aren't any!"

"But even if there were they wouldn't be poisonous."

"Just the sight of them is poisonous!" A look of disgust passed over her face.

"Look … I'll go first and scare them off. I promise!" I held up my hand as if in scout's honor.

"What about ticks?"

"I never had one yet." Well, I had gotten two on me once, the same day Freeman picked up three, but that was not the same as having one.

"If I ever had to cut my hair, I don't think I could live with myself!"

"Why would you have to do that?"

"Because of ticks! Why else?" She spoke like I was not too smart, and I wondered if maybe that's what girls do when they have ticks, though I'd never heard of it before.

Overall, I had to admit, her behavior was something of a disappointment. But then I realized she must have grown up without woods around her house and, after all, she was only a girl. On top of which I reckoned all her fears would vanish if I could just get her to the fort.

"There's nothing to be afraid of. Really! And there's a beautiful vacation home at the end, like I promised. And it's only about four or five more minutes!"

"Oh, all right! But if you're wrong about snakes, I'll scream so loud it will break your eardrums!"

We could not have gone more than ten feet farther when she screamed at the top of her lungs. I wheeled around to look and she was flapping her hands madly in the air, terrorized by something. My heart nearly stopped at the sight.

"What's the matter? What's the matter?" I asked frantically.

"A snake is biting my back! Get it off! Get it off!"

I looked closer to see what in the world she was talking about. "That's not a snake! It's a branch!" I reached behind her and snapped the scrub oak.

"Oh, good God! It felt just like a snake!"

"Snakes move on the ground," I pointed out.

"I thought it was one of those snakes that hang from trees and jump around your neck."

"Like in the movies?"

She nodded.

"That kind doesn't live around here."

"How should I know that?" she asked.

We started up and moved slowly, and she insisted I break off several branches ahead of her so they wouldn't snag or rip her clothing. "These clothes cost a lot of money and I have no intention of letting anything happen to them!"

Not much further along, she let out another scream after stubbing her toe on a root that crossed the trail. This was followed by a string of swear words that made me blush, while she did a jig and held her toe. I was a little surprised at her language, but on second thought I realized I'd be screaming too if I'd slammed a root with my toe. And after all, it was her first trip in.

"I'm really sorry I didn't tell you to wear sneakers."

"You really should get this paved, you know. This is the kind of thing sidewalks were made for. Look at that! I scratched my toenail polish!"

It seemed like a serious battle to keep her moving, and remarkably different from how I had pictured it—sneaking in late at night, her holding my hand, clinging to me for security, like a hero in a movie. But we arrived at last at the clearing. I marched proudly to the center of it and opened my arms wide.

"We're here!"

"This is the place?"

"Our vacation home!"

"So where's the home?" She looked around blankly.

"There!" I pointed to the fort that Freeman and I spent over half the summer making, risking our bodies and souls for and devoting buckets of blood, sweat, and tears to.

"This is it?"

I shook my head happily.

"You're pulling my leg! All I see is a pile of dirt!"

"No! Inside! You've got to go inside!"

I walked over and pushed the door in, inviting her to come and have a look.

"You have to be kidding!"

"About what?"

"About going inside that thing!"

"But this is it! It's the place I've been telling you about! Once you get inside, you'll see!"

"I wouldn't go in that thing for a million dollars! I'd be surprised if you could get a caveman to go in there!"

First I thought she was joking. But even with her sunglasses on I could tell from the lines around her mouth that she was scowling. My heart sank and a chilling despair came over me.

I walked to a grass bed and sat cross-legged upon it, facing her. I motioned for her to sit on the other bed, but she shook her head.

"Do you have a cigarette?" she asked.

"No. I um … I forgot to bring them."

"Why am I not surprised?" she said to herself, reaching into her blouse and producing a pack of her own.

"Please," I said as she lit her cigarette, without offering me one. "None of this is going right and I need to talk to you."

"About what?"

"About these!" I tilted sideways and pulled her two letters from my back pocket, then waved them in the air at her.

"What have you got there?" She exhaled a cloud of smoke.

"The letters you sent me!"

"Letters I sent you?" She sounded genuinely shocked. "I didn't even know your name till yesterday!"

It was then I realized that she had to be kidding about the letters, about the fort, about the snake, about everything. There was no other explanation! No other possible explanation! I suddenly felt relieved and lightheaded. This was the girl for me after all! What a keen sense of humor, I thought, and how long she can maintain it! I really like that in a person!

"C'mon! Just read them to me!" I said. "I've probably read them a hundred times myself, thinking of your voice while I did."

She looked at me like I'd lost my mind but I figured that too was part of the act. What else could it be?

"C'mon." I motioned again for her to sit down.

"You're nuts!" she said.

"But these are the most beautiful words I ever read in my life!" I replied. "How can you be embarrassed?"

"I'm not embarrassed. Except for being around you."

"C'mon! Just do it!" I smiled even though I had a terrible feeling that something was not quite right.

Finally she came over and sat on Freeman's bed. Without another word she held out one hand while she took a drag from her cigarette from the other. I passed over the first letter, which she proceeded to read aloud:

joseph simpson how i love you,
joseph simpson yes i do,
your gentle eyes they really send me,
and your words, how they thrill me!
your voice so soft,
takes me aloft,
for weeks on end.

She stopped to laugh, and to cough, and only after several moments did she stop laughing long enough to speak. "You are insane! You brought me here to show me a pile of dirt and have me read this … this little kid rhyme to you?"

I nodded, telling myself she must still be joking, even though in my heart I felt something was going rapidly in the wrong direction. She shook her head in disbelief, but proceeded just the same.

do you remember
our time together?
oh so sweet!
why don't we meet,
and try once more?
all my love,
your one and only

It took a minute for her to finish shaking her head and stop laughing and coughing a few more times, and by then I was cringing inside.

"You really think I wrote this to you?"

"You signed the other one! Remember?"

I persisted, even though I felt frantic and filled with profound anguish.

"What other one?"

I handed her the second note, which she took and read, stopping now and then to laugh to herself, and once to put her cigarette out.

hi joey! i saw you walking down the street, and my heart skipped a beat. you look so divine, i wish you were mine. so talk to me, can't you see? i'd do anything in the world, if you'd ask me to be your girl. love, me!

When she got done I pointed to the initials at the bottom.

"Those are my initials, but this is little kid stuff! I would never dream of writing such nonsense!"

"But you smiled at me in church! And in the grocery store!"

"I smile at lots of people! I'm a friendly person—usually. But I can't imagine that you'd think I'd write something like that to you!"

"You mean you really don't love me?" It was a last-ditch effort but I had to ask—no ifs, ands, or buts. There was nothing to lose and I had to know. I could see no other way.

"Love you? I don't even know you! You're pathetic!"

It was as if I'd been shot by a machine gun. My chest tightened up and I feared my breathing might stop. On the other hand, I almost hoped it would. How could this be? Was this really happening? I started to speak, to ask how come she even offered to see me if all this was true. But although my lips moved, I discovered I could not speak.

"You look like a dying fish!" she offered in a caustic tone for sympathy. "You're more pathetic than my brother-in-law! I thought I'd seen it all when that jerk tried to attack me. But you … you're a total basket case!"

I sat holding my head since I suddenly had a terrible, splitting headache, nearly as bad as when I had the hangover. The pressure behind my eyes was ferocious and I felt that if it got much worse I might go blind.

"I wish Vera was here to see this. She may be a fool but I think even she could appreciate this sight." Maggie stood up, lit another cigarette and walked in a small circle. "Thank God we'll be out of this stink hole in a week or so!"

I rocked back and forth holding my head, wishing this girl would just disappear and leave me alone. But she kept pacing in a circle, talking to herself, and smoking like a chimney, as if this was relieving her nerves.

"All 'cause of that jackass Mario! And then Vera going after JC for revenge. This has got to be the craziest town in the world!" She was moving her arms around and waving her cigarette in the air as she talked, looking at the ground, then at the sky, almost as if she was in as much pain as I was. She stopped pacing and again sat down on Freeman's bed, looking at me but still talking to herself.

"And now this little nitwit telling me he used to be JC's best friend and thinking I'm in love with him!"

My eyes widened as it slowly dawned on me who this girl must be. I felt like my head had been whacked in the side by a huge rubber mallet, in addition to my other problems.

"Mario! You … you're Vera's sister!"

"Of course I'm her sister. Did you think I was her brother?"

"You're the one she was talking about!"

"She's always talking about me, that jealous witch. Now she's even running around with JC because she thinks it'll make us even."

"Wait a minute! Wait a minute!" I put my hands on my ears, like a three-year-old, trying to believe what I was suddenly realizing, without hearing more. "You're saying Vera's been with JC to get even with you—because Mario … Mario … "

"Because Mario put his filthy paws all over me when he was drunk?" She looked at me as if to let the words sink in. "That's exactly what I'm saying. And I'd let her have JC in two seconds, except I can't let her get the upper hand."

I said nothing, just looked at her while shaking my head, and she did the same to me. A long while passed during which I tried to adjust to this harsh new picture of reality. I began to wonder what she was thinking now, and I asked myself how I could have ever thought of her the way I had. At the same time, I realized I still had no idea who did send those notes. I was so devastated and confused.

"Well," she rose to her feet and brushed pieces of dry grass from her skirt, "I guess there's no point hanging around here anymore. Though I must admit it's been entertaining. Truly entertaining!"

With that the girl who had been the love of my life for all those months, the object of my dreams day and night, the vision from heaven that kept me going, turned and began walking away.

"Don't you want me to show you the way out?"

"I can find my own way out."

"The trail is over there." I pointed to the trail in the opposite direction she was headed, and she turned and started that way.

"But aren't you afraid of snakes?"

"No."

So she had been lying all along, merely to get information from me about JC! I could hardly believe this was happening, but at the same time I breathed a huge sigh of relief to get rid of her. Oh, what a fool I'd been!

I sulked around my house for a day, laying in bed, staring at the ceiling, flipping through comics without reading them, even glancing at the covers of two books on my summer reading list. I was so depressed and beside myself that I said okay when Timmy asked me to play rummy with him. He beat me three times in a row, but I didn't even care.

"I wish you'd play with me more," he said. "It seems like all you ever do is hang out with Freddie Freeman these days."

"We have other interests. That's what happens when you get older."

"Yea, yea. Girls, girls, girls," he replied in disgust. "They're nothing but trouble, Joey."

"How would you know?"

"You'd be surprised how much I know. Real surprised."

It was the boasting of a little twerp, and it merely reminded me why I'd been so happy to have Freeman as a friend. I picked up the cards and made up my mind to go see Freeman. He hadn't made contact for the last twenty-four hours, reinforcing my belief that he was as depressed as I was. I thought maybe we could cheer each other up.

I found Matt and James on the floor in their living room but neither one knew where Freeman was.

"You should sit down and play Monopoly with us anyway." Matt pointed to a spot on the floor.

"Thanks, but I better figure out where that guy is and see what's going on." One part of me wanted to blurt out about Maggie, to explain what a wacko I'd fallen in love with, in hopes that talking would make me feel better about it; but another part of me wanted to tell absolutely no one about Maggie, not even Freeman, let alone Matt and James.

"He's been really strange the last two days," Matt acknowledged as he laid a utilities card on the board. "He doesn't talk that much anymore. All he does is mope around. What do you think's wrong with him anyway?"

"Yea, he won't even read comics to me!" exclaimed James, who seemed more interested in petting Doc than winning Monopoly.

"Must be that time of month," I joked. "Though it's hard to know what the guy is thinking."

Of course I was certain he was thinking exactly what I was thinking—that you have to be a damn fool to get all worked up about a female, and that it's a big, bad mistake to start dreaming about one in the first place. She'll probably never be what you thought, and in the end you'll feel nothing but depressed and miserable. Like I did that very moment. The whole thing is enough to drive a guy bonkers, and I had no doubt it was the same thoughts that were making Freeman appear so strange to his brothers.

"Good luck," said Matt. "I hope you've got some ideas to cheer him up. I've never seen him this bad."

"Me too!" echoed James. "You cheer us all up, Joey! You're just like Santa Claus!"

"I'll see what I can do, guys."

I finally found that dejected lump of flesh in the garage, plopped in a hammock, gaping at the ceiling like a corpse.

"How's everything?" I asked.

He didn't respond, didn't even move an inch, and I wondered if maybe he was dead.

"Screw 'em all, Freddie!" I said with more enthusiasm. "They're nothing but trouble!"

He continued staring at the ceiling, and I had to look closer to be sure he was still breathing. I pulled up a stool and sat beside him.

"We lived all our lives without 'em, Captain! We don't need 'em now! They're nothing but trouble anyway." It was a big fat lie and I despised the fact that I sounded so much like Timmy, but it was all I could think of.

"I wanna die, Joey. There's no point in livin' anymore. I'm gonna die right here in this hammock."

"You can't die from lying in a hammock."

"I will if I don't eat."

"It's just natural feelings," I consoled him. "Everyone goes through the same thing sometime in their life." I had no idea if this was so, but it seemed like it might be, and I had to tell him something.

"How would you know?" His gaze didn't move from the ceiling.

"You're not going to believe this, but I'm in the same boat, Freddie."

It took several moments for that to register, but then he sat up a bit and pointed a crooked finger at me. "You too?"

"Maggie is a bitch from hell, Captain. You won't believe what happened!"

He sat up all the way as I relayed most of what I could remember, what Maggie said about the fort, her attitude toward the woods, how she hadn't written the love notes. He showed even more interest when I explained who she was and her connection to Vera and Mario. Of course I wanted to tell the whole truth and nothing but the truth, but I couldn't quite bring myself to it. In fact, things got twisted quite a bit, even though it wasn't what I intended.

"So she made you read the love notes, even after she admitted she didn't write them?"

"She insisted! I think she would have attacked me if I'd said no."

"And she cried when you read them?"

"She said they actually made her love me, and she could easily understand how I thought they were from her."

It wasn't that I wanted to deceive him so much as the fact that his questions seemed to draw certain answers out of me. It's hard to explain, but I just kept spouting off whatever it seemed might perk him up, without making myself look too ridiculous. But the fact is I had no idea what might come out next.

"Well, if she loved you all of a sudden why didn't you make some moves?"

"I didn't need to; she tried to put the make on me!"

"What exactly did she do, anyway?"

"She put her hand on my leg and tried to kiss me."

"And?"

I was glad he was talking and showing some interest in living, instead of lying there all depressed. So I kept on going, despite the fact that I felt lowdown and despicable for lying like that.

"Of course it wasn't easy to call her off, but in the end I had to. There was no way I wanted any part of a girl who was used by Mario. Not to mention someone who didn't like our fort!"

"I told you we had to build it better!"

He seemed almost like himself again, and for a moment I forgot how depressed I was. "I don't think a better fort would have made a difference."

"Sounds like you had her in the palm of your hand!" He sounded both jealous and congratulatory, and I can't deny that I appreciated his attention.

"Maybe so. But who wants a girl who got felt up by a retard and goes out with a loser like JC, and is all concerned about getting even with her own sister?"

Of course I was referring to Maggie but he sat back in the hammock and breathed out deeply, as if this question somehow set him straight again. "I do, confound it! I'm in love with Vera! And it's why I wanna kill myself!"

"But it's just not worth it! There's gotta be a million other fish in the sea." I hoped I might convince myself along with him but the words sounded hollow even as I said them.

"I don't give a hoot about a million other fish! Or the sea either! All I care about is Vera, and she probably doesn't even remember my name!"

"Then count your blessings," I admonished, thinking of Sister Boneventure's endless lectures on the failure to do this being the major shortcoming of the human race. "You don't want any part of that woman—she'll make you as crazy as she's made those other two birds."

"I'd give my left nut just for one date with her."

"Yea? Then what about the second date? Not to mention the third."

I got off the stool and stood in front of him. "Look! You can't jump off a cliff just because some screwed-up female doesn't know what she's missing!"

It's hard to say what made me talk this way. It wasn't even close to how I felt. I wanted to jump off the Empire State Building myself, or Niagara Falls if I could be sure I'd land headfirst on a rock. I wanted to tell Freeman everything, to spill my guts and share every little bit of misery that I'd been through. But I just couldn't bring myself to do it. And here I was giving advice that I was not able to accept myself.

"I can't listen anymore, Joey. I just need to lay here until I die. That's all there is to it."

"Maybe you just need a smoke to soothe your nerves." I figured anything that might cheer Freeman up was worth a shot at this point.

"I even lost interest in those damned things! They're makin' me hack like a damn coal miner," he replied. "Plus my dad's doctor says he has to stop, cause he's getting nymphozyma or something like that. They took an x-ray and said his lungs are all gummed up. He's headed direct for lung cancer, if he doesn't stop now. Plus my mom agreed and said, 'No more!' Claims he stinks like a chimney and she's sick and tired of it.

"And if that wasn't enough, he asked me twice about a few missing packs. So that's one more idea I ought to hang myself over."

Well, maybe not, I thought to myself. I already was beginning to think about how I was going to announce my own quitting after my mom told me about my Uncle Tim having to quit for similar reasons. "That's a damn shame," I lied. "Seems like shit all rolls downhill at the same time."

"So mainly I wanna lie here and die, Joey. I can see no point in going on anymore."

He sounded beyond hope, and for a second I was all set to go away and give him the peace he seemed to need. But the realization that I could not stand being alone with my own thoughts, wallowing in my own bedroom thinking of Maggie, or bumping into Timmy or my mom around the house, made me change my mind. Plus I realized we were still just teenagers and probably had a few more years to go.

"Dang it, captain! You have got to drag your lazy ass out of this hammock! You're
squishing your brains in this smelly old thing, and you need to air them out somehow!"

"Like how? Jump off a bridge in my skivvies?"

"Never mind 'like what.' Just get up and follow me!" I said with all the authority I could muster.

I had no idea what I was doing but I grabbed his wrist hard and fairly yanked him from the hammock. We marched out of the garage and kept on marching, and I acted like I had a goal even though I didn't. But before I knew it we were downtown, sitting at a booth in Callaghan's, sipping Cokes that were purchased with my lawn mowing money.

"All right, look. I have a confession to make." I whispered as if we were in a real confessional. "Promise not to laugh and swear you won't tell a soul or even mention this again, and I'll tell you the truth about Maggie."

"I thought you already told me the truth."

"Only part of it."

"Of course I promise," he replied between sips, with a hint of life coming back in his eyes.

I rewound the story and told him everything, the whole truth and nothing but the truth; I spared nothing, and it wasn't long before that big goon was laughing and slapping the table, howling and shaking, and generally acting like his own normal self. Mr. Callaghan looked over and shook his head a couple of times, and I believe he was watching when Coke shot out Freeman's nose, after I explained how Maggie had said I looked like a dying fish after I asked if she loved me.

"That is a great one, Joey! I can't believe you did it! You got the biggest chabangas of anyone I know!"

"What else could I do? I had to find out for sure."

"You're right," he offered in sympathy when I got done. "She is a bitch from hell."

"And so's Vera. It runs in the family, Freddie, that's all there is to it. We should be happy to be rid of them."

I started to feel like I meant it, and it seemed that Freeman might be having similar feelings.

"Maybe there are other fish in the sea, Joey. I just want one to swim my way sometime."

How true that was, I thought. I was already thinking of Annabelle and how nice she had started looking, and how smart she was and how interesting, if you actually listened to the things she had to say. But I didn't mention this, partly because I feared Freeman might be having similar thoughts, and I didn't want competition.

"Hey! Aren't you the same kids who asked me about JC earlier this summer?" It was Mr. Callaghan, who was wiping the booth next to ours.

Freeman said, "Yes," while I nodded.

"I thought you two looked familiar. It just came to me. Did you guys hear the latest about JC?"

We shook our heads.

"His folks are finally sending him to some reform school upstate. He got accepted and he'll be gone in two weeks."

"Really?" Freeman's eyes got wide.

"Yea. It's about time they did something. This summer has been nothing but one problem after another with that kid."

I felt a surge of great relief. Imagine—no more worries about JC! It was hard to believe we were hearing right. It was as if a ball and chain had been taken off our ankles.

"Playing with a married woman is not something you ever want to do. What a disgrace to his family. But that stunt with wrecking his own car was the final straw. He's still saying it wasn't his fault, but he can't seem to pin the rap on anyone else."

"That is a doggone shame." Freeman spoke gravely, as if he'd just learned that his own mother had passed away.

"You really think so?"

"Actually … " Freeman glanced my way for support. "I think reform school is exactly what he needs." He spoke boldly, perhaps because I was nodding in affirmation even while a flash of guilt warmed my conscience.

"Well, that's what everyone thinks. Just keep an eye out for the next two weeks. You never know what that kid might do next. It's the main reason I think you ought to know," admonished Callaghan. "He never did seem to have much love for you two guys. Now's a real good time to stay away from him."

"Yahoo!" shouted Freeman on the way home, leaping in the air and kicking his feet.

"That SOB is finally goin' where he belongs! And to think it was our little joyride that put him away!"

"I only hope he doesn't come looking for us now."

"Who cares? Two weeks and he's out of here! We can survive that long no matter what he does." He paused and looked at me. "Can't we?"

I suspected he was right, though I dreaded the possibility he was wrong. But mainly I was glad Freeman seemed to be getting over Vera, and I seemed to be getting over Maggie, and I believed those two facts outweighed anything JC might do anyway.

"Of course we can survive," I boasted. "I'd almost like to see him try something now."

16

I soon forgot about JC, and that very night my mind went round in circles on another topic. A combination of factors set me to thinking, even though altogether they didn't add up to more than a hunch. Freeman had suggested the idea originally; my strange flying dream made me wonder; Timmy's statement that I'd be surprised about what he knew about girls enlarged my suspicions; and, of course, I had to find out sooner or later: Where did the love notes really come from?

Had Annabelle written them after all and was just too shy to admit it? It didn't seem likely. Was someone playing a joke, a malicious little prank, such as a kid brother might? Timmy always did good in school, and I suddenly remembered he'd once won a class poetry contest. There weren't a whole lot of options that I could imagine.

"Timmy," I said calmly as I walked up to his bed. He was almost asleep, but I really didn't care. "I need to ask you a question."

"You want me to go to the fort with you, huh?" He sat up and looked ready to go that very minute, pajamas or no.

"Well, maybe sometime. But not right now."

"Okay. Ask it."

"Is there any chance you might have written two letters to me earlier this summer?"

"Letters?" He paused and scratched his head, like I'd asked a difficult question.

"Don't mess around. Just tell me 'Yes' or 'No,' okay?"

"Letters? No."

A hesitation in his voice furthered my suspicions, though it was possible he was merely clearing his throat. In the darkness I was unable to read his face.

"All right. How about notes?"

"Notes? Like what kind of notes?"

"Look! Don't screw around! Just tell me if you wrote some notes, will you?"

"Notes, boats, goats, coats … No, I can't remember any notes."

I was getting fed up and feeling like he had something to hide.

"Stop acting stupid! Did you write me two poems?"

"Poems? You mean like short rhyming poems?"

He went quiet and I said nothing. It was the speed of his breathing and the long, guilty silence that gave the answer.

"You little bastard! You did it, didn't you?" My temperature rose, and I wanted to jump on his neck and throttle him with my bare hands.

"But you've been ignoring me, Joey! Ever since school got out! How else could I get your attention?" Anxiety filled his voice and he sounded ready to break down and cry.

"I only wanted you to do a few things with me!" he wailed.

I felt faint. And weak. Weak from knowing, weak from guilt about having ignored him, weak from anger, weak from having made such a fool of myself in front of Maggie. I thought of the times Freeman had tried to clue me in and how I had routinely ignored him. I pulled the chair from Timmy's desk and sat down, saying nothing for a long, long time.

"I can't believe you did it," I uttered finally.

"I just want you to play with me sometimes," he said, much as he'd been saying for the last several months.

"You listened to me and Freeman talking in his bedroom with the megaphone, didn't you?"

"I told you it worked real good. I could hear you in the garage, too."

"Why didn't you tell me about the notes after you'd had your little fun?"

"I was afraid you'd kill me. Though I did sign one 'me.'"

"If you had any idea what you put me through!" My voice rose angrily.

"I think Maggie's ugly anyway."

I took that in and I really couldn't disagree. I leaned numbly on the back of the chair.

"So … will you start playing with me once in a while now?"

"I'll see what I can do," I mumbled, standing up and heading back to my bed. I was worn out from my own emotions, flustered from realizing it was Timmy's little prank that had messed up my life so severely, exhausted from everything. I fell into a long, deep sleep, but a hundred years would not have seemed long enough.

Several hot, sunny days later Freeman and I splashed and swam about in the sump, and it was good to be back in the cool green water again. I was amazed at how good a swimmer Freeman had become in such a short time. Not that he was about to win any Olympic medals, but he could get around like a turtle, and he seemed to be completely over his fear of deep water.

"Watch me touch the bottom out here!" he shouted. He kicked his feet straight up, then he disappeared for a minute or so. He came up with a huge gob of mud and plopped it on his head, grinning. "It's pretty damn deep, Joey!"

"It looks like a horse took a poop on you! I don't blame him, either!"

Our nightmares over, Vera and Maggie were rapidly fading into the past, and I actually felt free and even relieved not to have to think about girls anymore. I realized we could clown around and have a great time without them, and it struck me pretty hard that we'd blown a good part of our summer getting all worked up over nothing.

"JC can have them all as far as I'm concerned!" I said as we laid in the warmth of the sun, covered from head to toe in brown muck.

"Except for Annabelle," Freeman was quick to remind me, though he didn't need to add that she was not available to either of us anymore.

As it turned out, Matt had had more on his mind than telescopes the day he asked me for Annabelle's last name. The very next day, according to Freeman, he had taken her to Callaghan's for ice cream; and the day after that they'd gone off to watch birds together. She even came by their house once, fortunately while I wasn't there, to show Matt her bird drawings.

"He was never interested in birds before," observed Freeman. "Girls either, for that matter."

"I'm glad for Matt," I said. "I think Annabelle is just right for him. And he seems okay for her."

326

"I gotta admit it makes me a bit jealous, to see him actually goin' out with a girl."

"Well, get over it. We need to forget about females for a while. That's what I say anyway."

"You're prob'ly right. Just one thing I keep wonderin' though: You think they're doin' more than bird watchin' at the fort?"

"No. That wouldn't be like Annabelle. It was a freak thing what she did with me at the junkyard." I pulled more mud onto my stomach and patted down the blob on my crotch.

"But I really don't care. I'm glad to see the fort being used one way or another."

"I told 'im it's ten comics every time he takes her there."

"You're one mean mother of a landlord."

"We're gettin' a mean mother of a comic collection too. Plus he's talkin' about puttin' in another support and a window in front." He breathed deep and the mass of mud covering him heaved and cracked.

"Can't complain about that."

"I hate to admit it, but that guy may be smarter than I thought. Annabelle sure fell for his invention, anyways. I heard her sayin' she thought it could be used to explore the oceans and might just be the best way of flying ever invented. Anyone who can hook a girl with a stupid contraption like that must know somethin' I don't know."

"Maybe it's not such a dumb idea after all."

"Maybe you and me are morons, too."

That was not a point I felt like arguing. We laid there basking in the warmth and the softness of the muck, enjoying the sounds of locusts and June bugs and dragonflies, and whatever else was out there, and the different birds singing and twittering and making calls of various sorts. Neither of us spoke for quite a while. It seemed like a good time to ask Freeman something I'd wanted to ask for several weeks.

"Do you believe in God?"

He thought for a few moments while he put two big gobs of mud on top of his nipples and began shaping them. "Which one?"

I thought for a second he was asking about his new boobs before I realized what he meant.

"You know. God, God."

"Well, it seems like there's a Protestant one and a Jewish one and a Catholic one ... "

I had never seriously thought of it that way, but I could see it would be a tough idea to argue with so I cut him off. "Okay, just the main one, then. You know, like the guy who made everything."

"I'm not sure, Joey. It's hard to imagine some real smart guy ma-kin' JC on purpose. Or Mario, or Maggie, or the nuns, or ... "

"Do you believe in hell?"

He thought for a minute while he admired his new anatomy. "I s'pose Mario's in hell. And we will be too, once school starts."

"What about heaven?"

He added a patch of mud to his right boob and patted it down. "Not really. Unless that's the name of a whorehouse somewhere. And if it is, I'd sure like to go to heaven, Joey!"

I watched clouds for a while and took all this in, feeling disappointed with Freeman's answers. I had thought if I could understand his outlook better it might help me be more like him and stop worrying about everything so much. But it wasn't much good so far.

"Then how the hell do you think we got here?" I asked, somewhat exasperated.

"We walked. Remember?"

"No! I mean how the hell do you think we got here on the earth?"

"Jeez, Joey. Didn't your dad ever tell ya nothin'?"

I didn't know if he was serious or pulling my leg. Or whether to continue questioning in either case. I laid there thinking and wondering what Freeman would be like if he'd gone to St. Frances since first grade, like I had. It was hard to imagine.

Right about then a small splash rose from the water, about ten feet away, which I saw out of the corner of my eye.

"Look at that, Freddie! It was a little fish over there!"

"Yea, I saw it too. I guess this place can't be too toxic."

Another splash went up, much larger, a short distance from the first one.

"Damn, there it is again," said Freeman.

"I wonder what kind of fish it is."

"Maybe there's sharks in here after all."

"There's something in here, I know that much."

The third splash was as large as the second, but we were both looking and it was no fish.

"Some asshole's throwin' rocks, Joey!"

"I saw it! What do we do now?"

We rolled over and looked around the perimeter of the place, but saw no signs of life along the fence.

"Some jerk's hidin' in the weeds," I said.

Right then another large rock, the size of a fist, landed between us in the mud, missing each of us by about six inches, splattering like you'd imagine a meteorite making a crater.

"Holy crap, Freddie! Someone's aimin' at us!"

"Get in the water, quick! Out near the middle!"

He jumped up and dove in and I followed, not wasting a second. Two more rocks came down, the size of large erasers; one hit the water while the other hit the mud, and they came from different directions.

We swam underwater to near the middle and popped up. I saw Hank Powers standing outside the fence, behind where the marker used to be.

"There's a bunch of 'em!" said Freeman.

I looked around the four sides of the sump; in addition to Powers, there was Billy Ferguson, Sandy Arnold, and Tony Angeli, who stood by JC, at the different sections of fence. We were surrounded, naked, and defenseless, with no way out!

"Look at the little kiddies, playin' in the mud," said Powers.

"Like polliwogs!" gloated Tony. "They're swimmin' in their own little pool!"

"Aw, dat's cute!" said Ferguson. "Dey don't even have deir wittle bathin' suits on!"

A splash came up behind us, a few feet away.

"What nice little targets for big boys with rocks!" said Powers.

"Keep facin' that way, Joey," Freeman whispered. "I'll look over here."

Three rocks came down at once, one about a foot from me, the other two maybe five feet away. The sizes were becoming hard to recognize, let alone remember, but it didn't matter; we were in serious danger no matter what, and there did not appear to be many options.

Powers clicked open a switchblade and the metal reflected in the sun.

"You guys are gonna be swimmin' for a long time, huh?"

I raised my middle finger as high as I could since I saw nothing to lose.

"No, no, Joey! You guys keep gettin' that backward!" Tony laughed as he heaved a large rock over.

"Five of you against two of us! And us out here in the water! That's real fair, ain't it?" Freeman said. "You're all a bunch of cowards!"

"Oooohhhh! You're the big boy with the bat, aren't you?" It was Ferguson, who Freeman was facing.

"I didn't swing the bat and you know it!" Freeman shouted.

"You made it happen, though, didn't you, Mr. Fred Boy Dead Boy?!" JC laughed and threw a rock as he spoke. It arched through the air toward us, spinning and whistling softly in the bright sun.

"Duck!" I shouted. We slipped under and emerged after the rock went down.

"Okay, guys! Let's see if we can sink the Bismarck all at once, now!" Powers laughed, then bent to pick up another rock. JC and Tony did likewise and it was clear the others were doing the same.

"On the count of three, let 'em have it!" said Powers. "Hey, you little girls down there wanna count for us?"

"Eat shit!" shouted Freeman.

"That's probably higher than they can count anyways," said Tony. "So we better help 'em out! One … two … three … "

Five rocks flew toward us at once; we dove quickly. The light green water was peaceful, quiet, and secure, and there was no reason for fear while we were under. I watched Freeman go up after about fifteen seconds, then followed. The moment we broke the surface another barrage of rocks came flying; we each took a quick breath, then ducked under.

Dang it! I thought. They'll keep this up until we can't hold our breath anymore! Freeman was facing me, and due to the high sun and being near the middle of the sump, the visibility into the water was not bad. I pointed with my arm toward the bank near Powers, hoping that blurry figure in front of me could make out what I meant. I figured if we could go under and come up below Powers, only Ferguson would have a clear line of fire, and he'd be too far away to do much damage. If Tony, JC, or Sandy threw rocks, we'd have a good chance to dodge them, plus the option of swimming along the weedy bank in the murky water to help confuse them all.

I dove deep, in hopes I couldn't be seen from above. Freeman had understood my message and followed close. But I soon came up for a gulp of air, lungs bursting.

"Sneaky bastards!" someone hollered as I drew a lungful and dove again, moving toward the steep bank below Powers.

We surfaced together near the bank, glanced at each other and then scrambled under the weeds growing off the muddy slope.

"This might be hell, too," Freeman observed as a rock from Ferguson landed some distance out, and another from Powers splashed about five feet in front of us.

"We may have to keep diving and coming up in different places till they go away," I whispered.

"I don't think goin' away is on their agenda. But you're right about divin' under. And we may need to swim in opposite directions to screw 'em up, back and forth along the edge here."

A large rock from Ferguson landed about two feet out.

"Go!" Freeman pointed for me to move toward JC and Tony in the weeds along the shore, while he traveled the other way. But even before we started JC and Tony had begun to climb up the gate, Ferguson and Arnold were making their way toward it, and I imagined Powers was headed there too.

"Shit, Freddie! They're coming in!"

"Stay put and see what they do. We may need to head toward the other side or back to the middle."

I took a whizz and felt better, even though JC and Tony had jumped down from the gate and were headed toward us. I tried to imagine what they had in mind then realized they probably had nothing in mind and were making things up as they went.

As JC and Tony came closer along our bank we swam out toward the far side. It appeared we could out swim them if they all stayed together, but we'd be in grave danger if they split up and continued throwing rocks.

And split up is exactly what they did. Powers, Arnold, and Ferguson scaled the gate in short order. Ferguson stayed near it while the other two spread out like before, except now they were inside the fence.

We got to the middle and the rock barrage began again, faster and more sustained, from all sides. If we went to a bank it was clear they'd move toward us and fire from a closer range. Freeman admonished me to swim in place with my back against his. "If one's comin' at us, move your back and I'll move with you! And feel for my back, too!"

Fortunately, we were able to see the rocks coming and had time to gauge their course; fortunately too, none of these guys was a very good shot and so holding still was usually all we needed to do. We swam in place and dodged back and forth in this manner, while rocks rained down and splashed around us. The hardest part was staying calm and not losing track of the rocks.

"Too bad a train don't come along now, huh, Joey?"

Two rocks flew toward us at once, from JC and Tony, and I couldn't decide which way to move. One missed my head by inches, while the other hit the water a short distance in front of me, slowed down, then bounced off my chest. Seconds later Freeman moved to my right and I followed as a fist-sized rock made a loud thumping sound right where our heads had been.

"They're gettin' better, Joey! I think we're gonna have to run for it and scale the fence!"

"But we don't even have clothes on!"

"That's the least of our worries! We're gonna have to go like hell!"

"I don't think it'll work!" I moved left, narrowly escaping a zinger from Tony that whistled as it spun into the water.

"Fuckers!" said Freeman, moving me further left as another rock slapped the water nearby. "Let's go under, come up beneath Arnold, and go after him. Then toss that twerp in before the others can get there!"

"And then what?" I asked.

"We'll figure that one out later!"

He hyperventilated and I did the same. We went below and moved toward Arnold's bank. When I came up, Freeman was already climbing the slope, his white, wet behind shining in the sun. Arnold was back in the weeds, behind the edge of the bank, and couldn't see us.

"Let's get 'im, Joey!"

I was there in a flash, scrambling up the bank behind him. In seconds we were over the top and face-to-face with Arnold, who was about a head shorter than Freeman and a fraction of his weight. But he had a switchblade and we had nothing, save the brief element of surprise. I looked for a rock to clobber him with, but saw none big enough.

"C'mon, ya little nudies! I'll cut 'em off now!" He posed with his knife, summing up the situation quickly.

Freeman hesitated a moment and Arnold moved in fast, slashing rapidly with his switchblade; in a matter of seconds he slashed Freeman's arm. Blood appeared instantly, but Freeman didn't stop to look. He lunged forward and put Arnold in a bear hug. There was a tremendous shuffling and a holler from Arnold; next I knew, Arnold and his knife were sailing through the air toward the water, Arnold kicking madly and flailing his arms as if trying to fly, with the knife traveling a few feet ahead of him. He landed a short way out in the water, where he went under headfirst. I imagined him sliding down the muddy bank underwater.

"Let's play 'Fly like a birdie' now!" hollered Freeman, putting his hand over the red gash on his arm.

"How bad is it?"

"Could be worse, but I'm gonna live. Watch out behind ya though!" He pointed as he shouted, urgency in his voice.

I turned and there was Ferguson, JC, and Tony nearly upon me, with knives out and unforgiving looks upon their faces.

"Get 'im!" shouted Ferguson to Tony, who was in the lead.

"Dive!" hollered Freeman as he took several giant steps down the bank then leapt far out into the sump.

I took one step down the bank and tripped somehow. From the corner of my eye I saw Tony leap toward me like a human spear. His knife missed my backside only because I had tripped. We both hit the slope and rolled till just before the bottom when I bounced to my feet and dove over Arnold, who was floundering in the slippery muck. I swam madly to catch up with Freeman.

Freeman was near the middle before I reached him. Adrenaline surged through me and everything seemed crystal clear. Rocks flew and splashed nearby; we dived on instinct, and swam underwater toward the other side. When we came up all of them except Arnold were coming around the sides. Arnold was still sliding around like a wet rat in the muck along the steep bank. We were perhaps three car lengths from where the truck ramp entered the water, and I made a quick guess as to who'd reach the gate first, them or us.

"Let's get out now!" I exclaimed, thinking this was the best chance we'd have. It would be close and we'd be leaving in our birthday suits, not even our undies, but what other choice was there?

"What the hell?" Freeman pointed toward the fence to the right of the gate, where the hinges were.

I looked beyond the weeds in that direction and saw the top of the fence leaning toward us, as if being pushed by some magical force. It was as though the whole scene was a strange dream and there was suddenly nothing to do but stop and watch.

Seconds later the shiny metal grille of the front end of a car appeared in the weeds, moving toward the water at the edge of the bank. It was a red car, and just as I recognized it was JC's convertible I heard JC shout hysterically, "What is that asshole doin?!"

The car kept coming to the edge of the bank where it protruded through the weeds; still it kept coming, until it leaned off the edge toward the sump, tottering like a seesaw. Only then did I see the huge bulldozer pushing from behind! Smoke from the exhaust pipes rose upward, and there sat Mario, smoking a cigar and driving just like the very first day we'd seen him, as if he were pushing a log across Cranberry Boulevard.

"Holy shit, Joey! The guy's lost his mind!"

"Maybe he found it," I suggested in total awe at the spectacle before us. "Let's move back so it doesn't land on us."

JC was quickly at the car, scrambling to get in the front seat as if he was going to be able start it up and drive away even as the vehicle nosed down the slope. The dozer kept pushing, gray smoke rising from Mario's cigar, black smoke racing from the exhaust pipes, Mario not moving at all, just sitting, looking down at the car and JC, who was now in the driver's seat, his hands on the wheel.

As the dozer itself tilted forward, Powers and Ferguson scrambled up the ladder in the back. Arnold had pulled himself together, and rather than stay for the show, now raced off through the demolished fence, dripping wet and headed for who knew where. Tony hesitated, evidently deciding what to do.

"Screw this shit!" he yelled to no one in particular, just before taking off like a frightened rabbit, close behind Arnold.

Ferguson and Powers scrambled about the dozer, descending like wolves after Mario then pouncing upon him. They pounded on his chest and beat his shoulders and neck with their fists; they must have dropped their switchblades to climb on board, though I wasn't sure. But they may as well have been flies pounding on a horse for it did no good; the dozer kept going and Mario sat like nothing was happening, calmly smoking his cigar and fixing his stare on the object that seemed to be consuming him.

The car broke the surface and started under but JC remained in place, as though he planned to drive around on the bottom of the sump.

"You bastard!" he hollered loudly, one fist waving in the air. He made me think of a cowboy atop a bucking bronco at a rodeo. "Ya can't do this to me!"

But his words were for naught. In another moment the car was up to the windshield and still going down.

"Get out!" screamed Freeman, hands cupped to his mouth. "You'll get trapped in there!"

"I can't swim!" JC replied, terror suddenly in his voice. His eyes met ours in that last instant before he went under as if pleading for help.

"Oh hell!" said Freeman as he started dog paddling toward the scene.

The car slid under till it was about halfway gone then dropped off quickly, vanishing from sight as if it had never been there in the first place.

Ferguson and Powers had given up trying to dislodge Mario from the driver's seat and were now monkeying with the controls. They had apparently put the thing in reverse, or else Mario had, as the treads were going backward. The dozer halted at the water's edge and hung as if in suspended animation, going neither up nor down, pulled by gravity and at the same time backing up hard in the mud. Mario sat like an immovable piece of the machine, blowing gray smoke from his cigar, and I wasn't sure now if he wanted to back up or follow the convertible to its watery grave.

Freeman, meanwhile, had paddled to about where JC might be and was pulling air, getting set to dive. He kicked up his legs and disappeared.

I swam into the vicinity and was there when Freeman came up sputtering.

"He's right here! But he's stuck, and I can't get him out! I'm holdin' his hair!"

I dove at once and followed JC's body down to his feet. I couldn't see much due to the murky water and had to feel my way down. It appeared one shoelace was somehow caught on the lucky dice that were tied to the rearview mirror. I tried to break the shoelace free but couldn't, so I slipped off JC's shoe instead. He started up, pulled by Freeman's powerful dog paddle.

Freeman floundered to the ramp now, pulling JC by the back of his shirt; I shoved his body as much as I could until we got him on the ramp.

"Put his head down the slope and push on his back!" JC wasn't breathing and I amazed myself by recalling this move from some Boy Scout movie I'd seen on water safety. Freeman did as I told him, but JC still didn't breathe. He lay still as if he were a corpse.

"Push on his back! Hard!"

Freeman did that several times, with no result.

"Move over!" I placed myself above JC's back and sat down hard. A large gush of water left his mouth, but still no breathing.

"Do it again, Joey!"

I did, and a second gush of water erupted.

"One more time!"

I did it a third time and no water came out, but as I moved off JC inhaled. Then he exhaled, and it looked for a moment like that might be his last breath. But no. He inhaled again, then exhaled, and after a few more cycles, began breathing almost normally.

I looked up and saw the dozer still hanging on the steep bank, treads going backward, the three passengers now slugging at each other in a free-for-all. But even as I looked, the dozer was beginning to slide forward.

"Get the hell out!" shouted Ferguson, jumping off the machine into the edge of the water, falling forward as he landed.

"The dumb bastard is tryin' to sink it!" shrieked Powers, just before Mario picked him up and flung him off, in a horizontal position. He flew a good way into the water, splashing down on his side.

Mario got back in the seat and played with the shift mechanism even though the dozer was already sliding slowly on its own. Now the treads went forward, as did the dozer, very rapidly. Mario sat there immoveable, as though nothing was wrong. He seemed perfectly content to follow the convertible to the bottom of the sump, and it dawned on me then that he might actually be trying to drown himself.

I had no doubt he was drunk, but this was beyond anything I could have possibly dreamed. The blade went under, and in another moment, all that remained was Mario's dark nipples, his shoulders, and his head.

The engine roared, the smokestacks belched, the treads turned; I thought of the lingering smile of the Cheshire cat, which was about all that was left of Mario. Then everything was gone.

Freeman was still attending to JC, watching to make sure he kept breathing. But now with no more noise from the Cat, he looked up.

"Where the hell's Mario?"

"He went under! Driving the Cat!"

"Go after 'im, Joey! I gotta keep an eye on this guy!"

So dumbfounded was I by the whole phenomenon it never occurred to me that I ought to make an effort to save Mario.

I dove back in and the momentum carried me to where the dozer ought to be. Just as I prepared to go under, Mario came up. His head broke the surface in front of mine, and his Diesel Power cap floated nearby.

"Help," was all he said, not shouting, not panicked, apparently not even concerned; not anything, except as drunk as I imagined he could be without passing out.

"Take my foot!"

I floated on my back and stuck my foot in his direction, again recalling a scene from that water safety movie. He grabbed it and I backstroked to shore. Freeman was there when I hit the bank with my back; he helped me pull Mario through the muck onto the ramp. We soon had him sitting, and he remained there in a daze, arms wrapped around his knees, muttering something about Vera. We let him be and went back to JC.

"Are ya gonna be all right?" asked Freeman.

JC shook his head ever so slightly, but Freeman ignored it. "Ya nearly died, JC. We just pulled ya out and saved your life. Ya understand that?"

He appeared too far gone to respond but at least he was still breathing. As we were getting our clothes on I heard a siren in the distance. Powers and Ferguson had taken off, though I saw them again shortly, along with Tony, in the backseat of a cop car. It turned out Arnold had had the presence of mind to call the police from the Goldman Electronics Factory.

Mario was soon in the backseat of a second cop car, wet and caked with mud, hands behind his back, mumbling to himself. The ambulance came not long thereafter and we watched as they loaded JC on the stretcher. As he passed by us I noticed a small wave of his hand as he motioned a thanks to Freeman.

Arnold, Freeman, and I were free to go after we told the end of the story about JC and his convertible. The cops believed Freeman when he claimed that we'd gone into the sump to get away from JC and Tony. With the dozer and the convertible underwater, this certainly sounded like a feasible part of the story. At least for the most part.

"Wait a minute." The cop looked up from his note taking, suddenly concerned the picture wasn't quite right. "How come your clothes are all dry now if you jumped in to get away from these guys?"

"I knew we couldn't swim too good with these things on," lied Freeman promptly, picking at the belly of his T-shirt. "And those guys were still on the other side of the fence. So me and Joey here stripped down in a hurry before divin' in."

The cop looked suspicious but accepted the story after Arnold said, "That's right, Officer. It surprised me too, but it was actually a pretty sensible thing to do. They never could have swam that good with their clothes on."

Neither of us looked at Arnold but I imagined he could feel the thanks I was emitting. It was that small piece of the story that just might be enough to clear me with my parents later on too.

"Don't you kids ever, ever go back in that place," admonished the cop. "You're lucky you didn't die from all the chemicals and crap they pump in there!"

A large wrecker had pulled the dozer onto the ramp, where it lay on its side, and the operator of the wrecker was trying to figure out how to hook onto JC's car when we left the sump for the last time.

Epilogue

Not long after school started, Freeman got a job from three o'clock till nine thirty at night during the week, and on Saturdays, as clerk and general operator of Callaghan's. His goal was to have enough money for a car by the middle of the next summer, which it looked like he might.

"We'll have a blast, Joey! Ya know how I love to drive!" he exclaimed, when he first got the job and I complained about not having anyone to hang out with. "It'll be a sports car, though I'm not sure which kind. But it ain't gonna be a convertible! And it ain't gonna be red!"

He got a girlfriend too, and she wrote to him often, telling him things that were going on in her life. He showed me one of the letters:

It's me again! You're still the most fun person I now. I think of you all the time. But I now you are busy so I will just keep riting letters. Do you remember how much fun we had getting crabs?

"If all else fails, I could just wait a few years and go out with her," he told me when he tossed the letter into the rest of the pile that Mary had sent.

I didn't see much of Freeman after that, except when I went to buy an occasional comic, and even then he was usually too busy working to talk very much. I'd see him once in a while on Sunday afternoons, but all we did was play Monopoly with Matt and James, and sometimes Timmy, and it was nothing like the olden days.

JC went to reform school somewhere upstate for the school year, and I was told by my mom, who learned from Helen, that they planned to evaluate things at the end of that time to see if he had improved enough to leave. I had little doubt that would be the case, and it occurred to me that he had already been reformed, at least as far as Freeman and I went.

340

Arnold's family moved away, and though Tony, Powers, and Ferguson still hung out together, they were seldom seen and they ceased to bother other kids, as far as I knew.

Herman informed us that Tony knew about the fort and had spied on us and was planning to wreck it, but that was before the underwater bulldozer adventure. I no longer worried about Tony.

Maggie and Vera went back to Hartford, hopefully forever, and Mario spent two months in the county jail, then got out on probation, which according to Herman meant mainly that he had to behave like a normal human being, go to some kind of alcohol meetings, and stay off the bottle. Herman said Mario got the dozer running again, and the convertible too, which JC's parents used on a trade-in for a new family car.

I played with Timmy more, not as much as years ago, but enough to shut him up and keep my mom reasonably content; and I was pleased that he finally developed an interest in girls, which gave us something to actually talk about.

James and Doc played together all the time, and every two weeks or so I'd go visit and take them both for a walk to the junkyard, sometimes with Freeman, sometimes with Timmy, and sometimes just James and Doc, which is when I had the most fun.

Matt and Annabelle kept seeing each other, and I often saw them going out on Friday night or bird watching on Saturday morning. They went in Matt's old pickup truck, that he bought for seventy-five dollars and powered with an engine he traded some junk for with a friend of Herman's.

I was jealous at first, but I got over it not long after school started. And I accepted that Matt was a much better man for Annabelle than I could ever be. Last I heard, they were both planning to enter the county science fair, her with a project on squirrels, him with his newfangled flying machine, which Annabelle had said was "the most remarkable invention ever to come out of Sunnyville." Freeman claimed she was "madly in love with a mad inventor," but I reckoned that Freeman was just mad period.

But I had more to concern myself with than Annabelle. I told Freeman about it one night at Callaghan's, when he and I were the only ones there and he had some time to spare. I had gotten used to his white cap and apron, though it still seemed a bit odd talking to him behind the counter while I sat on a stool like a customer.

"Turn the radio down first, will you?" It was blaring out that song I really hate, "Why Do Fools Fall in Love?"

He reached behind him and turned it down, and I broke out the good news.

"You wouldn't believe it, Freddie! She just moved in from Boston! Well, I think it was Boston, but it might have been Buffalo. Anyway, it was somewhere up there in New England. Well, I had gotten sent to the principal for sloughing American history, and there she was on an errand, getting something or other from the secretary. She turned around just as I came in, so I almost knocked her over. Our eyes met and *boom*! It was love at first ... "

"Wait a minute! Wait a cotton-pickin' minute, admiral!" He put his hand up and he waved it like a cop, directing traffic at a busy intersection. "Did she have green eyes?"

"No! But she had the most beautiful br ... "

"Joey! Joey! Joey!" He shook his hand more vigorously, indicating he did not want me to go on. "Listen to me, will ya? Did she smile at ya?"

He reached under the counter as he spoke.

"Yea, she did! How did you know?"

"Here ya go, lover boy!" He leaned forward and handed me a strawberry ice cream cone, as if to help me celebrate the start of my brand-new life, while he listened to the wonderful things I was eager to tell him, and help share the joy that was bursting from my heart. "It's on the house, Good Buddy!"

"Gee, thanks, Freddie!" I exclaimed to the best friend I ever had.

"Now eat it and shut up, will ya?" he said flatly, as proceeded to make a chocolate ice cream cone for himself.

The End

Author's note: It is my sincere hope that you enjoyed this story as much as I enjoyed writing it. My small request is that if you did like it, that you do what you can to let others know about it. For that, I thank you in advance. DG

About the Author

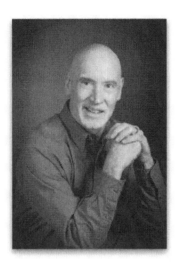

Daniel Geery has been writing since the seventies, mostly while teaching elementary school. He is now an inventor with two patents, the Aquaglider (described herein) and the Hyperblimp, easily Googled. He interviewed Robert Redford and likewise the late David Brower, Nobel Peace Prize Candidate and pioneer of the modern environmental movement. Geery has written countless letters to the editor on environmental topics, presented many speeches at environmental hearings, written a trail guide to the Wasatch Mountains, produced a self-help book, and wrote a "how-to" solar greenhouse book, along with articles for several outdoor magazines. He avidly studied and taught writing during his teaching career. Geery lived off-the-grid for fifteen years in an earth-sheltered, solar home that he designed and built. He now writes progressive political blogs and in 2012 ran for Federal Senator from Utah on the Justice Party ticket.

Made in the USA
Charleston, SC
24 May 2013